DEMYTHOLOGIZING LANGUAGE DIFFERENCE IN THE ACADEMY

Establishing Discipline-Based Writing Programs

DEMYTHOLOGIZING LANGUAGE DIFFERENCE IN THE ACADEMY

Establishing Discipline-Based Writing Programs

Mark L. Waldo
University of Nevada, Reno

 LAWRENCE ERLBAUM ASSOCIATES, PUBLISHERS

2004   Mahwah, New Jersey   London

Lawrence Erlbaum Associates, Inc., Publishers
10 Industrial Avenue
Mahwah, New Jersey 07430

Cover design by Sean Sciarrone

Cover artwork: The Tower Babel, Pieter Brueghel the Elder, 1563.

Library of Congress Cataloging-in-Publication Data

Waldo, Mark L.
Demythologizing language difference in the academy : establishing discipline-based
writing programs / Mark Waldo.
  p.   cm.
Includes bibliographical references and index.
ISBN 0-8058-4735-9 (cloth : alk. paper) — ISBN 0-8058-4736-7 (pbk. : alk. paper)
1. English language—Rhetoric—Study and teaching.   2. Academic writing—Study and
teaching (Higher).   3. Interdisciplinary approach in education.   4. Learning and
scholarship—Terminology.   5. Language and education.   I. Title.

PE1404.W3   2003
808′.042′0711—dc21   2003052858
                                                                           CIP

Books published by Lawrence Erlbaum Associates are printed on acid-free paper,
and their bindings are chosen for strength and durability.

Printed in the United States of America
10 9 8 7 6 5 4 3 2 1

Contents

Preface

This study in writing across the curriculum (WAC), writing centers, and writing assessment was mostly initiated by failures. In 1983, I was a first-year assistant professor and writing center director responsible for WAC at Montana State University. I brought a bulging box of tools, collected as a 10-year teacher and student of writing, to my first "how to use writing in your classes" workshop with Montana State's faculty. And I brought those tools with an evangelical fervor to use them.

During the early and mid-1970s, my thinking about how to teach writing was shaped by the work of Peter Elbow (1970), Ken Macrorie (1970), Donald Murray (1968), and Janet Emig (1971). My students grew and cooked their writing, understood and avoided "Engfish," conferenced with me and each other on their papers, and wrote "authentically" on topics of real interest to them in voices genuinely their own—not from "school" topics and voices. They shared their mimeographed work with their classmates and others outside the classroom to positive effect. The 1970s were heady times in composition, and so much of what these scholar/teachers were writing fit with obvious and intuited power into my own composition classes. As I grew as a composition teacher, many others became important, including James Britton (1972), Georges Gusdorf (1965), James Moffett (1968), Stephen Tchudi (then Judy, 1976), Ann Berthoff (1978), Mina Shaughnessy (1977), Jean Piaget (1959), and Lev Vygotsky (1962), to name a few. Many readers will acknowledge how these scholars have shaped their teaching and confirm their immense, continued influence on the way in which writing is taught. (Note the number of times they are cited as influences in *Living Rhetoric and*

Composition: Stories of the Discipline.) These scholars were the principal source for modern process-expressivist approaches to teaching writing, and they provided the initial challenge to what is commonly termed the current traditional paradigm.

They also strongly influenced WAC through its writing to learn component. WAC consultants have reportedly developed complementary methods for helping faculty do what they want with writing in their classrooms (learning to write in the disciplines) and do what the consultants want them to do with writing (writing to learn). Back in 1983, however, I had not developed such complementary methods. (I still have not developed them.)

About 15 teachers attended that workshop at Montana State. A couple of them were from the English Department, but the rest came from other fields: accounting, biology, engineering, forestry, history, philosophy, mathematics, and so on. I did not lack enthusiasm in presenting journal writing, freewriting, personal responses to text and course material, small-group work on drafts, writing as process, and expressive writing as viable, necessary pedagogies for the writing they assigned in their classes. I did not lack enthusiasm. As I said, I approached the task with evangelical fervor. Yet I did lack, I hope forgivably, a sense of audience. I believed I was talking about writing as it must be everywhere, not locally but globally. Almost all of these faculty members, however, had little interest in the techniques I successfully used in my own writing classes—techniques that were by then supported by an increasingly empathic literature (see, e.g., Knoblauch & Brannon, 1984). I did not completely alienate my audience. They nodded, chuckled, and seemed to like me, but they also asked me for ideas and materials relevant to writing in their courses and disciplines. Unprepared for their question, I had no ideas and materials.

That I had none was disconcerting to me on a variety of levels. I wondered how they could ask for relevant materials. Hadn't I provided them? After all I was a doctor of writing theory and practice (with instruments in hand), and I had taught writing for 10 years. I had presented everything that 90 minutes allowed. I wondered how they could think there was more, given that the principles and practices of process-expressivism were becoming so generally accepted, at least in my discipline. Presently, the problem seems obvious; in 1983, it was not obvious at all. I argue that even now it is not obvious to everyone. The world of writing in which I had lived and breathed for 10 years, in which I had taught with passionate commitment, and in which I had received a PhD was quite different, even alien to the worlds of writing of those in my audience. Readers now might ask how I could be so incompetent and underprepared. They will certainly raise their eyebrows when I admit that I tried almost the same workshop twice more.

Committed as I was to a particular set of principles and values for writing, I felt I had to make it work, and I worried, as a latter-day Romantic, that how my colleagues in the disciplines wanted to use writing would make their students engines, writing not as human beings but as disciplines, as Wordsworth decried in 1795.

Regardless of my passion and commitment, however, these workshops failed. My audiences were not antagonistic. They just were not much interested, and their numbers dwindled. The WAC effort at Montana State was voluntary. Nonetheless, I was hired with the idea that it would succeed and with the expectation not only that I would offer workshops, but that they would have some impact. (Imagine that.) I wanted to help teachers and their students, and, of course, I wanted to keep my job. Thus, at that point in 1983, I changed my approach. With Adelle Pittendrigh, another WAC consultant, I wrote a detailed series of questions I would follow at subsequent workshops (discussed in chap. 6). The first workshop was on assignment design, the second on paper grading, and the third on linking writing assignments to particular thinking skills. Over the years, the workshop offerings became increasingly diverse, but they had one feature in common. They depended on inquiry and dialogue as the basis of communication between me and the faculty volunteers attending the workshops. I put away the bag of tools completely, left my writing world, and entered theirs. For me, this meant keeping my values, purposes, and forms for writing to myself and seeking theirs. It meant helping them develop their writing pedagogies, not obliging (or even urging) them to adopt mine. This process succeeded for me and for WAC at Montana State. Writing remains a thriving enterprise there. At bottom, I think the success stemmed from a fundamental reality: There are dozens and even hundreds of different specialized languages operating on almost any university campus. Faculty speak, read, and write these languages, and they are paid to teach them to their students. WAC interaction based on inquiry and dialogue taps right into that reality, whereas WAC based in prescribing values does not, as I want to show. Instead, such WAC attempts to impose its own reality on everyone else. Faculty—university faculty anyway—are not very tolerant of imposition.

I acknowledge that what works for one program or person may not work for another. Almost any WAC process or activity may also be defended as effective. The process I describe here has succeeded at two second-tier public universities—Montana State University and the University of Nevada, Reno (UNR). Outside of using writing center statistics, we did not measure the degree of success generated by the WAC program at Montana State nor the quality of writing its students were doing. By 1989, we knew that writing assignments were being required in several classes in every department. In many departments, all of the classes required writing. I probably could not have explained then why the rewritten program of workshops succeeded as well as it did there. Yet at UNR, we have kept 13 years of writing center statistics, we have interviewed hundreds of faculty and graduating seniors from every department, and we have conducted discipline-based assessment of upper division student writers in eight disciplines. (Program assessment is detailed in chap. 7.) We have ample evidence demonstrating UNR's WAC/writing center success. I think now that I can explain the theoretical basis for it.

The majority of this book describes a program that may essentially be termed discipline-based WAC and writing assessment, housed in writing centers but belonging to faculty and students in every department. It argues the importance of comprehensive writing centers to the WAC endeavor. It explains tutor training and faculty consultancy, and it includes many of the best assignments generated by UNR's faculty. It discusses a multilayered assessment program. As part of the assessment project, we ask faculty to share their own and their discipline's values for writing, and each of those lists is included in chapter 7. These lists suggest the reasons for the argument that makes up the remainder of this text, particularly in its first two chapters. Each list is different from the other, although seven of the eight share two characteristics—student writing should improve critical thinking and include minimal sentence-level errors. Yet there are striking differences, the most relevant of which is between the English Department's list and every other department's list. This difference has important implications, at least to me, for campuses where WAC, writing centers, composition specialists, and rhetoric and composition graduate programs are housed in English departments; where first-year composition is taught to all students by English; and where writing assessment is conducted by English.

Because I find the implications disturbing, I may be perceived by some readers as biting the proverbial hand that feeds me. Certainly, several graduate students who have heard these arguments in my seminar on WAC theory and practice have thought and told me so. They also remark on the potential elimination of composition jobs that the argument, in one sense, implies. Perhaps I do bite the hand that feeds me, although I feel no adversarial relationship with my own English Department or English studies generally. All of the English Department graduate students who have worked closely with the WAC/writing center program at UNR have received tenure-track positions in WAC/writing centers elsewhere. Since 1996, this amounts to 12 people—a substantial percentage of our MA and PhD graduates. My own appointment is 50% in UNR's English Department, where I am a tenured professor, and 50% in the Writing Center. My teaching and research are reviewed for merit by the Department's Personnel Committee. The one performance ambiguity

I have experienced stems from review of my writing center responsibilities, which are campuswide. Sometimes the English Department reviews and rewards this work; sometimes no one does. Yet my rewards at UNR have been substantial, and I have few complaints.

Over the years, I have taught mostly graduate courses as well as several upper division and first-year courses. If readers glanced at the values English faculty offered for writing (voice, the expression of the writer's self in the piece of writing; independence, thinking demonstrated in the writing that distinguishes it from the writing of others; meta-consciousness of language; originality; etc.—chap. 1) and then looked at course calendars for my writing classes, they would see many shared values. I support voice, independence, and originality for writing courses in English and encourage them in my own writing courses. My complaint arises when they are thought of not as reflecting good writing in English courses, but as good writing period. Readers may argue that an imposition of values does not happen (anymore). I argue that it certainly does, at least through the teaching of first-year writing and through the writing to learn component of WAC. It also happens in writing assessment. An Old Testament quality exists in thinking that one language and one imagination is the most desirable condition for human beings. It is a thinking that does not accommodate universities as they are or should be.

ACKNOWLEDGMENTS

A section of chapter 5 appeared in "The Last Best Place for Writing Across the Curriculum: The Writing Center." *Writing Program Administration (16)3*, 1993, pp. 15–27.

Sections of chapter 6 appeared in "Finding Common Ground When WAC Writing Center Directors Meet Neurotic Pride." In Robert Barnett & Jacob Blumner (Eds.), *Writing Centers and Writing Across the Curriculum: Building Interdisciplinary Partnerships* (Westport, CT: Greenwood Publishing, 1999) and "Linking Paper Grading to Assignment Design in Classes on Cultural Diversity." In Phyllis Kahaney and Judith Liu (Eds.), *Contested Terrain: Exploring Cultural Diversity Through Writing* (Ann Arbor, University of Michigan Press, 2001).

All are reprinted with permission of the publisher.

—*Mark Waldo*

Introduction: How Universities Are Towers of Babel and How They Are Not

> 5   And the LORD came down to see the city and the tower, which the children of men builded.
>
> 6   And the LORD said, Behold, the people is one, and they have all one language; and this they begin to do: and now nothing will be restrained from them, which they have imagined to do.
>
> 7   Go to, let us go down, and there confound their language, that they may not understand one another's speech.
>
> 8   So the LORD scattered them abroad from thence upon the face of all the earth: and they left off to build the city.
>
> 9   Therefore is the name of it called Babel; because the LORD did there confound the language of all the earth: and from thence did the LORD scatter them to all parts of the earth.
>
> —Genesis 11: 5–9

Outside of these few lines quoted from Genesis, the Tower of Babel receives little biblical mention or treatment. Yet as a myth with a lesson for humans, it carries singular weight. According to the myth, the Lord beholds a unified people, with one language and one imagination; and in that condition, they can do anything that they set out to do. ("And the LORD said, Behold, the people is one, and they have all one language; and this they begin to do [to build the Tower]: and now nothing will be restrained from them, which they have imagined to do.") The Lord, however, is unhappy with the Tower builders because they are not only constructing it to reach Him, but also to be as He is, demonstrating an unacceptable hubris. So He brings humans low by confounding their language and scattering them abroad, creating multiple

1

languages and imaginations. Evidently, one of the severest punishments to be leveled against people is that they "may not understand one another's speech," which goes some distance to explain the myth's negative implications for universities. By presenting its opposite, the Babel myth invokes the dream of a unified, nonalienated world—a return to the garden before knowledge of good and evil. It renders what people had, one language/one imagination, inaccessible to them while demonizing their multiple languages/imaginations. People find themselves on the sharp horns of a cosmic dilemma. They are denied one language for their activities because it makes them Godlike, but they must despise their multiple language condition because that condition further divides them from God and each other. This is powerful stuff. It becomes easy to see how a longing to return to one language would develop and be sustained. Yet the Babel myth ignores a fundamental reality.

As complex a project as the building of the Tower of Babel would be, one language and imagination could not achieve it. For people, its building would require multiple languages and imagined activities: architecture; stone-hauling and stone-masonry; levels and balances; drainage; the carpentry of braces, forms, wood, straw, and mud; and political and social organization, to name a few. Stone masons, then and now, talk the work they do; if Vygotsky is to be accepted, they think their talk, and the language they use as professionals in a real sense guides their activities. The same is true of architects, plumbers, and carpenters. Although it might not be as true for tower builders then as it is now, certainly specialists would have been necessary then as they are now. Without them, the Tower could never have been conceived, let alone built. Also required would be some collaborative language, a means through which specialists communicate with each other, as the Tower is being conceived and constructed.

Of course these observations ignore the point of the myth: People should not build towers to reach God and lose themselves (and God) in the process. Yet the comments mean to introduce another point. Only in a prefallen world would one language/one imagination suitably manage human affairs, problems, and projects. In Paradise, without much to know or do except bask in joy, without tasks much more complicated than plucking the sweetest apple (being careful which one), people and their problems would seem to require little language and imagination at all. Yet the Tower, of course, was begun in a postfallen world. The Genesis writers may have missed that point. The postfallen world and perhaps especially the postmodern world, full as it is of complex problems, projects, and dangers, demands specialists and their languages.

The conflicted message sent by the Babel myth is as contradictory for professionals within the academy as it is for the general population to which it originally referred. For the purposes of my text, no one label, except perhaps the *Ivory Tower*, has been more frequently applied to our colleges and universities than the *Tower of Babel*. They are, indeed, composed of numerous disciplinary voices—voices that often seem unable to communicate with one another. Even within the same academic hallways and departments, linguists baffle literary critics; conservation biologists confuse evolutionary biologists; and music theorists befuddle musicians—principally because of separations between professional discourses. These voices are close disciplinary neighbors. Yet when we expand the neighborhood to include biologists conversing with English teachers, marketing teachers with those in mining engineering, and so on, and doing so in the language of their work, we find the possibility of communication diminishing to a point akin to English speakers seeking a public restroom in Hanoi. As English speakers, they may have to find, double fast, another place for relief.

The lesson of the Tower of Babel appears evident everywhere in postsecondary education. As academics we *are* mostly unable to talk to one another, at least in the languages of our work. And, if we abide by the Babel lesson, this condition is not a good thing. Because of the metaphor's implications for chaos, cacophony, and arrogance, and because of its traditional Christian and Hebraic interpretations, it is almost always applied to postsecondary systems in a negative way: "That money-wasting Tower of Babel up there on the hill is full of jargon-spouting prima donnas who, by the way, only work fifteen hours a week." I have some sympathy for the myth's lesson of what we have lost—the one language and one imagination. A part of me—perhaps the Wordsworth devotee—wishes we could somehow return to such a condition in the academy and beyond. However, I acknowledge that we cannot and that we must discontinue trying. Consequently, I want to propose a revision of the Tower of Babel's lesson as it is applied to the postsecondary academy, making its application much more positive.

Unflattering applications of the Babel metaphor to colleges and universities may amuse, but they can hardly be termed *fair*. The arena (and reality) of these institutions is disciplinization and development of expertise. They must, through the teaching and research of their faculty, ritualize the word and fix roles for speakers (Foucault, 1972). Specialization, as David Russell (1991) observed, has become "the fundamental organizing principle of modern education and, behind that, of modern knowledge itself" (p. 31). As institutions, their activities might generally be termed *higher order problem solving*, and complex problem solving requires the assimilation of complex languages. This process of assimilation, taking a system into the mind and thoroughly comprehending it, may not separate us too much. For example, it is easier to become a waiter than a music theorist, easier to become an auto mechanic (maybe not—who understands what their mechanics are telling them?) than a chemical physicist. The lower down on the *specialist food chain* (and I do not use this term accidently; prestige, power, impact, and money often depend on one's placement on the specialist food chain), the more possible common communication becomes. Yet the problems, projects, and dangers with which I am concerned here, and the people trained to address them, are high on the chain. As teachers and researchers, they speak, write, and think in languages that separate and even isolate them into smaller and smaller groups. As a critical requirement of their jobs, they teach their students to speak, write, and think in these languages, helping them to develop increasingly sophisticated cognitive behaviors. Perhaps proportionately, the more evolved the expertise, the smaller the group with which it can be shared.

"Abstract Triple Proportion" or "First Excited Singlet"

I offer here two examples—the first a paragraph from the *Journal of Music Theory* and the second from *Chemical Physics Letters*—to amplify the point of separation and isolation. They were originally selected at random from the periodicals section of the University of Nevada library to help introduce the concept of difference between the languages of disciplines to my graduate students in our WAC theory and practice course. The reader need only scan a few sentences of each.

The first is from the *Journal of Music Theory*:

> Example 6a observes that set 5 is the T5-transpose of set 4, just as set 2 is the T5-transpose of set 1, just as set 1 is the T5-transpose of set 3: the I-labels then follow, given that sets 4 and 5 are inversions of sets 1-2-3. The left-to-right aspect of the visual display conflicts with the chronological order in which sets 1-2-3 are projected by the music. The particular display for example 6a was constructed so as to emphasize as strongly as possible the abstract triple proportion among sets 3, 1 and 2, making the T5-relation a consistent visual motif. Just so, one could arrange nodes marked "dominant," "tonic" and "subdominant" in left-to-right visual order on the page, even though some actual music which these categories addressed in an analysis proceed I IV V in chronological time, rather than V I IV. The structuring effect of T5 here is suggestive in connection with the T5 interval for the aborted sequence within the chorale, a sequence which will later be unleashed as described in note 3. (Lewin, 1994, p. 82)

If this music theory paragraph is readily accessible to my readers, if the paragraph sings for them, I offer now the chemistry paragraph, which, I have been told by more than one chemist, is from a generalist journal. Here is the article's opening paragraph and a quarter:

> There is much current interest in large molecule photodissociation dynamics involving many degrees of freedom and multiple electronic potential energy surfaces. The photofragmentation of the nitrosoalkanes provides an experimentally accessible class of molecules for which the influences of structural and electronic complexity can be investigated in a systematic way. The general features of the gas- and condensed-phase photochemistry of alkyl nitroso compounds are well understood [1-5]. Excitation of the S S (n) transition of the alkyl nitroso compounds in the 600-700 nm wavelength region leads to dissociation to nitric oxide and an alkyl radical fragment. The lowest, metastable vibrational levels of the first excited singlet electronic state of the nitrosoalkanes have a high fluorescence quantum yield and are only weakly predissociative; excitation at shorter wavelengths results in dissociation with a high quantum yield.
>
> Previous spectroscopic studies of gas-phase (CH), CNO, CF, NO, and CCIF NO near their S S origins show resolvable vibrational structure primarily involving C-N-O bending and torsional motions. This vibrational structure disappears at shorter wavelengths as dissociation becomes the dominant relaxation pathway. (Tomer, Wall, Reid, & Cline, 1993, p. 286)

I am sure that most readers had trouble reading even a few sentences of these paragraphs. Although the words are English, each paragraph requires people to absorb a highly specialized discourse to understand it. Note in the music paragraph, for example, the words "constructed so as to emphasize as strongly as possible the abstract triple proportion among sets 3, 1 and 2," or from the chemistry paragraph, "vibrational levels of the first excited singlet electronic state." These quotes are from simpler sentences. The words by themselves have meaning for the reader, of course. Yet when one word is combined with only two more words (e.g., *abstract triple proportion* or *first excited singlet*), they become more obscure and community based. Could someone from outside the discipline imitate these languages? Probably, but that imitation would not be more meaningful than a non-German speaker imitating Bavarian German. He or she might say the words and combine them, but do not let a native speaker ask a question. To those who do not use and think in the language, the paragraphs probably appear so alien in their diction and syntax, so agglutinated in their conceptual presentation, as to become incomprehensible. (Appendix A has five more examples that demonstrate the same effect out of literally thousands of pages readily available.)

To bring the discussion closer to home, three questions surface. First, are these passages actually doing the work of their disciplines or merely, as Peter

Elbow (1998) might have characterized them, doing "academic jive" (p. 162)? Second, could these writers do their work in a plainer, more personally emphatic language, say, in Elbow's "street language" (p. 162)? For now the answer to the first question is enfolded in the second. It took a composition graduate student working in collaboration with one of the writers of the chemistry article 11 double-spaced pages to represent the last sentence quoted ("This vibrational structure disappears at shorter wavelengths as dissociation becomes the dominant relaxation pathway," given the context of what comes before and after) in a way that might be understood beyond the discipline. They both agreed, after their grueling effort, that the translation did not do the same work as the paragraph does.

The third question is, do readers view these paragraphs as good writing? My own answer is that they probably do not if they judge the paragraphs by the values offered by UNR's English Department assessment committee, discussed in chapters 1 and 7, or by the values forwarded in the text *What Makes Writing Good* (Coles & Vopat, 1985). Composition specialists might have genuine difficulty labeling the writing *good*, whatever else they might call it. This suggests a problem I address in the text's first chapter. What makes writing good in one discipline certainly does not make it good in another. If composition is developing the experts in writing theory and pedagogy, members of an emerging field as Stephen North entitled it in 1987; if composition often teaches first-year writing to all students; if it houses WAC and writing assessment programs, then it should be highly conscious that its values, purposes, and forms for writing are community-based, not universal. It should teach its graduate students that those values are community-based, not universal.

My audience for the WAC seminar is usually MA and PhD candidates in English's rhetoric and composition program, fresh with enthusiasm for studying and teaching writing, committed in varying degrees to the theories and practices provided by their mentors. Generally, they have received no information concerning difference in disciplinary languages, and they cheerfully enter the composition community believing (or not caring or insisting) that what they teach in their composition classes translates into the writing world out there. Largely, they have no idea about the operations of universities, which ultimately lead students to the diction, syntax, and codification of such paragraphs as the music and chemistry paragraphs. Nor can they believe or accept (not, at least, on the first day of the seminar) that universities should be leading their students to write these paragraphs. They believe, not surprisingly, that universities should not be doing so.

Outside one group, even within the institution, expressions of expertise must sound much like babel to another group. They are condemned as such by some members of the composition community and elsewhere. Not only are these languages railed against as babel, but as despoilers of a student's real self and voice, as students conform to the dictates of a particular literacy education. Consequently, the Genesis dilemma for postsecondary institutions occurs when they do what they are designed to do and then are demonized from the inside and out for doing it. Accompanying this condition of demonization is the mythologizing or valorizing of the one language/one imagination scenario with a disjointed effort to return institutions to *one voice fits all* through many first-year writing sequences, some writing across the curriculum programs, and almost all writing assessment instruments.

Rethinking the Myth of the Tower of Babel

The time spent railing against this tower, designing programs to tear it down and build another, would be better spent accepting specialized languages not as demons, but as a reality and necessity. Should colleges and universities create specialists? The question is moot. To do so is the desire, design, and purpose of these institutions. This process, beyond its reality, is necessary for solving serious and threatening problems. For example, we cannot hope to disarm a nuclear missile safely without the specialized languages approaching the complexity necessary to build it. In an example closer to my home, we cannot hope to design and create tunnels in Nevada's Yucca Mountain, meant to store the nation's nuclear waste safely, without the languages of hydrology, engineering, biology, chemistry, mining, plumbing, and welding (the list is far longer) *and* without at least an awareness of the languages that generate those wastes. As I revise this chapter after September 11, we cannot hope to dismantle terrorist structures without the particularly applied languages of international politics, sociology, and the military (among many others), and without at least some awareness of the language and culture of terrorism. Application of specialized languages has created many of the problems we face, it is true. Yet it is at least as true that only application of specialized languages will solve them. To continue to build through these languages without a venue of collaboration and conscious reflection, however, will lead to profoundly unattractive consequences, just as conscious reflection without the expertise of a discipline will lead to equally unattractive (or no) results.

Hence, I propose a rethinking of the myth of the Tower of Babel when applied to postsecondary educational systems. As a cross-curricular writing consultant, I accept these systems for what they are, and I will do what I can to nourish their discourse activities. I want to help faculty to design assignments that fit within their classes, disciplines, and cultures. I also want to promote collaborative discourse within and between disciplines beneath an umbrella of conscious reflection.

Collaboration is a basic pedagogic technique in writing classrooms. Since (and before) Kenneth Bruffee's (1984) influential article "Collaborative Learning and the 'Conversation of Mankind,'" compositionists have used group projects and problem-solving activities. So important has the pedagogy of collaboration become that it has expanded into a school of composition (Howard, 2001). Most compositionists recognize that, in the world of professional activity, collaboration is the norm and often produces better results than individual activity. What is not recognized as a norm is the notion of *conscious reflection*. In a simplified sense, this means that the developing specialist might reflect, "I know how to build it; I have the language to do so. But whose help do I require to do it well? And then, should I be doing it at all? What will the consequences be to me, to my field, to those beyond me and my field? Do the benefits of what I now do outweigh its deficits to me, to us, and to those in the future?" There exist only a few disciplinary contexts, only a few programmatic endeavors, that ask the question seriously, "Should I be doing it?"

I point here briefly to one disciplinary context—engineering—that makes an effort to instill reflective consciousness in its students. I quote the substance of its fundamental canons now with the promise of developing it in chapter 8, my book's conclusion:

The Fundamental Canons

1. Engineers shall hold paramount the safety, health, and welfare of the public in the performance of their professional duties.
2. Engineers shall perform services only in the areas of their competence.
3. Engineers shall continue their professional development throughout their careers and shall provide opportunities for the professional and ethical development of those engineers under their supervision.
4. Engineers shall act in professional matters for each employer or client as faithful agents or trustees, and shall avoid conflicts of interest or the appearance of conflicts of interest.
5. Engineers shall build their professional reputation on the merit of their services and shall not compete unfairly with others.
6. Engineers shall associate only with reputable persons or organizations.
7. Engineers shall issue public statements only in an objective and truthful manner.
8. Engineers shall consider environmental impact in the performance of their professional duties.

Three points rise in importance for me among these eight: one ("the safety, health, and welfare of the public"), three (the ongoing professional and ethical development of engineers), and eight ("environmental impact in the performance of their duties"). The engineering student who gave me these canons claimed that they receive emphatic treatment in a variety of contexts and classes. Yet I make no claim that all, or even most, engineers abide by these principles in doing their work. My claim now is only that a formal, programmatic effort is being made and that any thinking about ethical behavior is better than no thinking. All academic disciplines need to consider the creation of a Fundamental Canon governing their behaviors.

Writing to Learn Versus Learning to Write

The metaphor of the Tower of Babel means to tantalize us with what we have lost through our own hubris—the one language and imagination that makes all things possible, except becoming as God. Although people might desire this condition, it is hardly the basis on which to run a university or develop secular knowledge in the contemporary world. Yet this urge for one language has not declined. It makes disciplinary languages the objects of babel myths and metaphors. What should specialists in rhetoric and composition, specialists in writing centers, writing across the curriculum, and writing assessment be doing given that they face towers of babel—institutions within which often seemingly insurmountable differences in expertise and its expression exist between disciplines? What should they be doing given that the values, purposes, and forms for writing differ? It is helpful when composition studies expands its image of the writing world beyond a field-limited perspective, looking beyond its singular frames for writing process and product. A tendency exists in a limited field to view values for writing as givens, to mistake the particular in writing for the general, and that tendency can lead to an imposition of values. It is helpful when experts in writing pedagogy resist imposing their values for writing on faculty in other disciplines and search instead for the values and goals of their colleagues. Imposing values and even languages across the curriculum has a Jehovah-like quality—people return themselves to one language community, when the writers of Genesis mandated that they could not and global reality mitigates against it. Such an event has little hope of succeeding now, not at least before the planet is decimated by overpopulation, fuel source depletion, pollution infringement, political disagreements large and small, and, if not those, then planetary heat. Hence, composition specialists, WAC, and writing assessment personnel would be prudent to let go of their own image of what is right for language and writing and begin to

act more globally and collectively. They should develop their own Fundamental Canons.

I admire McLeod and Maimon (2000) in their "Clearing the Air: WAC
Myths and Realities." Yet I think their article also points to one of the most
significant problems with WAC as it is generally practiced today. McLeod
and Maimon countered Daniel Mahala's "claims that WAC theory is not but
should be involved in a profound 'institutional critique' of knowledge and
curricula in practice, bringing about a challenge to 'prevailing institutional
divisions, faculty interests, and dominant forms of knowledge-making' " (p.
578). Mahala endorsed a one-language/one-imagination scenario for WAC
by arguing that its main purpose should be to critique and challenge the institutional structures it was actually designed to support. Whatever its appeal,
Mahala's argument pursues a lost cause. As McLeod and Maimon pointed
out, it is the wrong purpose for WAC. His WAC, with its heavy-handed
ideological agenda, amounts to storming the Tower's barricades. As with
other WAC programs with such agendas, it must alienate more than invite
faculty into the writing enterprise across campus. Mahala argued from a field-
limited perspective; whatever his vision of WAC proposes to do, it will not
cross the curriculum. Thus, I admire McLeod's and Maimon's insistence that
WAC interaction with faculty take place not through force of arms, but from
the grassroots: "as any agent of change knows, change cannot be forced; faculty are independent agents with their own agendas" (p. 578); faculty engage
in WAC workshops because "they want to improve their teaching, because
they want to help their students . . ." (p. 578). Taking some risks in this argument, the McLeod/Maimon article largely reflected institutional reality and
faculty motivation for engaging in WAC, which happens when faculty perceive WAC to help them and their students.

Nonetheless, I note the tone with which McLeod and Maimon (2000) began and then proceeded in their essay: "As pioneers in the field, we know the
WAC territory because we have explored and helped to map it inch by inch."
"We know," they repeated mere words later, "the field" (p. 573). Maybe they
do, but they are clearly angry with the upstart Mahala, as any reader of tone
will hear, and other demons of his ilk. Because of their experience and history
with WAC, they represent their approach as *the* approach to WAC interaction with faculty in the disciplines. After their opening, in an immodest example of irony, they do what Mahala did, promoting an ideological agenda
for WAC, although theirs fits within composition studies much more comfortably than his. Explaining what they determine is Mahala's false
dichotomizing of the " 'American WAC theory,' which he divides into
'expressivist' and 'formalist' schools," they insisted that "these two categories
are misrepresentations of the two complementary rather than competing

views of WAC in the literature . . . —what we have called in this essay 'writing to learn' and 'learning to write in the discipline' " (p. 577).

Many WAC scholars support this notion of complementarity between these views in the sense that they believe writing to learn supplies what learning to write in the disciplines lacks, or that the former completes the latter. What I hope to show is that, although the two may not be contradictory, they are not complementary. Writing to learn has it roots in *process-expressivism*, defined by its combination of "journal writing, workshops, in-class free writing, expressive writing, writing as process" (Jones & Comprone, 1993, p. 66) and exercises requiring personal, authentic, and creative responses to course and material (Bean, 1996). Learning to write in the *disciplines*, if the term is understood to subsume "learning discipline-specific discourse conventions," means learning and writing in the language of the student's discipline with its own values, purposes, and forms for writing. Learning to write, by definition, belongs to all disciplines. Writing to learn is a set of values for writing developed largely in the context of the discipline of composition studies. It belongs mostly to one discipline. Not shared across the disciplines, it cannot complement learning to write. When our assessment program asked faculty in eight departments to list their values for writing, none but English listed any of the values that can be characterized as process-expressivist. For example, *voice* only appeared on the English list.

In "Where Do We Go Next in Writing Across the Curriculum," which I examine in some detail in chapter 3, Jones and Comprone (1993) more than implied that if we want to sustain process-expressivist values for writing across campus, they may have to be forced into classes, and Jones and Comprone seemed to advocate force. In WAC workshops, the effort to oblige writing to learn to complement learning to write produces mixed results at best, and opens disciplinary conflicts at worst. Thus, I wish to situate this text at a point of edge where "learning to write in the disciplines" nudges "writing to learn" off the Tower and out of WAC practice or perhaps less emphatically stated: to make "writing to learn" an option rather than a requirement for faculty who want to assign writing. Beyond that, I want to show how WAC programs can be developed by engaging faculty at the point of their primary interests: their own goals for learning in their classes and the relationship of that learning to the broader interests of their disciplines.

As a now identifiable field, composition should open itself to the need for multiple languages and the possibility of their positive consequences. At least with regard to WAC, it should work not from its own agenda, but within the writing agendas of the disciplines. Composition is well placed to do so given the increasing acknowledgment of its expertise. It is also situated to consider how some formal application of a language of collaboration and consequence, of stewardship and agency, might be created within a healthy Tower of Babel. Given that composition appears intent on building its own section in the Tower, its own specialization, however, the question becomes, Will it reach beyond its values for writing in working with others? The answer is, as yet, unknown. At present, composition studies appears regrettably homebound, focused on creating its own disciplinary specialization. This process could mark the end of it—not as Stephen North prophesied from internal struggles between specialists, but because of the irrelevance of those struggles to other disciplines and the immediate need for problem solving overall.

1

First-Year English, Graduate Programs in Composition Studies, and Writing Across the Curriculum: In the Tower Wobbling

Imagine that you are a biology teacher interested in including a writing assignment in one of your courses. You go to a workshop on effective assignment design offered by a panel of experts in writing theory and pedagogy from the English Department. As a new faculty member, you are nervous because, although you have heard about the value of writing to learning and are committed (vaguely) to that concept, you do not know much about assigning and grading writing. You also worry that assigning writing may affect your teaching time and especially your research time, thus potentially compromising your tenure. Settling into the room, you hear by way of introduction the following from one member of the panel: "I often work professionally with those in other disciplines, but I confess that my PhD in English literature has so confirmed a particular discourse community that I routinely . . . find it hard to respect the scholarship of nonliterary communities" (White, 1990, p. 191). From another you hear that "discipline-specific writing [the writing you want your students to do] encourages both conformity and submission" (Spellmeyer, 1989, p. 266), leading to "a pervasive lack of commitment" (p. 271) because it does not allow students "to enter a discipline by finding their own voices" (p. 275). Students might work hard, this speaker continues, to comply with your community's "rules and fulfill its expectations," but too often are left with "nothing of [their] own to say" (p. 271).

Your third and fourth consultants tell you that, in your biology course, the writing experience should combine "journal writing, workshops, in-class free writing, expressive writing" with "discipline-specific discourse conventions"

(Jones & Comprone, 1993, p. 66). Others endorse that point of view by asserting that writing to learn practices complement learning to write in your discipline (McLeod & Maimon, 2000). The most esteemed member of this panel tells you that academic discourse is "author-evacuated prose" (p. 157) and continues emphatically: "Putting it crassly, students can do academic work even in street language—and indeed using the vernacular helps show whether the student is doing real intellectual work or just using academic jive" (Elbow, 1991, p. 162). Academic writing, he asserts, is not writing that does "real intellectual work." Instead, it is *academic jive*. It is "stylistic conventions" and "surface features" (p. 163). The last consultant explains to you why these experts are the best folks to be telling you what to do. She observes that English departments should control WAC because of their "expertise in the study of the construction and the reception of texts" (Smith, 1988, p. 391). English faculty, she continues, understand and care about the writing process more than you do. They have informed themselves in composition theory, and, because of your lack of expertise, your efforts will be "blundering" (Smith, 1988, p. 391).

These quotes suggest a degree of field-limited vision, which calls even their authenticity into question. Although I have made up the context, the quotes are real. Each of them appears in articles published in journals that rarely reach an audience beyond literary/composition specialists, and so none of the writers would expect to have these sentiments read by those who might emphatically disagree or feel discounted by them. Each of these writers does WAC consulting work with faculty across the disciplines, although few would speak this directly to you, as a biology teacher, at one of their workshops.

If you heard these comments in your effort to include writing in your biology class or classes, would you feel inspirited and enfranchised to use writing? The answer is, probably not. You would rightly feel alienated because some of the opinions are offensive to you and the values are inconsistent with those of your discipline. Within the context of this fictional scenario, the workshop leaders do not seem much aware of these qualities *as* values or, aware of them as values, they endorse them as universal. If form were the only matter of concern here, if "discipline-specific discourse conventions" were the only difference between these experts and you to be negotiated, the issue would be serious enough. However, the differences lay much deeper than that. They reflect, as anthropologist Geertz (1983) argued, "ways of being in the world" (p. 155). Maturing in a discipline, he observed, evolves "varieties of noetic experience" or "forms of life" (p. 155). To do the work of a discipline "is not just to take up a technical task but to take on a cultural frame that defines a great part of one's life" (p. 155). As a biology teacher, you may not be conscious that professional/academic biology is a defining cultural frame—a way of being in the world, a form of life. You are probably not aware that your workshop leaders have also taken on a defining cultural frame that guides their interaction with you. Nonetheless, you know that something is wrong and that they do not seem to be speaking to you.

I recognize the subjectiveness of removing quotes from their context and inserting them into a fictional scenario, but I do so to make a point. As WAC consultants and trainers of potential WAC consultants, we have a serious responsibility to acknowledge the differences in languages, and in the values, purposes, and forms for writing our clientele may have, and to organize our consultancy in ways that address those differences.

The Case for Difference and Its Implications for WAC

The fact of difference evidences itself regularly to me and other Writing Center personnel as we conduct our discipline-based writing assessment project at UNR. This project tracks the writing that junior and then senior students (the project's apparatus, process, and results are described in chap. 7) from selected departments during a 2-year period. The first three semesters are devoted to reading and ranking individual papers, the last semester to papers collected in portfolios. Yet at the beginning of every interaction with a new department, after explaining the project, the first question we ask of committee members is to list their own and their discipline's values for academic/professional writing. The project is obviously labor intensive, and thus far we have worked with only eight departments: Criminal Justice, Electrical Engineering, Political Science, Accounting/Computer Science, Curriculum and Instruction, Nursing, Biology, and English. I want to focus here on English and Biology and their respective values for writing.

When asked to share their values, English Department assessment committee members offered the following:

- Voice—the expression of the writer's self in the piece of writing
- Independence—thinking demonstrated in the writing that distinguishes it from the writing of others (students "take their own stand," one faculty member said, "articulate their own view of things.")
- Meta-consciousness of language (intentional use of diction, syntax, and rhetorical figures, etc.)
- Vividness of detail; originality
- Awareness of rhetorical purpose and audience

- Evidence of thinking critically (effective summary, interpretation, analysis, argumentation)
- Few or no sentence-level problems

For me and my Center colleague on the committee, this list was powerful. We felt at home with it, and it is consistent with the values discussed in the work of many scholar/teachers in composition studies deservedly admired (including Murray, Emig, Harris, Elbow, Newkirk, Ronald).

Yet it is quite different from what we heard from the Biology committee, which values:

- Clarity in statement of purpose (the paper's abstract includes a clearly stated hypothesis)
- Adherence to appropriate form (report writing contains the following sections: abstract, introduction, methods and materials, discussion, and conclusion) and placement of correct material in pertinent sections
- Coherent integration of secondary sources
- Accurate citation of secondary sources
- Accurate depiction of graphs and tables
- Evidence of thinking critically (problem solving, data analysis and interpretation, argumentation)
- Evident commitment to experiment and to written description
- Few or no sentence-level errors

The biologists want writing that is clear in its statement of purpose. They expect formulaic writing, accurate citations and graphs, and few or no sentence-level problems. Shared between these lists are three abstractions: commitment, coherence, and thinking critically; and one specific: few or no sentence-level errors. What really distinguishes the lists are their differences: emphasis on voice, independence, intentionality, and originality in the English list; and emphasis on clarity, formula, and accuracy in the Biology list. Without a doubt, I prefer English's values, and I teach to them in my writing classes. As a WAC consultant, however, I acknowledge these differences as values inherent to communities, with one list not superior to another. To return, briefly, to the scenario of the biologist seeking help from the panel of writing experts, I ask the reader to consider herself, as an English teacher, in the biologist's position. If Biology held sway over writing on campus, how would she feel attending a workshop and hearing that her "students' writing must adhere to the appropriate form" and "it needs accurate depictions of graphs and tables"? "What?", she might respond, just as the biologist might to her. Our work in tutoring, cross-curricular writing consultancy, and assess-ment confirms, unqualifiedly, that "Finding ways to harness the efforts of the disciplines—where the faculty's primary loyalty and interest lie—will per-haps achieve more in the long run than structurally separate programs, no matter how well intentioned and financed" (Russell, 1991, p. 304).

The questions the lists imply, among many others, include the following: Is there a theory for cross-curricular writing consultancy that accommodates these differences? If so, what is that theory? Given the differences, is there a home for WAC? If so, where is that home? Given the differences and politi-cal pressure for testing, is there a model for standards and assessment that re-flects growth in disciplines while still measuring the effectiveness of student writing? This study argues the merits of a particular assessment strategy—one that reflects what postsecondary institutions (and the professions to which they send students) obviously are, differing language communities with dif-fering values for writing; and it strenuously opposes assessment models that judge student writers based on the mistaken notion that one instrument fits all—models that legislatures are likely to favor. Yet I also want to define a model for writing across the curriculum that precipitated a swelling use of writing assignments at two midlevel, public universities (Montana State and the University of Nevada–Reno), where, in the latter, writing is required in more than 90% of the undergraduate classes (phone survey of 400 faculty rep-resenting a third of the teachers from every department; see chap. 7). How did writing take hold? The answer lies in acknowledging, as Russell (1991) asserted, that differences "are not only inevitable but also, if we understand them correctly, invaluable as a means of constructing curricula and writing pedagogies that are responsive to the nuances and complexities of modern knowledge and social organization" (p. 33). The WAC programs at each of these schools was built out of a curriculum of accepting difference. A WAC curriculum of difference is becoming amply supported by the burgeoning re-search into writing communities undertaken by numerous scholars.

For example, Dias, Freedman, and Medway (1999) cited Lave and Wenger (1991), who described "a process called 'legitimate peripheral participation' to explain how newcomers 'inevitably participate in communities of practi-tioners and the mastery of knowledge and skill requires newcomers to move toward full participation in the sociocultural practices of the community' " (p. 30). In moving toward their own thesis, they also cited Brown et al. (1993), who argued "that by 'participating in the practices of scholarly re-search [children] should be enculturated into the community of scholars dur-ing their 12 or more years of apprenticeship in school settings' " (p. 30). The thesis of Dias et al. then affirms their research: "In the analysis that follows, we show how in writing specific genres elicited in their university classes, student writers came to adopt the intellectual postures (e.g., the modes of argumentation, the constructions of reality) of scholars in that field; in this sense the writing was epistemic—enabling students to see the world, and to categorize reality, in new ways and ways characteristic of specific disciplines" (p. 48). Locating their study, they observed, "Insights into this learning were provided both through textual analysis of student essays as well as through analyses of taped composing sessions . . ." (p. 48). Berkenkotter and Huckin (1995) observed, in another example, that "Learning the genres of disciplinary or professional discourse [is] similar to second language acquisition, requiring immersion into the culture and a lengthy period of apprenticeship and inculturation" (p. 13).

Some writers want students to have some influence on this process of appropriation of discourse. For example, Prior (1998) observed that his "microhistory of mediated authorship suggests how relative newcomers to disciplines change as they appropriate discourses and practices . . . but it also suggests how such newcomers, especially at such key sites like major research institutions, might exert their own centripetal force as their ideologies are dialogically received and accommodated as well as offered" (p. 243). Newcomers to disciplines inevitably *change* as they appropriate discourses and practices. Prior suggested that students might have something important to say as they change: Students "might exert their own centripetal force as their ideologies are dialogically received and accommodated." Beginning her chapter "Literacy and the Nature of Expertise" in *Academic Literacy and the Nature of Expertise*, Geisler (1994) remarked on the surprising difference, with regard to academic writing, between the practices of experts and novices. She and her colleagues expected to find "a developmental continuum with professional practices at one end and student practices spread out across the other." What they found, however, suggests that "the two sets of practices are substantially different in character" (p. 81), with experts creating and transforming knowledge and novices "getting and displaying" knowledge. Dias et al. asserted that the social motive of student writing is twofold: On the one hand, it is epistemic—enabling students to learn to use language "in ways valorized in specific disciplines" (p. 47). "Because disciplines differ," they continued, "disciplinary courses tend to elicit writing that is at once homogenous (within that class) and also distinctive (as compared to the writing of the same students for other courses)" (p. 47). The epistemic motive, however, is complicated by "the existence of another motive for eliciting writing," the sorting and ranking of students. According to Dias et al., "the two impulses often exist in uneasy tension" (p. 47).

Geisler and Dias suggested a bifurcation in the use of writing in the academy. First, writing becomes an essential medium for entering the cognitive life of a discipline; second, in the case of Geisler, there appears to be a cognitive disconnect between what experts do with writing and what they expect their students to be doing with it. By implication at least, she would like that disconnection to end. For Dias et al., student writing is often used to rank and sort students within disciplines, and such a ranking and sorting motive exists in "uneasy tension," a nice phrase, with the motive to bring the work of the discipline cognitively to life for students. I agree with Prior that students, if located in dialogic situations, have much to say as they evolve in their disciplines. I agree with Geisler that what faculty expect of student writing is too often disconnected from their own use of it, and sometimes in ways (because assignments fail to acknowledge their linguistic and cognitive levels) that place students at a severe disadvantage. I also agree with Dias et al. that, along with admirable and necessary motives, writing is often used to rank and sort.

I further accept that entry into the language and culture of a discipline may be a fear-inspiring activity. One of the subjects of Kirsch's (1993) study of *Women Writing the Academy*, "a full professor of anthropology," remarked of moving into the writing and reading life of another discipline:

> When you're working in an interdisciplinary area such as I am trying to do, you have to become like a child in the other field. I may be an adult in anthropology, but I am a child in the field of technology innovation. So I'm trying to learn that field and incorporate its theory with anthropological theory and reflect it back to experts in a way that seems authoritative. *It scares me. I'm constantly uncomfortable.* I have to read more and more sources. It leads to an overload [of reading] in order to establish authority in a new field. (p. 106)

By extension, when students enter a disciplinary context, their experience is akin to second language acquisition. If a full professor is scared and uncomfortable with such movement, students must be especially so. This recent research confirms that (a) learning to write leads students to the language and cognitive behaviors of their chosen disciplines; (b) learning to write almost always includes the goal of assimilation, but it may be inconsistent in how it attempts to achieve that goal or it may serve to rank and sort; (c) people are afraid as they enter a new language community; and (d) any WAC/writing assessment program must incorporate these findings into its practice. The programs at Montana State and UNR confirm the accuracy of this literature. WAC should recognize the inevitability of specialization and its desirability.

It should also encourage more consistency between experts and novices, helping to establish a developmental continuum and lessening the use of writing to rank and sort students. These practices can ensure students' growth in the language and cognitive behaviors of a discipline while alleviating the fear such growth engenders.

What is meant here by the term *language?* How do all of these distinct language communities evolve? Language in this context is the system of diction, syntax, and usages shared by people as they speak, write, read, and so on in a particular academic discipline or profession. It is further the cognitive structures, critical thinking, and (even) affective patterns, the "ways of making meaning in the world," that emerge as a consequence of the individual's assimilation of language in a discipline or profession, its shared activities, history, and culture. Developmental psychology helps us understand how so many distinct disciplinary languages evolve.

Much groundwork has been laid to support the premise that language precedes thought. The most influential explanation of this sequence still comes from Vygotsky (1962), whose work builds on that of Piaget. Piaget, through intense observation of hundreds of children, documented the running commentary of infancy and childhood, the system of vocalization that the child assimilates from those in his or her environment and accompanies virtually all activity: play, familial interaction, and problem solving. As parents, few of us can ignore this commentary, listening to our young children talk as they move their toys from one position to another or try to explain to themselves how clouds rain, fire heats, and toilets flush. Those of us more wicked or playful have interrupted their commentary: "Hey, who are you talking to over there?" For our interference we have received severe rebukes. (In an extraordinary bit of comedy and evident insight into cognitive and language development, Steve Martin spoofed that parents should use the wrong words for things in their own conversation around the home, forever baffling their infants.) According to Piaget, when social speech develops in children, this running commentary—this egocentric speech—atrophies and fades away because it is no longer needed.

Vygotsky (1962) described an alternative outcome for the running commentary—an alternative profound in its implications for the teaching of writing generally and WAC particularly. Instead of atrophying, the running commentary turns inward, becoming an abbreviated and individuated code—the basis, Vygotsky argued, for all acts of cognition: "the decreasing vocalization of egocentric speech denotes a developing abstraction from sound, the child's new faculty to 'think words' instead of pronouncing them" (p. 135). His observations not only qualify Piaget, but they permanently counter the classical, traditional view of the relationship between language and thinking—a view that places thought before language, meaning and knowledge as elements "out there" to be clothed by language. Under this model, which, with few fits and starts, dominated notions of style, rhetoric, reading, writing, and speaking in the Western world for 2,000 years, language is subsidiary to thinking.

Vygotsky's (1962) findings demonstrate the primacy of language to thinking and the critical link between community and the growth of individual consciousness. They have been widely referenced by scholars in nearly every discipline, including composition studies. Yet it was Bazerman (1988), in a singular application of Vygotsky's work, who made it possible to see the language-into-thought perspective within its academic disciplinary context. I refer to his description of the developing chemistry major: "An important moment in the child's development for Vygotsky," Bazerman wrote,

> is when the child starts to develop an internal language so that these self-instructions, regulating the child's behavior, go underground becoming invisible to the observers and even eventually to the child. In this way, gradually the neophyte [chemistry major] becomes socialized into the semiotic-behavioral-perceptual system of the [chemistry] community with language taking a major and multivalent role in the organization of that system. . . . (pp. 306–307)

Specialized languages surround novices entering a community and, appropriated by them, eventually become abbreviated and individuated codes, the basis for their thinking in particular contexts. Of course, this process begins with the family. Yet by an extension Bazerman made obvious, it continues into every significant group to which the individual belongs, including academic disciplines.

Faculty are already immersed in a specific language as teachers and researchers within their discipline. As one of their professional duties, they guide students (declared majors certainly but in often confusing ways, nonmajors as well) into their specializations through many activities, including lecture, one-on-one dialogue and critique, classroom interaction, writing and reading assignments, individual and collaborative problem solving, and so on. To a large degree, the ability to mentor students determines a faculty person's success, and the ability to assimilate determines a declared major's success. This point is hardly controversial to anyone in the academy, at least on its surface.

Yet the lists of values for writing expressed by those in English and Biology suggest potential barriers and difficulties. At the top of the English list is "voice, the expression of the writer's self in a piece of writing" and second is "independence, thinking demonstrated in the writing which distinguishes it from the writing of others." At the top of the list for Biology is "clarity in statement of purpose" and then "adherence to appropriate form." The contrasts between these lists suggest many questions—questions that Vygotsky's explorations into the relationship of language to thinking begin to answer. For example, how could there be such disparity given that Biology and English are neighbors on the same campus? Do they each speak and write in English? Can we all write and speak in a way that is understandable to all of us? More abstractly, can we all think and solve problems in the same language? Most particularly, if each discipline has evolved its own participatory language, how can one discipline be responsible for the writing activities of all?

In large part, the contrast can be explained by the fact that the faculty members offering the lists have spent so many years within their respective disciplines. For these UNR committee members: as undergraduates (2–4 years plus), as graduate students (5–9 years plus), and as teachers and professionals (1–20 years plus). Becoming immersed, if we follow Vygotsky's reasoning, they have abbreviated and individuated their discipline's language. Their conceptions of writing have become ingrained, home-bound, and submerged beneath the level of critical consciousness.

Thus, a broad-minded and community-oriented biologist might tell a composition teacher, equally broad-minded and community-oriented, that her students seem to learn nothing about writing in first-year composition. She may also observe, "that first-year writing wants students to write in ways different from the way I want them to write." I do not doubt that students will learn something in general about writing in even the most value-laden of writing circumstances. Depending on the context of her comment, however, the biologist may be right. She does not list the development of voice as a quality she esteems in academic writing. If the composition classroom's primary focus is the development of voice, independence, and creativity, and the composition classroom is viewed within the English Department and the institution as a whole as preparing students to write across the curriculum, the biologist would not only be right in her comments, but right in registering a formal complaint. However, let us reverse the situation—have Biology with its list of values teach the university's writing course(s). Would the English Department then have reason to complain? To be sure. "Adherence to form," Biology's second criterion, means that essay writing must begin with an abstract, followed by an introduction, methods and materials section, discussion, and then conclusion. Few English teachers would find this pattern palatable having just, within the last 30 years, reversed the tradition of formulaic essay writing.

However, qualifiers are appropriate at this point. These lists are generated by faculty at only one university. (I encourage readers of this text to try a simple experiment: Gather two or more faculty from a given discipline and ask them for a list of characteristics they and their discipline value for student, academic, and professional writing. My hypothesis is that they will receive lists similar to those we have developed; similar or not, I would like to hear the results at waldo@unr.edu.) Other campuses may have composition programs that more closely approximate Biology's list and biology programs that approximate English's list. If I had shared the lists between committees at UNR, placed the two groups together, and insisted on consensus, such could probably be achieved (although how genuine it would be is open to debate). In other words, these lists are not inflexible commandments. I believe that one group could come closer to the other. Nonetheless, I hope the reader understands my point. As academics, we have spent an impressive number of years working with our discipline's language, using it in class and with each other, reading it in texts and writing it ourselves, and that process has specialized us—separated us. This fact, before any other, must be at the base of writing across the curriculum. If developmental psychology is right, if the burgeoning research into writing communities tells us anything, it is that WAC cannot treat everyone to the same set of values and expect lasting results. For lasting results, WAC needs to do what does not feel natural—leave its own community-based expectations at home and discover expectations in other communities.

One of the primary reasons for the existence of WAC, many used to observe, was that English departments could not be solely responsible for teaching writing. For students to improve as writers, responsibility must widen across campus. This observation, assuredly correct, mainly asserted how comparatively little writing students would do if limited to English classes, and it was meant to counter the wrong-headed notions that "teaching writing is English's job," "they're the experts." With the current understanding of faculty immersion into specialized languages and student initiation into them, the idea of English taking responsibility for teaching writing becomes not just wrong, but disarmingly naive. Composition teachers cannot teach biology students to write biology, chemistry students to write chemistry, accounting students accounting, or even history students history because they have not internalized the language, values, purposes, and forms for writing to do so. Clearly, faculty within those disciplines must teach their own students because they do have the language. Now what does this mean for developing a WAC program that insists on complementing learning to write with writing to learn, or a writing assessment program that measures the quality of student writing from one set of values or rubrics? It means that neither can be done with the kind of success for which we hope.

Writing Programs Housed in English Departments

Further, what does the preceding assertion mean to writing programs usually housed within English departments? To me the issue seems complicated and politically charged. It is complicated by such matters as requiring a first-year writing sequence and, at many institutions, advanced expository, technical, and professional writing courses. It is complicated by the advent of MA and PhD programs in rhetoric and composition, and by experts with English degrees teaching writing courses in other disciplines. It is politically charged by such questions as, Should first-year and other writing courses be required? Should English teachers be teaching "writing in engineering," "writing in the natural sciences," or "writing in business"? The least treated and most recent question is, What are all those successful MA and PhD programs in composition studies training their professionals to do? Given the real basis of WAC, where are those programs bound?

First-year writing programs may be clear about their sense of self and community. They may say directly that they have their own goals for the development of student writers; for example, that they want to return students to their selves and voices and not prepare them to write within the context of some other discipline (for a stimulating treatment of this argument, see Spellmeyer, 1989). They may acknowledge an agenda of their own, even that they have their own values, purposes, and forms for writing, and openly teach the art of the personal essay. Saying so, first-year writing frees itself from being what it cannot be—all skills in writing to all disciplines; and it counters its reputation as a service course. Yet doing so, it opens itself to other conflicts and questions: If it is its own course, then why teach it to every student, especially if it teaches from its own agenda? As an alternative, first-year writing may admit an agenda to itself: training its teachers and students in that context while not volunteering information about this process to the remainder of the campus. Of course, although widely practiced, this alternative may seem a little insidious. Another alternative is to attempt to mold the composition program in a way that crosses the curriculum.

In a recent definition of critical thinking, Bean (1996) made two compelling points: "To a large extent, these mental habits are discipline-specific, since each discipline poses its own kind of problems and conducts inquiries, uses data, and makes arguments in its own characteristic fashion. But some aspects of critical thinking are also generic across disciplines" (p. 3). In the early 1980s at Montana State University, John Bean and John Ramage put the abstraction "some aspects of critical thinking are also generic across disciplines" to the test by establishing a first-year writing program that publicly focused assignments on critical thinking. Students used writing to solve problems, analyze processes and information, examine opposing points of view, and make arguments.

As the amount of writing increased at Montana State into many hundreds of classes each term, veteran faculty suggested eliminating the first-year course as a requirement. Such a course was easy to defend, however, as relevant to students in all majors—because of its critical thinking emphasis. Other composition programs and courses are designed, through a critical thinking emphasis, to cross the curriculum (see Kirscht et al., 1994).

That some critical thinking skills "are generic across disciplines" is open to debate. Thinking in particular languages must certainly be the condition Bean had in mind when he remarked that "these mental habits are discipline-specific," and that process is more local than general. Yet some critical thinking behaviors may be generic across disciplines, as he also remarked. Whether these mental habits cross the disciplines or not, however, teachers in the disciplines largely think that they do. Including the Geography Department at UNR, eight lists of values for writing generated in the assessment project so far have included the development of critical thinking. If critical thinking crosses disciplines as a value for writing, then composition programs promoting it are certainly defensible. These types of courses, however, were not the norm then or now. If there is a norm for composition programs, it probably remains closer to the values of process–expressivism than any other: "Though radical departures for the time, many of these methods now constitute mainstream writing instruction" (Burnham, 2001, p. 22).

Faigley's detailed treatment of *What Makes Writing Good* (Coles & Vopat, 1985) suggests this difficulty; in creating this text, the editors "asked forty-eight teachers to contribute one example of student writing that 'in some way demonstrates excellence,' along with the writing assignment and a commentary explaining how the example is distinguished" (Faigley, 1995, p. 120). Faigley commented on the "range of student writing" considered. Thirty-eight of the essays picked by the contributors are either personal experience essays (30) or include "writing about the writer" (8). In his effort to explain the strong preference for expressive writing, he quoted several of the commentaries, which repeatedly emphasize that good writing is "honest," is expressed in an "authentic voice," and possesses "integrity"; good writing assumes that "individuals have a 'true self' and that the true self can be expressed in discourse" (p. 122). Faigley's summary statement about the autobiographical preferences of the contributors, "recognizing the sources of contradictory and incompatible discourses in student writing runs squarely against both the expressivist and rationalist traditions of teaching writing that deny the role of language in constructing selves" (p. 128), might be reconstituted this way: Expressivists believe in an authentic self—a self that exists before, independent of voice; good writing develops and expresses that self, its voice. Contradictory and incompatible discourses stifle and perhaps repel that voice. Therefore, those discourses become, to put it kindly, less good. Harris (1996) is more pointed than Faigley in his treatment of *What Makes Writing Good*. He observed that several of the essays "seem to have been chosen precisely because they conform so closely and well to that familiar genre of school prose, the personal essay" (p. 33). Very soon after, in an assertion relevant to WAC, he remarked that personal essays "are all as much *social* [his emphasis] forms as the business letter, the scholarly article, and the five paragraph theme" (p. 34). I assume Harris' term *social* means that these essays are generated by a communal language and way of making meaning in the world, not, as may be hoped or pretended, an individual one.

The problems suggested by Faigley and Harris, I hope, are evident. First, the book implies that what it defines as good writing is not only good for English teachers, but good for everyone. Second, the 48 teachers chosen to make their selections and commentaries are an influential group within English studies generally and composition studies particularly. They include Corbett, Britton, Lunsford, Murray, Bleich, D'Angelo, Irmsher, Shor, Young, Lindemann, and Tchudi. Even within the context of teaching writing in English composition courses, the exclusivity of their definition of good writing strikes me as debatable. Yet their opinions extend deeply and broadly into an emerged specialization—composition studies. They are writers of composition scholarship and readers of it. They teach composition, and they train novice writing teachers.

Training composition teachers meant something different 30 years ago than it does now. In the past, their training was less systematic perhaps because composition teaching was considered drudgery, beneath the serious attention of literature faculty and their graduate students (Hirsch, 1982). Training did exist, but I think it is safe to say that composition teachers and their classrooms were then less focused on student writing (and more focused on literature) than they are now. Now novice composition teachers are trained by seasoned specialists, and the training suggests some significant concerns. If these specialists train them in the limited perspective suggested by *What Makes Writing Good*, largely process-expressivist, then writing teachers in English will ask for and grade on values different from other disciplines. In other words, their course will not cross the curriculum. Should it, can it, cross the disciplines? If composition is, in fact, training students out of its own set of values, then why should it be required of all students?

Before answering, I want to further compound the problem, in its already unfortunate complexity, by inserting two more issues: the creation of advanced degrees in composition studies and the unique position English holds to act on its values. Advanced degrees in rhetoric and composition require the assimilation of a particular language that generates a specialized approach to writing and its teaching. It has institutionalized a nomenclature and created a new academic culture. Over the years, hundreds of terms such as *current-traditional, organic* and *mechanic, process approach, expressive, experiential, cognitive, social rhetorical, the five-star theme, growing and cooking, Engfish, recursive, metacognitive, writing to learn, learning to write, writing for the self, the other, voice,* and *originality* have become saturated with meaning with regard to the teaching of writing. As is necessary to establish an academic culture, this nomenclature became abbreviated and individuated in the professional, in his or her ability to think words instead of pronouncing them. Hence, as a specialization in composition studies evolved, first-year writing became the laboratory for the new discipline to test its assumptions. In most cases, it was a *fait accompli* that these assumptions would cross the curriculum in a practical sense because of the requirement of the first-year writing sequence. It is certainly questionable whether these assumptions cross the curriculum in any other sense, as I hope the lists of values held by differing disciplines shows in chapter 7.

As Harris (1996) remarked in his treatment of voice in A *Teaching Subject*: "we should not downplay the extent to which work in our field has long been infected with a kind of missionary zeal" (p. 25). I think Harris is talking mainly about a zeal within the rhetoric/composition/English community, but certainly the point applies, and with greater force of consequence, across the curriculum. From my perspective, there is little wrong with the deployment of composition's values for writing within the English community. When the deployment extends into WAC theory and practice, and then with a missionary zeal, it becomes problematic. In the academy, we remain confused about this issue.

English departments and their faculty members have long held primacy as experts in writing. They believe in that primacy themselves, and they are often endorsed in it, if back-handedly, by their colleagues in other departments. As I want to explain in some detail in chapter 6, the difference between English and other departments lies in its pride of ownership of writing and its position to act on that pride. Specialists in English, and especially in composition studies, believe they know what good writing is and how to teach it, their perception often extending beyond their discipline's boundaries into the WAC enterprise.

Given the reality of difference in disciplinary languages, however, a WAC that imposes its own values or processes for teaching writing silences many faculty and students, falling barely short of colonization. Yet the error extends beyond (nearly) colonizing another department. It may extend into critical thinking itself, with the consequence of muddying it. Globally, we suffer from immensely complex and dangerous social, political, and environmental problems—problems that threaten all of us. To progress toward solutions to these problems, the disciplines need to do what they can potentially do best—create an atmosphere for clarity of critical thinking within their own contexts. WAC programs are well situated to help advance this kind of specialized activity, but they are also well situated to counter it.

As I explain in the second chapter, some WAC practices actually oppose specialization. They do so sometimes to alert students to serious gatekeeping inequities in the disciplines or to challenge "prevailing institutional divisions, faculty interests, and dominant forms of knowledge-making" (Mahala, 1991). Most often, however, opposition to specialization is meant to preserve a student writer's authentic self and voice. Writing to learn—journal writing, free writing, expressive writing, writing as process—prevails as a large part of most WAC programs because of the influence of process-expressivists, who want to face down the conformity and submission (Spellmeyer, 1989), the academic jive making (Elbow, 1991), they believe student writers will experience as they learn to write in the disciplines. Do students face conformity and submission in writing in their disciplines? To some degree, yes, but no more so than when they write to, and then are graded by, the standards of compositionists. In the sense I want to forward here, each discipline writes in its own (often multiple) voice(s). To learn to write in the voice endorsed by process-expressivists in English departments will usually be quite a different matter than to learn to write in the voice endorsed by conservation biologists. Neither one of these voices, however, is intrinsically better than the other; each reflects some quality of self, and each does its own work. Do individuals, in adopting the language of a discipline other than English composition, become somehow less authentic, less honest, and less spontaneous? Certainly such a claim could never be proved. Because of that fact, it should never be made without the most serious qualifiers. Granting the proposition that every facility must be provided for students to grow in their disciplines may require a rethinking of the terms *authentic* self and *voice*, but it does not require denying them.

Thus, to return to the question of requiring a first-year writing course or courses focusing on voice, filling the cavity of being with language (as Elbow has put it), I say "yes," require such a course. It is the only course that will have student writing as its content, the only one that will favor writing over reading, and the only one in which questions of the writing process and expressivism may be central. If it works as it should, the course will demonstrate how writing makes meaning, how writing affirms or changes writers' minds about themselves through revision, how sharing writing with others challenges their own impressions, and how good writing takes time. Should composition courses alert students to diversity issues, feminist issues, issues of the environment, or issues of gatekeeping? I answer, "yes, certainly." These agendas suggest important knowledge-making activities in which students should engage. However, whatever happens in such a course or courses must be made publicly evident. That is, composition teachers and directors need to explain to students and their colleagues in other departments that they are forwarding a course that abides by its own values, not necessarily designed to cross the curriculum into other disciplines.

As to the question of English teachers teaching writing in the natural sciences, writing in business, or writing in engineering, pertinent issues apply. In my experience, I have never known an English teacher who could write engineering (although I acknowledge that there must be such professionals), but I have known English teachers who can teach writing to potential engineers. In the University of Nevada's English Department, there are several faculty members who capably teach Engineering 301, the Engineering College's introductory writing course. This capability is, at once, positive and negative. Because of their expertise and enthusiasm, these teachers often bring a part of writing in engineering to life for students.

It is also negative because of its effectiveness. This course cannot hope to do more than introduce writing to engineering students; the more advanced, specialized work of engineering is always left to other courses. Nonetheless, the 301 course makes it possible for faculty to abdicate responsibility for teaching writing in their courses—a problem which I have witnessed coming from teachers who have said, at times, "why should I use writing in my course; students get their writing in 301." Recognizing the importance of writing, the nation's engineering accrediting agency (ABET) has mandated that writing must play an important role in undergraduate engineering education. The mandate may, as I understand it, be satisfied by a course such as 301. Yet in an unusual (and appropriate) alternative to requiring a single course, ABET accepts and applauds programs that require writing throughout their curriculum, such as Montana State's program. So I am ambivalent about English teachers teaching writing courses in other disciplines. I recognize that they may teach introductory writing courses in the general specializations or colleges effectively. However, I also know that writing has the greatest impact for thinking when it is sequenced in context—in most or all engineering courses. As with first-year English, I would encourage a climate in which forums are created for discussing such questions and courses openly.

With regard to the emerged specialization in rhetoric and composition studies, I believe there must be a semester-long forum, probably a more public and lengthier forum, for discussing the following issues: that disciplines are separate language communities with their own values, purposes, and forms for writing, with one set of values not superior to another; that this equality has important implications for WAC consultancy: Noninvasive techniques for WAC interaction with faculty should be developed and employed; that writing assessment instruments should measure writing quality within the context in which students mostly do it, their majors; and, finally, that processes should be encouraged for collaboration between disciplines and reflective thinking about consequences within them. We are, as a profession in rhetoric and composition studies, in a potentially claustrophobic world confined to first-year writing, perhaps a required course in advanced expository or technical writing, and courses we teach in writing in the sciences, business, engineering. WAC activity opens our profession into a vastly broader world of writing. However, it is important to think about how we interact with that world, if evangelistically, then learning to write in the disciplines as our colleagues value it and not writing to learn as we value it. The next chapter explores the emphatic nature of writing to learn and its sources for a crusadelike thrust from first-year writing courses into writing across the curriculum.

2

Saving Wordsworth's Poet

Poetry is the image of man and nature. The obstacles which stand in the way of the fidelity of the Biographer and Historian, and of their consequent utility, are incalculably greater than those which are to be encountered by the Poet who comprehends the dignity of his art. The Poet writes under one restriction only, namely, the necessity of giving immediate pleasure to a human Being possessed of that information which may be expected from him, not as a lawyer, a physician, a mariner, an astronomer, or a natural philosopher, but as a Man. Except this one restriction, there is no object standing between the Poet and the image of things; between this, and the Biographer and Historian, there are a thousand.

—Wordsworth's "Preface to the Lyrical Ballads" (1800/1965, p. 454)

When Wordsworth (1800/1965) asserted that "The Poet writes under one restriction only, namely, the necessity of giving immediate pleasure to a human Being possessed of that information which may be expected of him, not as a lawyer, a physician, a mariner, an astronomer, or a natural philosopher, but as a Man" (p. 454), he probably alienated a few of his readers—at least those who were lawyers, physicians, or mariners. According to his "Preface," the obstacles that stand in the way of professionals as they write are far more debilitating than those "encountered by the Poet." They are debilitating because of the limiting vision that defines each of the professional contexts and the limited expression these contexts oblige. Because poets belong to the "discipline of Man" and not other disciplines, they write without a profession's language between them and the image of things. Language, in the poet's hands, *is* the image of things; it mirrors and shapes the self while rendering the experience of the other. The poet's clarity of personal vision, elevated purpose, relational imagination, and unlimited professional context raise him or her to the top of Wordsworth's rhetorical system.

Wordsworth's proclamations seemed elitist and exclusionary to a few readers then and might continue to seem so to (perhaps more than) a few now. Yet the arrogance suggested by these lines, and the extreme elevation of the Poet's status, is mitigated somewhat by Wordsworth's notion of which people can become poets. Much of Wordsworth's canon, including his "Preface," "Tintern Abbey," "Intimations Ode," large parts of *The Prelude,* and his prose, wants to show how all people, with the right conditions for development, can become poets ("what one is, / Why may not millions be?" *Prelude,* Book XIII, lines 88–89), restricted only by potential. Wordsworth's rhetorical theory, his educational proposals for full lives in language, intends to lead to this poet, but not in the singular sense of the inspired genius visited by the muse, writing in one sitting the most penetrating and universal insights. Instead, Wordsworth represents himself as an everyman figure, a person it is true, of uncommon intellect and feeling, but a person in the general sense among many millions of others, receiving an education others could receive, toiling as a writer as others toil, revising his work and then revising it again, viewing the whole process as, in his term, *organic,* and claiming language as the source and shaper of thought and not merely its clothing ("Epitaph Three"). He wishes the growth of his mind to be a model for the growth of everyone's and that all might experience the conditions of development he describes for literacy education. Taken as a whole, the prose and poetry from Wordsworth's acknowledged decade of excellence, from 1795 to 1805, would constitute a good theory for teaching writing in a particular way and then a good agenda of practice for doing so. In fact, Wordsworth's ideas did influence future teachers of writing, most strikingly scholars such as Elbow, Murray, and Britton, who acknowledges Wordsworth's influence in his *Language and Learning.* The thinking and spirit of the Romantics, especially Wordsworth and Coleridge, has been essential to the development of the modern process–expressivist movement in composition studies and teaching, as has now been frequently explained by composition scholars (Berlin, 1988; Faigley, 1986; Gradin, 1995; Waldo, 1986).

I felt much excitement in 1980 when I discovered the connection between the expressivist theory of composition and Wordsworth's and Coleridge's extensive commentary about writing, language, and psychology. I wrote my dissertation (*The Rhetoric of Wordsworth and Coleridge: Its Place in Current Composition Theory,* 1982) about that connection. Writing the dissertation did not feel (much) like work to me. It was mostly pleasurable. I had loved to read the British Romantics since undergraduate school—since high school, really. I had loved to teach writing since 1973. This project linked the two. Because what I studied in the poets' canon was so consistent with my own transformation as a writing teacher and with what I was reading in composition theory, sociology, psychology, and linguistics, I became a passionate convert—a process-expressivist evangelist. Given the right literacy education and circumstances for development, I believed that all students could become poets—not verse writers necessarily, but fully alive in the language of the self and its experience of the other. I believed, as Elbow remarked in 1995, that "all my students could . . . feel themselves as writers . . ." and then "as academics" (Bartholomae, 1995, p. 490). Yet the problem with my evangelism, and Elbow's, lurks ominously in Wordsworth's quote.

Prophetically, Wordsworth got it right in terms of postmodern notions of people living in differentiated, even fractured communities and the immense shaping influence these communities have on their writing and thinking. He also got it right in terms of modernism (being one of the inventors of it)— that all people have inner selves that can be nourished or lost, and that they can write the voices of their inner selves with authenticity, spontaneity, and originality. The problem is and remains his obvious belief that the two positions are incompatible—that the latter becomes so desirable, whereas the former so heinous. The educational and cultural backgrounds of those in various professions make them see the world differently, and Wordsworth more than implies that something is seriously wrong with their seeing, with the written visions of the lawyer, doctor, astronomer, mariner, and natural philosopher. Such people appear, from his perspective, to be lost souls—people pounded by outside "intermeddler[s]" into "the pinfold of [their] own conceit" (*The Prelude*, V, line 336). A directive and mechanic educational experience, which in Wordsworth's view prevailed during his day, makes them become as engines. People who become poets, in contrast, are found souls, masters of themselves and their language. Their *organic* educational experience fosters the growth of their inner selves and voices.

Coleridge, Wordsworth's colleague and collaborator during much of the decade of excellence, held similar views about organic and mechanic education, but Coleridge had a broader view of the poet than did Wordsworth. Anyone who exercises the "secondary imagination," dissolving, diffusing, and dissipating reality to re-create it (a willed and therefore conscious activity), is a poet; and this person might readily be a member of a profession other than Wordsworth's Poetcraft. Nonetheless, Coleridge observed that, although "all people are poets, most people are damned bad ones." For him, a damned bad poet is one whose language obscures the vision, the re-creation becoming muddled by linguistic infelicity. For Wordsworth, a nonpoet is one who writes not authentically from the self, but in the voice of the other. Among many others, Wordsworth's notions of inner self, authentic voice, organic literacy training, spontaneity, originality, and language as thought (and "not the clothing for thought") have had profound philosophical, practical, and intuited appeal in the modern world of composition studies. These notions, nonetheless, deny postmodern conditions. However much Wordsworth longs for all people to become poets, he also excludes everyone who is not him or does not enter the community of poets with him.

I do not mean, with the remainder of this chapter, to expand much on the notions of Wordsworth's Poet or the connection between the Romantics and modern composition theory (for that, the reader again might turn to Gradin, 1995; Waldo, 1986). What I intended with these first few pages, instead, was to suggest the either/or character of Wordsworth's position and the evangelical fervor of its expression. A similar either/or condition exists in the work of recent compositionists, particularly that of process-expressivists, and their tone might certainly be (has been) termed *evangelical*. As I said in the Preface to this book, my own tone had been evangelical. I want to discuss some of that work—not to insult it, but to suggest how it found its way into the WAC enterprise mainly in the form of writing to learn. Romantic, expressivist thinking does have a profound appeal to many compositionists, of course, because it has succeeded in their own writing classes, but also because it stems from a literary tradition with which, as English teachers, they feel familiar and comfortable. From my perspective, that appeal should have influence in the world of writing, but not in arenas where it is not valued. Saving Wordsworth's Poet belongs in some contexts but not in all.

Process Evangelism

The either/or position and its evangelical tone is reflected in Knoblauch and Brannon's (1984) edgy and controversial book, *Rhetorical Traditions and the Teaching of Writing*. At the time of its publication, *organic* and *mechanic* were current terms. The *classical* teaching of writing opposed the *modern* perspective. And the modern perspective was emphatically preferable to them. In their book, Knoblauch and Brannon seem, as much as anything, to be writing the compositionist call to arms, urging the new thinking organicists to overthrow the mechanicists, locked as they were in their classical rhetorical teaching postures:

> The shift from ancient to modern perspective has not been a matter of gradual and slight conceptual adjustment, modern rhetoric growing naturally, imperceptibly, out of its ancient earlier tradition. Instead, the two traditions are es-

sentially opposed, representing a disjunction in intellectual history because they derive from two different and incompatible epistemologies, two irreconcilable views of the nature of knowledge and the functions of discourse. Teachers will not see a slow modification of familiar ideas when they look at the history of rhetoric after the seventeenth, and especially after the nineteenth, century. Rather they see the displacement of one system of concepts by another, unrelated system, and they will have to struggle somewhat to comprehend the new system without reference to the old. (Knoblauch & Brannon, 1984, p. 78)

That Knoblauch and Brannon call the two systems *irreconcilable*, without qualifying their terms, and that writing teacher/observers would "see the displacement of one system of concepts by another, unrelated system" suggest the passion they and many others felt, generated from the struggle to replace the ancient with the modern, the current-traditional with the process-expressive. Now when I teach *Rhetorical Traditions*, the authors' unequivocal position prompts much discussion, particularly about their book's treatment of classical rhetoric. That treatment, under the guise of being a chapter on classical rhetoric's history and influence, becomes an ideological display of its perceived faults. A few reviewers of the book noticed the distinct bias when the book was first published (see Gage's, 1984, review). I knew of these dissenting voices, but I dismissed them as current-traditional sour grapes.

Initially reading their book, I was enthralled. These scholars, acknowledging the Romantics, had given a summary voice to the personal struggle in which I had been engaged for 10 years. Many other teacher/scholars, I think, viewed their book not only as an ardent endorsement of process-expressivist pedagogy, which it certainly was, but as historical and theoretical evidence legitimizing their pedagogy. The importance of composition studies and teaching continued to evolve. Yet Knoblauch and Brannon included hints of trouble to come inside composition studies, at least for WAC, when they observed that "the conditions for meaningfulness reside *within* particular discourses and need not be the same for all of them" (p. 59). I have not seen this comment quoted anywhere in composition or WAC literature, but for this text it matters.

The notion that writers can become either found selves or lost souls is also present in the work of many other eloquent process-expressivists, including Spellmeyer (1989), Elbow (1991), and Newkirk (1997). Spellmeyer, for example, argued that the "prevailing tradition of discipline-specific writing instruction encourages both conformity and submission . . ." (p. 110). Its "admonition to suppress feelings and beliefs for the sake of public approval encourages an attitude of calculating alienation" (p. 111), which comes from the student imitating "the language of the academy without gaining an ability to use that language on her own behalf" (p. 119). Writing must be used instead, he argued, "as the means of discovering an enlarging horizon that every discourse can open to her view, [which will allow her gradually to] enter the community of 'knowers' while retaining her own voice in the process" (p. 119). "The writers we most admire," Spellmeyer concluded, "are typically those who have learned to reinstate their voices within the language of a discipline: or rather, they have learned to enter a discipline by finding their own voices" (p. 120).

Elbow is even more adamant about the protection of student voice and the phoniness of student writing in the disciplines. In an essay published in 1991, Elbow made writing in the disciplines an activity "that academics use when they publish for other academics" (p. 145). This is writing that explains; it does not render experience. Teaching writing in the disciplines, Elbow later acknowledged, is the work of faculty in the disciplines: "In short, [composition teachers] are not qualified to teach most kinds of academic discourse" (p. 148). He cited Bizzell (1986) and Harris (1989), "who write thoughtfully about the differences among communities of discourse" (p. 148). Yet after this acknowledgment, in a noteworthy reduction, Elbow maintained that, "Maybe it's not, then, the intellectual stance or task that distinguishes academic discourse but certain stylistic or mechanical conventions—not the deep structure but certain surface features" (p. 154). If only surface features are different, then deep structure might be taught by compositionists, whereas specialists teach conventions. He appeals to his audience by separating language from thought in an extraordinary reversion to classicism: "If we have to learn a new intellectual stance or take on difficult intellectual goals, we'll probably have better luck if we don't at the same time have to do it in a new language and style and voice" (p. 162). This if/then structure opens Elbow to the conclusion that, "students can do academic work even in street language" (p. 162). Vygotsky, however, had long before made the separation between language and thought virtually impossible, inextricably connecting language to thinking and thinking to community. Students learn to think in disciplinary contexts by writing in them. Thus, Elbow struggled to sustain English department expressivism in every form of discourse.

Newkirk (1997) asserted, in an eloquent expression of values, that:

> expressivist pedagogy *is* [his emphasis] romantic, that romanticism is deeply imbedded in American literary traditions (and I would wager into the actual belief system of even its critics). This romanticism has extraordinary resonance with young writers. It is empowering for students—for all of us—to believe:
>
> • that we can imagine ourselves as coherent selves with coherent histories and can therefore create stories about ourselves

- that this coherence, the "identity," allows for a sense of agency, a trajectory into the future
- that we each see the world in a distinctive way and have the ability to make a distinctive contribution to it
- that human beings share an essence that allows the "I" of the writer to become a mirror for us all
- that knowing entails feeling, and that discourse becomes sterile if it shuts out emotion
- that openness to the particularity of the natural world, what Lawrence Buell calls an "environmental imagination," serves as a check to human egotism and can create a sense of stewardship. (p. 98)

Many readers would feel at home with any of these scholars' passages and view them more as points of fact than assertions of opinion. With Spellmeyer, they might well accept as fact the notions of personal voice, that writing in the disciplines charges students to imitate without owning a language, and that this process alienates students from their voices and selves. They might applaud the idea that students must enter the community of knowers while retaining their own voices because the writing most admired reinstates the writer's voice within the language of a discipline. With Elbow, they may agree that writing in the disciplines is academic jive—the writing academics do for each other. And with Newkirk, that students have coherent identities that empower them to become individual agents acting for good in their worlds.

I used to accept these positions more as fact than opinion. I do not any longer. For me, Spellmeyer's position cannot be more than intuitively attractive, which it certainly is, because he can only claim, not prove, that students "who enter the community of 'knowers' " lose their authentic voices in the process. To array such proof, he would have to establish that his values for voice are correct and universal, whereas other values are not, and therefore students entering disciplines with other voices lose the one correct voice. Spellmeyer cannot establish the validity of any one of these conditions or its consequences. He cannot prove that adopting the voice of a discipline means that writers lose authentic voice or that the voice in a discipline is not authentic. Beyond saying that this process of conformity and submission occurs, a process that is as true (under the conditions described here) for students in composition courses as in any other courses, Spellmeyer and others will have trouble proceeding. Encouraging discipline-based languages through WAC may involve moving away from voice in the process-expressive sense and toward voice in the disciplinary sense, although there is irony in some compositionists' surprisingly singular view of voice.

Spellmeyer celebrated a reinstatement of voice on the part of academics who write. Yet often those who have reinstated their compositionist voices do so when they write *about* their work, after they have fully established themselves as professionals, not when they are *doing* it, as can be graphically illustrated by the writing of such academics as Gould or Sagan. As compositionists, we may admire their creative nonfiction more than their professional papers, but that does not make the creative nonfiction any more effective. From my perspective, creative nonfiction does a different type of work, not a better type. Spellmeyer said nothing about the relationship of language to the activities of a discipline, nor the personal passion and commitment that academics in the disciplines have for their work.

Passionate commitment is not limited to personal and autobiographical writing. It is found in all disciplines to which people often seem drawn by some preinclination, perhaps their own senses of self, community, and style, in Richard Lanham's terms. When I ask faculty about the time they became interested in their subject matter, they often express surprisingly young ages. For example, Jeanie Yamamura, an accounting professor, told me that her family would take on sales projects, gathering or making items they would then market to neighbors. Her much cherished responsibility in this process, at 4 years old, was to count the money received. Was Jeanie's becoming an accounting major, an accountant, and then an accounting professor a denial of her voice and self or the expression of them? As another example, my friend in biology, Al Gubanich, told me that his interest began developing at age 6, when he wished he could get into the psyches of animals, become them, and then report back about what that existence was like. Was Al's becoming a biology major, a biologist, and then a biology professor a denial of his voice and self or the expression of them? The obvious and sustained energy these people have for their work and lives, the urgency with which they talk about both, suggests the latter. Anyone who talks and listens seriously to most faculty about their work in their disciplines and their commitment to student learning cannot mistake their passion for either.

Al Gubanich was an early participant in UNR's WAC workshops in assignment design and paper evaluation, and his assignments on how birds fly and why birds sing have become among the best we have shared nationwide. (They appear as appendixes in this text.) I decided to interview Al, with basic expressivist principles as the touchstone points for the interview. I wanted to know if he *felt* that expressivist principles fit in his discipline. His responses consistently endorsed his colleagues and their students as emphatically (personally) committed to their activities—in conception, process, and expression. Their composing about these activities is decidedly different from that in composition, but in conception and process their activities meet or exceed any expressivist mandate. The expression of these activities does not make it any less authentic in voice or any other arena. It must be done in their language and with their values, purposes, and forms for writing in mind, just as expression must be done in the compositionist arena. Al and I have shared this interview at a variety of conferences to enthusiastic audiences. (I do not provide the text of this interview or its interpretations here, but I invite readers to ask for copies at waldo@unr.edu.) Women and men alike, from the widest variety of disciplines (even when their interest begins later or they are besieged by political problems inherent to the academy), voice their passion for their work, projects, teaching, and research.

Elbow (1991/1998) appeared uncharacteristically zealous in his remarks about academic writing in the article I quoted, more acerbic than say in his more recent discussions with David Bartholomae. There are few points that Elbow makes in this 1995 article with which I would disagree, and his argument "that virtually every . . . course" other than first-year composition "privileges reading over writing," and that no other course has the students' writing as its content, seem the most persuasive points for sustaining composition in its process-expressive orientation. Yet his claim in 1991 that academic writing is the jive that academics do for one another and that it can, and should, be done in the street vernacular is disconcertingly naive, akin to saying that we can frame and solve the global warming problem with the language of first-year composition. Until we live life in the disciplinary culture we choose, we cannot speak, write, read, or think in its language. However appealing street vernacular may be to the poet in us, it cannot solve the problems even Elbow sets out to solve in his own articles, which are written in an accessible language, but nonetheless based in a discipline far from any street on which I have walked.

I think Newkirk precisely described the nuances of appeal in the process-expressivist position. It does have "extraordinary resonance with young writers," and each of his bulleted items is empowering "for all of us," or at least for those interested in composition as a discipline. I have been trying to make the point that values are not givens, but when I read a claim like this one, "that knowing entails feeling, and that discourse becomes sterile if it shuts out emotion," it is hard for me to resist crying out "Bravo." I want to strike the tents and march on biology, so busy molding even its first-year students into writing and thinking as biologists, writing and thinking formulaically. The trouble is, of course, that Newkirk's scheme ignores the emotional commitment of students learning and teachers teaching biology and their in-place commitment to stewardship. A movement to change the biology faculty's ways with regard to teaching writing *would* amount to "striking the tents" and marching on them, given that they are as committed to their values as Newkirk is to his.

Commitment to agency and stewardship, important to Newkirk's criteria, becomes significant to my argument as well. I agree that every person needs an openness to the natural world, an *environmental imagination*. Everyone must become an agent *and* steward because both are essential to our collective well-being. Further, every discipline must play a role in developing agents and stewards. However, it is also important to acknowledge that effective stewardship requires expertise, and that one discipline's language will be better suited to touching certain parts of reality than another discipline's. For example, conservation biologists are usually better at the project of preserving wetlands than musicians, who are better at writing and singing songs about the need for preservation. Medical personnel are better at treating the AIDS-afflicted in Africa and elsewhere than sociologists, who are better at describing the impact of AIDS on the local and global community. Automobile engineers are better at designing cars that achieve 70 miles per gallon than advertisers, who are better at marketing such cars. English teachers are better at interpreting *The Jungle* than federal food inspectors, who may want to use that novel in support of their own work. The list of who is better at what activity is nearly limitless—as limitless as the Tower of Babel metaphor suggests. Even so, all of these voices should be viewed as necessary and equal. As appealing as Newkirk's call for agency and stewardship is, and it is appealing to me, it offers no explanation of how expressivist pedagogy creates professionals who know how to do the work of expert stewards and agents, making a mistake similar to Wordsworth's position on the "Poet": If everyone is a Poet, then who argues law, mends patients, reads stars, or saves, preserves, and restores natural resources?

Process-expressivists, and those such as Wordsworth who precede them, celebrate the writer's individuality, personality, self-awareness, and voice. They caution against thrusting people into writing situations that force them to speak like institutions because of a fear that their voices and selves will eventually take shape out of those institutions. For Wordsworth, they become not only less than poets, but also less than human, "like engines" (*The Prelude* V, line 358). As compelling as his rejection of conformist-literacy education is and as inspiriting his declaration for universal poethood, they open Wordsworth to the obvious complaint that if all of us become poets no one will be left to do the work (if we acknowledge that the work of a profession is done principally through its language). Many process-expressivists open themselves to the same complaint. Nonetheless, the observations of professionals such as Elbow, Spellmeyer, and Newkirk have extraordinary resonance within the composition community.

There have been a few bumps for process-expressivist pedagogy over the years. Questions about the quality of student writing have long been with us. As Russell (1991) showed in his critical history of writing instruction in the United States, complaints about student writing have spanned at least the last century. No one date or event focuses these complaints or the attempts to answer them, but one date and event did have particular dramatic force—the publishing of "Why Johnny Can't Write" in *Newsweek* on December 8, 1975. "Can't Write," as virtually everyone involved in literacy studies during the time knows, had an impact far beyond its merits. It fueled the back-to-basics movement, spawned many more "Why Johnny Can't . . ." and then "Why Johnny and Jane Can't . . ." articles, and shamed many writing teachers in the schools. Apocalyptically, the article's first paragraph begins with, "If your children are attending college, the chances are that when they graduate they will be unable to write ordinary, expository English with any real degree of structure and lucidity." That same paragraph ends with "Willy-nilly, the US educational system is spawning a generation of semiliterates" (p. 58). As its guiding point, the article claimed that a new, less rigorous, more student-centered writing pedagogy had replaced a more hard-nosed skills-and-drills pedagogy, thus initiating the drastic decline in writing abilities. The evidence the article offers supporting its claims is skimpy (mostly some bad sentences quoted in its margins and teacher complaints). Its solution to the problem is laughably cosmetic (return to drill). However, composition studies and process-expressivist pedagogy more than weathered *Newsweek*'s assault. Ironically, the article even benefited writing teachers, increasing their training, funding, and status within English departments. It benefited WAC by observing that teachers in departments other than English (e.g., a professor of economics) felt the need to help students with their writing because English was failing to do its job. It stimulated the growth of graduate programs in rhetoric and composition. Why? Because it concentrated massive media attention on what amounted to largely a contrived literacy crisis, and because composition appeared to be the closest vehicle for addressing that crisis.

I believe that the continued back-to-basics movement and writing assessment also began largely as responses to process-expressivist pedagogy. Lockstep grammar and punctuation tests and timed essays have always been easier to measure for quality than essays drafted over time, written in authentic voice on topics of real interest to students, and reviewed by peers. Producing more bumps in the road, there are also many other ideological agendas now competing for dominance in the composition classroom.

The coincidence of timing and need has made many agendas possible for composition studies, including process-expressivist theory, social constructivist theory, cognitivist theory, greenist theory, feminist theory, alternative-lifestyle theory, multicultural theory, postmodern theory, whole-language theory, reader/writer response theory, and, of course, cross-curricular writing theory. All have flourished without much external political influence because, as the discipline has evolved, it appears to be the primary hope for improving the writing of students, and few young disciplines attract intense political and public attention anyway. These remarks do not imply that I support conservative critics or that varying approaches do not belong in writing classes. I align myself to some degree with several perspectives, particularly expressivist, socialist, feminist, greenist, and, of course, cross-curricular theory, and I teach thematic and topical courses in composition. I agree with the purposes of composition teachers who teach writing from an agenda or under the umbrella of one of the perspectives listed earlier. I just do not agree with the agenda or perspective being imposed across the curriculum.

The intent of this chapter was to characterize the either/or quality of expressivist thinking, its missionary zeal, and its impact on the teaching of writing in English departments particularly. That impact has been profound. For the teaching of writing, process-expressivism did (as *Newsweek* ignorantly surmised) become the basis for the new writing paradigm, and its power and appeal helped, in part, to overturn the current-traditional paradigm (see Hairston, 1982). This act occurred within the history of composition and literacy studies during a three-decade period marked roughly in its beginning by the Dartmouth Conference (1966) and continuing to this day despite the rabid march into standards, conservative curricular reform, and testing. During this period, many English composition (grammar) teachers found themselves on extremely unstable ground—ground that Kuhn (1970) claimed will develop as one paradigm for acting within a discipline gives way to another. Those left behind discover their worlds suddenly lack much relevance. For example, writing teachers out of the current-traditional mode—with its attention to learning particular rhetorical techniques, lecture and teacher-led discussions dealing with concepts to be learned and applied, the study of models and other materials that explain and illustrate concepts, specific assignments or exercises that generally involve imitating a pattern or following rules that have been previously discussed, and teacher-based feedback on writing (Hillocks, 1986)—were challenged and increasingly displaced by the emerging model with its own set of values and rules.

In 1987, North predicted the demise of composition studies as a discipline. He devoted a long, early chapter to lamenting, with questionable sincerity, how the practitioners in the field, mostly important process-expressivists,

were being dismissed as credible researchers because what they published reflected classroom practice: what works and why it does, what does not work,
and why it does not. They have, he explained in an interesting metaphor,
built a "House of Lore," which would be dismantled by the more serious researchers to come. Yet North clearly underestimated the emotional strength
in the arms building and the articulate people inhabiting that house. He also
partly and sometimes nearly wholly discredited every other research arena he
categorized as important to the emerging field mainly on two grounds: that
the research methods were impure and that the research made competing
(ideological) arguments about teaching writing as much as it reported results.
He thus undermined the credibility of those he claimed would counter practi-
tioner influence. These practitioners continue to thrive in publication and
practice, and their influence must be acknowledged as not only strong, but
pervasive in composition teaching because of the extraordinary resonance
their ideas have with students and writing teachers. However far the variety
of agendas that appear in composition classes has extended, it is process-
expressivist thinking that remains dominant in practice.

3

Wordsworth's Poet Conducts WAC Workshops, or the Influence of Writing to Learn on the Cross-Curricular Writing Enterprise

> *In writing classes in the United States I found that I had to reprogram my mind, to redefine some of the basic concepts and values that I had about myself, about society, and about the universe, values that had been imprinted and reinforced in my mind by my cultural background, and that had been part of me all my life.*
>
> *Rule number one in English composition is: Be yourself. (More than one composition instructor has told me, "Just write what you think.") The values behind this rule, it seems to me, are based on the principle of protecting and promoting individuality (and private property) in this country. The instruction was probably crystal clear to students raised on these values, but, as a guideline of composition, it was not very clear or useful to me when I first heard it.*
>
> —Fan Shen (1989, p. 123)

For WAC, process-expressivist thinking manifests itself in a way that is perhaps at once peculiar and predictable. That position has, according to much of the literature, been foundational to WAC programs. For example, Fulweiler and Young (1990) observed that most institutions "base their programs on a common core of language theorists, most often including some mix of James Britton, Don Murray, Janet Emig, and Peter Elbow; and promote similar process-oriented pedagogy" (pp. 1–2). Russell (1991) remarked that, "Such theorists as Peter Elbow, Ken Macrorie, Donald Graves and James Moffett . . . gave the WAC movement its focus on the classroom as community; its student-centered pedagogy, often with a subversive tinge; and its neoromantic, expressivist assumptions . . ." (p. 273). Smith (1988) accepted as givens that teachers in the disciplines must "apply similar assumptions and questions to professionals' and students' processes of composing" and will succeed to the extent that they "have informed themselves in composition theory" (p. 392). If readers think that this agenda has departed over the years from the WAC enterprise, they need only return to the McLeod/ Maimon (2000) article, where the expressivist and formalist are "complementary rather than competing views of WAC" (p. 577), or to Detweiler's (2000) remarks about writing in occupational therapy: "If the occupational therapy program hires a non-occupational therapy faculty member to teach the writing course, consider engaging a writing specialist. . . . Writing teachers are just a little more focused on writing than you are, obviously and necessarily, and they have a bit more practice with teaching this learning process" (p. 56).

If anything, English's grip on WAC seems to have tightened rather than loosened in the decade following Russell's remarks. The pronounced presence of process-expressivist notions in WAC literature and presumably in WAC programs may be explained when we think of where most WAC practitioners come from—English department writing programs. Those practitioners may have trouble letting go of their own hard-won and cherished tenets for teaching writing. More likely, as members of what Kuhn (1970) termed a *received paradigm*, within which "professionalization leads . . . to an immense restriction of [their] vision and to a considerable resistance to paradigm change" (p. 64), they view as givens (writing to learn) what are really values for writing. Having gone native in the discipline, their vision becomes restricted by their community; thus they preach abroad what they believe at home. To explain the presence of process-expressivist assumptions in WAC literature and programs may be easy. It is harder to explain how these pedagogies succeed in WAC practice with faculty in other disciplines, unless it is through "a conversion experience which cannot be forced" (Kuhn, 1970, p. 151) as Fishman (1992), philosophy teacher, seems to have experienced.

Yet these conversion experiences must be exceedingly rare—a fact implied by Jones and Comprone (1993) in their article, "Where Do We Go Next in Writing Across the Curriculum?" They answered their title's question by offering a combination of process-expressivist assumptions with discipline-specific discourse conventions: "Writing-to-learn strategies—journal writing, workshops, in-class free writing, expressive writing—[need] to be combined with the course material and conventions" (p. 66). (I take the term *conventions* to mean that psychology students write using surface features different from English students who write using surface features different from biology students, etc. *Convention* means qualities distinguished by discipline and learned within disciplines, say, formulas for organizing papers; *convention*, however, does not mean that languages differ between disciplines; because of those differences, ways of thinking and making meaning differ.) Early in their article, Jones and Comprone offered a narrative about a graduate student at Michigan Tech who reports, controversially, that WAC practices based on "writing as learning, expressive discourse, and faculty workshops" worked better with humanities than with engineering faculty, although they had not managed to motivate even a small group of teachers from any of the disciplines into a secure programmatic base. Jones and Comprone (1993) continued,

> By far the most controversial of her comments was, however, that the emphasis by the English teachers who had developed Tech's writing-as-learning WAC program, well known WAC experts and practitioners such as Toby Fulwiler and Art Young, had never been appropriately supported by research into the kind of writing that goes on in different discourse communities. In fact, Brown suggested, emphasizing writing as learning without looking closely into what actually goes on in the writing of different academic communities may actually have harmed the cross-disciplinary movement by making it into a general-education revision rather than a systematic look at how and why writing was actually done in different disciplines. (p. 60)

These observations suggest that, as far as the graduate student was concerned, a disconnect existed between what experts in WAC, English teachers, presented to faculty and what those faculty were willing to internalize or even accept as useful. That disconnect occurred because, and the diction is vague here, their emphasis (focus of their workshops on writing to learn and expressive-writing techniques?) "had never been appropriately supported by research" (had little relevance?) "to the kind of writing that goes on in different discourse communities" (to the real world of writers in their disciplines?). I acknowledge that I do not know whether that is what the sentence means, but the last one in the paragraph is clearer. It voices a complaint that faculty in the disciplines have regarding WAC workshops run by English faculty. Those workshops promote a form of writing for students appropriate to general education revision or to English departments, but not to faculty in the disciplines. This failure to understand the writing that actually goes on in the disciplines, outside the humanities at least, may actually "have harmed the cross-disciplinary movement."

Without amplifying the implications of that finding, Jones and Comprone built on it, supporting and undermining it simultaneously. They immediately observed that, "This little Michigan Tech vignette connects very nicely with a good deal of what recent expert commentators . . . have said about WAC at comprehensive universities." They quoted Bazerman and McLeod, who wanted to link WAC with "research into the discourses of different academic disciplines" (p. 62). Research into those discourses sounds like a direction

Jones and Comprone believed would be good for WAC, "intense and open searching into the rhetoric of disciplines" (p. 60). Yet then they undermine that direction by asserting that "writing to learn and expressive writing techniques, including the keeping of journals, the emphasis on personal perspectives on generic conventions, and the inclusion of language-intensive approaches" are, "of course, essential" (p. 63). Their conclusion is that, "writing faculty and those from other disciplines [must] meet halfway," thus the combination they offer for the new WAC direction.

There is some vagueness and confusion in their writing, particularly in that which explains and surrounds the graduate student vignette perhaps because of Jones and Comprone's ambivalence about where WAC goes next. The point of most relevance here is that what at first is "research into the discourse of different academic disciplines" then becomes instead acceptance of "conventions of writing." The discourse of different academic disciplines does not in the end seem to impact WAC practice, as offered in their proposal, whereas the conventions of writing do. Why? I think the answer lies in the power and resonance of process-expressive pedagogy. If you really base WAC practice on research into the discourse of different academic disciplines, would there be room for or compatibility with expressive writing techniques, keeping journals, or personal perspectives? The answer is minimally "not necessarily" and more likely "usually not." If the answer is usually not, then Wordsworth's Poet fades.

Although Jones and Comprone did not mean to put their finger on one of the central issues dividing WAC from English departments (they are among the camp that argues WAC will flounder anywhere but in English or another humanities department) in their article, they nonetheless have done so. As composition experts and teachers, they "know that teaching process in a writing class in one part of an institution cannot ultimately be successful unless the writing in that one course is reinforced by the same kind of approach to learning in other courses" (p. 59). They perceive writing to learn and expressive writing techniques to be "essential" (p. 63). At the same time, their research "into the definition and function of genre in different academic and professional fields has made [them] aware of just how problematic the whole question of synthesizing form and context in the writing processes common to different disciplines really is" (p. 59). This contradiction between their WAC convictions and their research remains undeveloped in their article and in the main even unrecognized as a contradiction. Just how problematic the situation Jones and Comprone described is implied in the growing difficulties with adopting the neat programs of cognitivists, who sometimes assert that one good writing process exists and, once uncovered through protocol analyses, can be imitated by novices. Berlin (1988) pointed out the attractiveness of cognitivist approaches to industrial constituents, who want the quick fix of the best process quickly discovered and deployed. Even the uniformity of the writing process, however, is now being challenged by important work within composition studies (Kent, 1999).

The equation, in the Jones and Comprone article, works itself out in something like the following way: Process-expressivist approaches are fundamental to the teaching of writing and to WAC activity; ways must be found to synthesize form and context in the writing processes of different disciplines so that process-expressivist approaches may be met halfway by disciplines across the curriculum. Nonetheless, it is hard to synthesize so many diverse processes; WAC could be compromised because of that diversity; therefore difference must be understood as nothing more than rhetorical or stylistic conventions. The implication is that if process-expressivism is essential, it may have to be force-fed across the curriculum, *reinforced* in their terms. The two arenas into which Jones and Comprone did not enter are (a) to offer any proofs for their claims that writing as process must be taught by everyone to succeed and that process-expressivist approaches are essential to WAC, and (b) to acknowledge that WAC programs might be constructed out of the difference between language communities on a campus. Difference to them seems in the end far from a positive feature, but particularly abhorrent—something to be overcome through reinforcement of the same kind of approach to teaching writing in every course. This position is ironic because Comprone himself has contributed to the literature of difference.

Jones and Comprone cited many scholars whose publications call into question their own conclusions about the direction for WAC. For example, how can one read Bazerman's application of Vygotsky's theory of cognitive and linguistic growth in children to the development of a chemistry major and not extrapolate from it at least one crucial point: That languages, and not rhetorical conventions, are the basis for developing as a major in a discipline? How can one read Berkenkotter, Huckin, and Ackerman's article, "Social Context and Socially Constructed Texts," about the severe difficulties a graduate student has moving from a philosophy major to a concentration in rhetoric and composition (two seemingly similar communities) and not acknowledge the importance of maturing in a language to one's success in an academic community? How can one read Russell's (1991) conclusions in *Writing in the Academic Disciplines* "about finding ways to harness the efforts of the disciplines—where the faculty's primary loyalty and interest lie" in the development of WAC programs (p. 304) and ignore the need for WAC to pay attention to community-based language? Again these are scholars whom Jones and Comprone cited.

There are many others who published before 1993, the publication date of their article, including Knoblauch and Brannon (1984), who stated that "the conditions for meaningfulness reside *within* particular discourses and need not be the same for all of them" (p. 59). Some, on whom Jones and Comprone could have called, are outside composition. For example, Kuhn (1970) made a strong case for how professionals develop through their assimilation of language, the inexorable movement toward specialization that allows one to do the work of the discipline: "To translate a theory or world view into one's own language is not to make it one's own. For that one must go native, discover that one is thinking and working in, not simply translating out of, a language that was previously foreign" (p. 204). Geertz (1983) argued the similarity of academic cultures to Amazonian tribes: "In the same way that Papuans or Amazonians inhabit the world they imagine, so do high energy physicists or historians of the Mediterranean in the age of Phillip II—or so, at least, an anthropologist imagines" (p. 155). Growth and work in a discipline, Geertz argued, "is not just to take up a technical task but to take on a cultural frame that defines a great part of one's life," and thus an ethnography of "modern thought begins to seem an imperative project" (p. 155). Langer (1957) repeatedly and persuasively argued that language is heuristic: "It is essentially an organic, functioning system" (p. 35), which "interpenetrates with experience" (p. 126), and whose forms tend to integrate and make complex patterns. We see the world, Langer argued, as we use and think in language. Germane to this issue, the writing of Foucault, who despised any gatekeeping inherent in entering various academic language communities, articulated the point, basically, of universities: "What is an educational system, after all, if not a ritualisation of the word; if not a qualification of some fixing of roles for speakers . . . if not a distribution and appropriation of discourse, with all its learning and powers?" (p. 227). The work of these writer/teachers suggests the reason for the ambivalence of the graduate student about the effectiveness of the WAC program at Michigan Tech—that program was not integrating itself with the community-based motives of its audience. Why not?

Again, I hope my presentation in these two chapters explains "why not?" If we acknowledge the importance of difference in language between communities, we fear we lose the poet, at least Wordsworth's Poet. We lose that person whose language is grounded in the self, in authenticity, spontaneity, and feeling, creating instead a sterile discourse and person. We do not want that outcome, and I include myself in that we, and so we struggle to counter it, although I no longer continue to do so.

In the mid-1970s, I learned about how to teach writing by teaching it. The same is true about my becoming a writing center director and WAC consultant in 1983; I learned those roles by doing them. After 10 years as a teacher and student of writing, I came to my new job as Montana State's writing center director a confirmed, zealous expressivist. I believed in writing as process; I believed in writing from the self in authentic voice, in writing vividly and originally, with striking imagery and active verbs—writing that combined passion with reason. I believed in journal writing, free writing, small-group work on drafts, and large-group critique of published student essays. As I adopted them in my writing classes, these principles and techniques resonated with me and many of my students. They also resonated with me, as a PhD candidate, studying them in the late 1970s and early 1980s, as I read the publications of so many eloquent researchers and proponents of voice, authenticity, and cognitive and linguistic development.

The differences between writing in disciplines *had to be*, as Jones and Comprone asserted, mainly rhetorical convention and form, learned not lived. Writing to learn *had to* complement learning to write. The personal voices—the feeling voices of students—could sing in any paper. The response to my early WAC workshops at Montana State University, however, reflected that of the faculty at Michigan Tech. Before I began to address my workshops to the needs and concerns of faculty and their disciplines, my audience was interested and had fun, but their commitment was minimal and nothing much happened.

As a WAC consultant in 1983, I did not insist that faculty adopt and practice my values for teaching writing, but these values saturated my discussion, particularly the Jones/Comprone combination of journal writing, workshops, in-class free writing, and expressive writing with discipline-specific discourse conventions. Jones and Comprone did not publish their article until 10 years later, but I know this combination seemed right to me, as I think it did to many of us, and I know I wanted it to be right. Why? In my new position, I was troubled by a dilemma. My training and teaching had immersed me in an especially process-expressivist attitude. I worried that too much formulaic writing and speaking might not only mechanize discourse, but mechanize the personality, might lead to Spellmeyer's notions of conformity and submission to a discipline's discourse rather than the student's real voice. I worried that helping faculty to design writing assignments for students in their courses might make them engines.

The Darker Side

There remains an undeniable dark side to our multiple language condition. Language has often been used to obscure what individuals and organizations have done or are doing. Perhaps as much obscuring occurs as ethical creativity, perhaps more, and compositionists are well positioned to know how this adverse application of language works. Often the display of how obfuscation takes place becomes a large part of composition courses. Lawyers baffle their clients with legalese; doctors remove themselves from their patients with diagnostics on purpose. Plumbers disable their clients while describing the pipes or toilets in their homes; auto mechanics disarm their customers through the way in which they talk about problems with their brake systems; tobacconists blow smoke about the damage done by tobacco smoke on purpose. That is, they use language to achieve the distance they desire between themselves and their audience. They do this partly to increase the importance of their specializations—the amount of prestige and/or money they receive for their activities. They do it to avoid responsibility for errors, when the consequences large or small are clearly negative. (They also do it because they are what they speak and cannot help it.) There exists, perhaps arguably, no one individual or group on the planet that has not at some time used language to obscure, if the individual or group has matured to the point where linguistic manipulation becomes possible.

Euphemism and passive voice (generally) and militaryspeak (specifically) lessen the impact of war, attempting to render it less heinous and more acceptable. The 24th Bomber Group did not drop bombs on jungles, villages, and people, but "ordnance was delivered on pre-determined coordinates"; it did not fly bombing missions, but "sorties were flown"; young Marines did not crawl into the bush to receive fire from unseen enemies, but "fire missions were deployed." As a young composition teacher just following the Vietnam War, I was convinced of the intentionality of this language—that it was meant to distance, deceive, and depersonalize. I taught it to my composition students that way. I still believe militaryspeak was and is distancing, deceiving, and depersonalizing.

Further, without critically conscious behavior monitoring their use, specialized languages will continue to generate as many problems as they do solutions. Sport utility vehicles (SUVs), city-sized casinos, and nuclear defense shields will continue to be built as will other aberrations. Evidently it has become technologically possible to put advertising in space, in the form of mile-long, half-mile-wide billboards orbiting the earth. If unreflectively thrown up there, this rancid pollutant would repeatedly cry out, say, COKE!, to nearly everyone on the planet on a regular schedule. One of its promoters described this project on the *Today* show several years ago to the expressed (and admirable) horror of both Bryant Gumbel and Katie Couric. It has not resurfaced as an idea or a reality, that I know, since. I would like to believe that reflective thinking played some role in its disappearance: "We know how to build advertising in space; we have the language and technology to do so. But should we build it?" "Nah, because it presents an inescapable visual pollutant, seriously damaging the planet's environment"; or perhaps it is more likely that government agencies with more authority than the promoters might have said, "They know how to build billboards in space; they have the language to do so. But are we going to let them build it? Nah." (Important to this study is that the builders decide themselves not to build it, whatever it is, after deep reflection and collaboration, understanding that the potential consequences for bad outweigh those for good.) A third possibility exists. The person representing the technology on the *Today* show may have overstated its readiness, and we may still see it.

What we used to call the military-industrial complex is driven by specialized languages. Natural phenomena threaten our existence on the planet. Comets strike, volcanoes blow, and earthquakes crack. Yet it is not much of an exaggeration to say that the largest threats to meeting human needs—controlling population, generating comfort, (even) sustaining life by protecting the planet—come from humans. These threats are language made. Composition studies is ideally placed to examine and expose all of these issues in its courses and help students develop a critical consciousness about their activities as potential specialists.

For me, the notion that language perpetuates conflict and depletion, in the technical as well as the political sense; that it has made possible machines and technology constantly threatening to the population and the environment; that it has divided us from ourselves and conquered us in so many ways is the most serious objection to discipline-based writing across the curriculum. How can anyone, in good conscience, devise techniques to improve the linguistic capability of those nebulous organizations that seem unreflective of the consequences of their activities and those individuals who speak and write within them? What of the authentic voice of these individuals? How can anyone improve the conditions by which students lose their own voices in assimilating those of their disciplines and professions? These questions are difficult to answer, and I would not be asking them if discipline-based WAC were not so effective.

The answer to them has developed practically and theoretically for me during two decades of WAC work. Practically speaking, I am expected not only to collaborate with faculty from all disciplines, but to do so successfully. Confining WAC workshops to process-expressivist values or any one external set of values has not been effective for me, did not "motivate even a small group of teachers from any of the disciplines into a secure programmatic base." Many faculty view such confinement as imposition and then resist it; even softening my workshop approach, I found, by combining expressive principles with discipline-specific discourse conventions did not come close to the heart of the matter for WAC:

> If writing is to become a central focus of pedagogy, then it must be structurally linked to the values, goals, and activities of the disciplines; faculty must see a connection between encouraging better writing among their students and advancing the value and status of their disciplines—and their own individual careers. (Russell, 1991, p. 302)

Both of Russell's claims in this quote have resonated with me for two decades—that writing must be structurally linked to the disciplines and faculty must see its advantages to them and their students. The results of the programs at Montana State and UNR elevate his claims to warrants in the Toulmin sense of argumentation. Linking WAC workshops to the disciplines and faculty teaching within them is effective, resulting in numbers of undergraduate classes requiring writing exceeding 90%. Perhaps given the dark side to specialized language use, however, one might ask whether we want WAC to be effective.

For me the answer is "yes" because we need to encourage the development of the best problem solvers we can. To put it in plain but timely examples, we need the languages of climatology, chemistry, physics, and biology (among others) to measure the rate at which the earth heats and to design programs to arrest that process. We need the languages of sociology, political science, and education (among others) to understand the dynamics and consequences of poverty, overpopulation, or what Freire (1990) termed the *banking system of education*. We need the languages of veterinary science, range management, and conservation (among others) to explain how to collect sheep excrement in Montana and how such collection may interpret the health and direction of the herd. We need specialized languages to determine the most efficient turning of pistons in freighters hauling petroleum from Saudi Arabia to the United States or Alaskan timber to Japan, and how to develop, in any proactive sense, alternative fuel sources and building materials. As a local and global people, we have immediate concerns and needs. Mary Shelley, then a teenager, must have understood something of the notion of technology loose in and battering around garden Earth or at least garden England. She certainly represented it in her *Frankenstein*. Victor Frankenstein longs to return to pastoral innocence after he has built his creature, but it was too late for him then. It is far too late for us now. We must risk, I believe, the dark side of specialized languages to get the best that they may offer us and the best thinkers in those languages. Consequently, I chose the discipline-based ap-

proach to WAC because agenda-based approaches did not succeed and because, despite their dark underside, specialized languages are necessary to
solving specialized problems.

The list of what the language of English composition courses cannot do is
long. It cannot do climatology, chemistry, physics, biology, sociology, political science, or history. However, what it can do is important: It can talk
about the work, how it is done, and whether it should be done at all. As part
of its pedagogy, the composition sequence can provide one important forum
for the development of critical consciousness—a place where students can
talk about historic language events, technological advances, and their consequences (such as global warming). The sequence can talk about voice in
its varying personal and communal contexts. It can talk about the relationship of expertise to stewardship and agency. The composition sequence is a
promising location (although not a necessary one) for this kind of reflective
thinking as students begin their careers as specialists. In the context of this
argument, agency and stewardship mean individuals knowing first how to
act within their disciplines and then how to act for the better—using the
discipline and its language to access pieces of reality to save, preserve, or improve them. Such exertion, in the context of this study, is voice in one of its
highest forms.

Even the most eloquent proponent of expressivism, Georges Gusdorf
(1965), devoted much space to articulating the relationship of expression
and communication. Expression without communication is solipsism or
psychosis; communication without expression is mere "coin of the realm."
Gusdorf favored a benign blend of the two, and he implied that such a blend
occurs in almost every discourse act because almost no one purely expresses
or communicates, almost no one is exclusively self or other. I certainly agree
with Gusdorf, and I extend his conceptual implications to the practical—
that biologists, sociologists, educationists, or any of us entering into or operating within the disciplines does so as a self and an other. If we find the discipline's voice consistent with ourselves and our voice, we stick with it. If
not, we have the choice not to. The fact that students can choose has created a comfortable space for me to engage in WAC activities, but it seems
ignored by those compositionists who assert that people lose their authentic
selves as they write in the disciplines. The problem with this position is its
arrogance, assuming without any proof that one voice is superior to all others. I have given up on that assumption in favor of another: Many faculty
have found, and many students can find, authentic voice in the disciplines
they choose. Compositionists, rhetoricians, and WAC and writing center
professionals are in the best position to staff WAC programs which encourage these language users.

Composition, however, has just reached academic respectability and is experiencing a frenzy of delight in its burgeoning field. Note its numerous, imaginative courses in writing theory and practice at the undergraduate and graduate levels, its flurry of scholarly articles and books, its broadening attention to literacy education in various underattended-to communities, and its placement of graduate students in teaching positions in a long-withered English studies market. Composition studies has become a discipline acknowledged as providing the expertise in writing not only for students within its first-, second-, and third-year courses, but the discipline that provides expertise for everyone. There is reason to celebrate and understand why this success might translate into a vision for writing that transcends the boundaries of one discipline, becoming what that discipline hopes to be the vision for all. As a global population, we are in a race to the end now, however seemingly invisible. Without specialized languages, we make this race one-legged.

The Lighter Side

Between 1993 (when "Where Do We Go Next in Writing Across the Curriculum?" was published) and 2002, the term *discipline-specific discourse conventions* evolved into the term *learning to write in the disciplines*. In other words, learning to write in the disciplines (instead of discipline-specific discourse conventions) now complements *writing to learn* in the WAC lexicon. This is certainly an improvement because discipline-specific discourse conventions only touches the surface of difference between disciplines. The term eliminated the most serious cause of separation between disciplines, their specialized languages, and made it easier for experts in composition studies to dominate writing pedagogy in other fields. After all, if the language in which we write is the same, then one set of principles can guide writing practice. The experts from the discipline of composition studies, of course, would know those principles better than anybody else.

The term *learning to write in the disciplines* complicates this situation. It implies that a more intimate and complex connection exists between writing and disciplinarity, and that there is *reason* to learn to write in a discipline. That is, learning to write in biology is going to differ from learning to write in English; if you are an aspiring biologist, it is probably not going to do you much good to learn to write in the English Department. You are no doubt going to want to learn to write from biologists. "Learning to write in the disciplines" brings WAC closer to the condition in which universities actually exist as multiple discourse communities employing specialists who train novices. As much of an improvement over discipline-specific discourse conventions as it is, however, the term also remains linked to writing to learn, which is based in composition studies. The problem for WAC has been to disentangle a particularly nasty knot: (a) writing to learn supports a specific context for writing; (b) this context is no less important than others, but no more important either and certainly not universal; (c) the values for writing it supports are not shared across the curriculum as the lists of values generated by UNR's assessment project demonstrate; (d) nonetheless, WAC personnel are usually composition specialists who support writing to learn, and they want writing to learn to complement learning to write; and thus (e) their workshops, which try to establish this complementary relationship, become in part irrelevant and in some cases antagonistic to faculty in the disciplines.

This chapter's purpose has been to demonstrate how WAC theory and practice may carry the stamp of one department, program, or social and political agenda, and how that stamp may alienate those encountering it. This process of departmentally based activity does not necessarily limit itself to English departments and their writing programs, although English departments, and perhaps compositionists particularly, usually feel a pronounced pride of ownership of writing. English is almost always the only department mandated to teach writing to students across campus. These conditions ripen the potential for English to view its values for writing as givens and turn its own experience of writing into the universal experience. Other departments, often out of a head-in-the-sand urge to avoid the work of requiring writing, may support the claim that teaching writing is English's job. To assert that one department must do its job of teaching writing to all, however, is to beg some critical questions stemming from the academy's separateness. If you are a biologist, psychologist, chemist, or historian, if you are a member of any department at the typical comprehensive postsecondary institution who insists that English composition "do its job," those questions become: How could any one department, given its faculty's predispositions and specializations, be expected to teach writing in another discipline? How can any department expect another department to know or respect the profound nuances of language and cognitive activity its students must assimilate? How might any department be expected to synthesize form and context between disciplines when form and context are so individual to disciplines? The answer is, no one department can or should be expected to do so.

This answer suggests another serious difficulty, however: If no one department can comfortably be the home for WAC, where can the consciousness of difference and its implications for WAC theory be promoted? Where can the theory of difference best be applied, consciously, in practice? The best location from my perspective is the WAC writing center. Writing centers intrinsically become the only place to describe and accommodate difference, the best place to house writing across the curriculum programs. *Intrinsically* is not an accidental term. Writing centers potentially align themselves within the academy in ways that no other department does because they have no language of their own in the disciplinary sense outside of a language meant to aid student writers from any course and at any level of instruction. Again potentially they have no impulse to change faculty members into assignment makers and graders in their own image, favoring one set of values, purposes, and forms for writing over any other. Instead they want to draw from student writers what the writers hope their drafts will do (and help them do it); they want to draw from faculty what learning faculty hope their assignments will produce (and help them achieve it). WAC writing centers do not, or perhaps I should say must not, have the rhetorical agenda common to individual departments—an agenda that, if my basic premises are accepted, goes underground as individuals evolve as thinkers in the language of a discipline. Their agenda is cross-curricular, and that means helping students and faculty in the context of their own multiple languages not only because that multiplicity is a reality, but because it is necessary.

Wordsworth's biographer, historian, physician, lawyer, mariner, and natural scientist may be *engines* in his rhetorical scheme, but they need to be thought of as poets in ours. As a people, we need these professionals and their disciplinary voices—not to obscure their activities through language, but to do the problem-solving work their language makes possible and necessary. The more carefully they do their work and express its doing, the more prophetically they envision its consequences and persuasively offer them, the more they become poets.

4

WAC Administration Reduced to English-Only, Writing-Intensive, or Discipline-Based Models

There are many models for writing across the curriculum—perhaps as many as there are institutions that include WAC programs. A reading, say, of *Programs That Work* or *Writing Centers and Writing Across the Curriculum* demonstrates the multiplicity of models evolved over the last two decades. In an effort to render them manageable, I reduce their administrative foundations to three. In the first model, composition becomes endorsed as an English department endeavor, and English is charged to teach writing to all students in its first-year English sequence—even going so far as to designate writing courses for the humanities, business, social and natural sciences, and so on. English is funded to hire advanced and technical writing specialists to offer upper division composition courses, and the Department supervises the teaching activity in these courses. In the second model, upper administrators and departmental supervisors tell faculty where and how to teach writing, and selected courses within departments are designated as *writing-intensive*. In the third model, WAC activity bases itself in the disciplines, with the faculty members deciding where and how writing might be used in their courses and disciplines. It would be pointless for me to ignore that nearly every WAC program attempts to include some degree of each of these features as they will almost uniformly claim; it would also be nearly pointless not to affirm that the third model is my choice and that my life in WAC work is based on that choice. My argument here depends on how my readers perceive writing across the curriculum: as writing in English departments, writing in one or two contexts within disciplines, or writing that occurs when faculty want it to because they see its value to themselves, their disciplines, and the students they teach. The

58

question is biased, to be sure, but given these general approaches to WAC, which have a basis in existing programs, where should WAC be housed to be most effective?

Under the first scenario, WAC is housed exclusively in English. Not many English department faculty members would acknowledge it as their role, exclusively, to teach students how to write. They may believe that their values for writing are superior to those in other departments, but when faced with the immense responsibility for teaching all students to write, they would rightly balk. Their mission to teach literature might certainly be compromised by such a focus, as might their own philosophy of composition. The issue, however, is complicated by English's urges toward ownership of composition, as I explain in chapter 6, and by the faculty at large, which wants English to teach writing: first because history and the prospering discipline of composition studies support it, and second because including writing takes time away from their own teaching and research, challenging them in ways they may not want to be challenged. If English teaches it, they may not have to. Another complication stems from the seeming ease with which WAC may be brought to campus by making it English's responsibility. Refocus the composition program, which is already in place, hire a few (hundred?) advanced and technical writing specialists, create a comprehensive course sequence at more advanced levels, and, presto, a WAC program.

There are, of course, many problems with this scenario. First, funding such a program must be costly. It would be folly to hire one or two advanced and technical writing specialists in English, offer writing courses at the upper division level, and not expect nearly every department to send its students as a requirement into these courses. UNR's English Department, for example, offered an advanced expository writing course to its junior majors and a few others for several semesters before it was discovered by the Colleges of Education, Business, and Engineering. Once discovered, the course was overwhelmed by hundreds of students from these colleges, which began to require it. At first the English Department tried to meet the demand with full-time faculty, letters of appointment, and teaching fellows. However, it was not being funded for teaching this course across the curriculum and finally took the only action it could—dropping the number of sections it offered down to two and restricting enrollment. The faculty in other departments may not and probably will not want to teach writing while still recognizing its value to their students. Upper division writing classes in English satisfy their desires in multiple ways. They can abdicate responsibility while believing that it is being met elsewhere. They can insist that English is doing its job while they are doing theirs. Obviously, one or two of these writing teachers will not be able to cover the demands on such classes; the number of technical writing people and the number of courses offered will have to be dramatically increased. Thus, the program becomes expensive.

The second problem comes from the notion that first-year composition can design itself to teach writing in the disciplines, with courses designated for various majors (e.g., first-year writing for science, business, or humanities majors). The impracticality of this program has already been shown at a few comprehensive universities, which assertively attempted to institute it. Students registered for classes in massive numbers not because of any applicability to their intended majors, but because of convenience of time and availability, causing many potential engineers to register, say, for composition courses emphasizing business and many potential biologists to register for courses emphasizing humanities. Some readers may observe, "Well fine, students cannot be hurt by these multiple, sometimes contrary presentations of writing and reading." They may be right. Yet their perspective denies the point of such courses: to help students enter the writing communities of their disciplines. If students register for the wrong composition courses, they can and do complain about irrelevance to their own interests, although they were the ones to sign up for these courses, and the difficulty of pertinence creates profound and expensive registration problems.

These kinds of composition courses also pretend to do what they cannot do. They pretend to prepare students for the writing work of a discipline when all they can hope for is to prepare students to write about the work done in the disciplines. That is, first-year composition teachers, often teaching assistants in English, cannot teach the real writing of a discipline or make the writing or reading assignments that evidence the work. They cannot do so because their own specialization limits their entry into other specializations unless they have appropriated other languages. Naturally, they want a closeness to their own disciplinary contexts, and their writing and reading assignments reflect that desire. My point is that even if postsecondary institutions could somehow place their students in the right composition courses, they would not get what they want: writers prepared to write in the disciplines.

The problem with first-year composition attempting to prepare students for writing in the disciplines hints at a third problem: the difficulty with advanced and technical writing experts bearing responsibility for teaching writing across the curriculum. If one accepts that writing cannot be taught across the curriculum by the first-year English sequence, and I hope my readers do, then one must at least wonder about how technical writing experts may teach writing to every discipline. How will they design the courses? How will they accommodate the varied languages and teach the values, purposes, and forms for writing to students from such a disparate group of academic communities? How, without being members of the communities to which their students belong, can they render the writing experience authentic? Each of these questions suggests the problems with blanketing the writing curriculum with one type of context, rather than with the reality of writing in the multiple contexts presented by the academy. Such a blanketing does not readily stretch itself to include the academy's many languages and its multiple values, purposes, and forms for writing. It leaves students at a disadvantage because it will probably lessen their opportunities to write within their disciplines.

Computers and Composition: A Marriage Made in Heaven?

It is appropriate here to discuss the new urges to teach writing through the rapidly evolving computer-generated technologies, and the acknowledged expertise in this arena of technical writing professionals housed in English departments, composition programs, and writing centers. This is a formidable movement, causing McLeod (2001) to refer to WAC as "Electronic Communication Across the Curriculum" (ECAC; p. 62). McLeod intentionally overstated, but certainly technology has become seductive in itself for its steamy expansion in numerous directions: word processing, databasing, page making, to be sure; but also e-mail, the World Wide Web, online teaching and tutoring, the out-sourcing of teaching and tutoring, distance learning, wired classrooms, electronic portfolio and presentation making, and Web page design. I published an article in *Collegiate Microcomputer* many years ago about the issue of computers and composition (Waldo, 1985), in which I argued that word processing was the only viable use for computer technology and writing. My article rejected, as worthwhile uses, grammar worksheet and invention programs. The realities of computer technology, then, pale when compared with those now. However, I continue to stand by my claim, although I am slowly accommodating some changes. Our writing center, for example, has its own Web page, along with online tutoring capability. We have not yet unleashed this tutoring capability for fear of being buried by requests for it, when we now tutor to the limits of our budget in person one on one. (I note that Colorado State's Writing Center, heavily Webbed and online, discontinued online tutoring for 3 months because it could not afford the tutoring traffic [CSU Web site, December 1999].) I am aware of the attraction that upper administrators feel for these technologies and their potential for increasing full-time equivalencies without increasing teaching staff. Extremely popular inside and outside the institution, computer technology is a track of which nearly everyone approves and administrators support; it is a track that writing programs and centers may follow without political speed bumps while so many other tracks they follow may shovel bumps up and, as such, it is valu-able. Nonetheless, I emphasize the same point I made in my article.

Whatever technology may be able to do, it cannot (yet) write and think critically for students or their teachers. It still remains only possible to do the work of a discipline by appropriating and using its language. That takes peo-ple writing, reading, listening, talking, interacting, mentoring, and being mentored within disciplinary contexts. No matter what technology can do, and I recognize it can do much to provide specialized data and synthesize it, present all or most of the arguments on a given issue, and even create interac-tive situations for people to work collaboratively on projects, its main purpose remains to bank text for withdrawal and supply writing tools. It fails to make the imaginative connections that solve problems, synthesize data, analyze op-posing points of view, and make arguments in a way that people committed with full heart and mind can.

Risking exposure as a Luddite, I hope technology will always fail to do so. Perhaps one day programs may be able to think and write critically for us—perhaps they may not only display the textual scenario surrounding a prob-lem, say, the Yucca Mountain nuclear waste dump, but then also frame the problem and propose its best solution. Without ignoring the potential here for special interests to include chips that forward their own solutions to prob-lems (with their own products supplied as essential), a feeling I admit is some-what paranoid, I worry about professionals thinking (again, my paranoia?) that computers can develop the kind of critical behaviors described by Freire (1990) in his *Education for Critical Consciousness*. They cannot.

At present, one may access data to help solve problems. Yet the process must be recognized, at bottom, as a trip to the library without the walking; the results of that trip may be shared with collaborators without the delay and inconvenience of the Post Office or Federal Express, but the experience must be understood as a means to an end and not the end itself. We may use com-puter technology to help us solve our problems, but not to solve our problems for us. Everyone reading this text may agree to this point about computer technology, even those committed unreflectively to it. However, as I look at the job descriptions in the MLA, as I read the chat room correspondence for writing programs and writing centers, and as I listen to my own upper admin-istrators, the real problem emerges: Computer-generated research and writing technology may not be able to think and write for us, but we may begin to be-lieve that they can. We may start to celebrate the technology for itself. Writ-ing centers must be particularly wary of this process, but so too writing pro-grams, because their tenuousness to the institution at large encourages them to latch onto any new vehicle for support and permanence.

During November 1999, I received a call from a northeastern college president. His college, primarily devoted to engineering and the professional schools, was to advertise a position as Director of the Center for Communication Excellence, a technopalace only to be dreamed of by those who love machines. After hearing the job description, I wondered about recommending people to apply—the main reason for his call. He had mentioned nothing about the director working with students or faculty beyond the technology— helping students develop as critical thinkers or the faculty as assignment designers and graders. No one I could recommend would be satisfied in his or her position admiring technology only, however enticing. Should a college president be guided by these considerations while initiating such a grand communications center? In my opinion, without a doubt. He or she must want the jobs that graduates do to be done well, and this means thinking, speaking, and writing the language of a discipline. Yet he or she must also hope that they will think ethically about what they are doing. I know this person who called me is one to consider all these matters, to relish the possibility of a cutting-edge technological center, but also, as the months and years pass, to consider whether these graduates understand, beyond the immediate, what they are doing. Nonetheless, the opportunity for a purely technological center was too appealing for him to mention other considerations at the time. Why should he think beyond such a center? It is what it is, where much FTE now seems to be made, where the prestige seems to be made, and where the alumni money seems to be made. It is, or might be, its own self-fulfilling prophecy. One must climb on this train, the new steam engine(?), or be left to ride a bike. This, in part, is what we face now as teachers of writing and as writing center directors—the opportunity (unsympathetically) to cash in on what college upper administrators want, however obscurely, from technology, research, and writing. It is what it is—too alluring not to become a focal point of our endeavors. It must not, however, become *the* focal point of our endeavors.

I believe, as I did in 1985 when I published the article, that the publicity lauding computer technology and writing far exceeds its grasp, but I also celebrate its potential for accelerating the students' growth as writers by increasing their opportunities to write and receive feedback on their writing. That potential rests in the following areas:

- word processing—the more efficient and comprehensive the programs the better;
- e-mail correspondence—if the telephone replaced letter writing, perhaps e-mail will replace the telephone, at least for much personal corre-

spondence, and now classroom correspondence, each increasing the writing and thinking its users do;

- wired classrooms—in which students and teachers can review each other's work in progress, not just in English department writing classes, but everywhere;

- online tutoring and teaching—although I am more enthusiastic about the teaching, as Faigley (1995) demonstrated effectively in his technology chapter in *Fragments of Rationality*, than the tutoring, which no one has shown to be as cost- or quality-effective as tutoring one on one; and

- research gathering on the Web—although I worry about the enhanced environment for plagiarism; nonetheless, to gather research banked by computer libraries and Webs affords a readiness of access, and doing so may improve writing and thinking in given communities.

These five arenas are consistent with Moran's (2001) survey of computer technologies for writers and teachers (pp. 207–214), and they all share one important condition: people using tools and not tools using people.

As writing centers and programs move into helping students prepare their electronic portfolios, wired classroom presentations, and Web sites, not to ignore grammar exercise programs and rhetorics on disk, they begin to lose the focus that makes them institutionally effective: working with students and faculty in developing critical thinking behaviors that cause people to work productively within the disciplines to be sure, but also to think consciously about their work and disciplines. If they have to ride this steam engine to survive, they should perhaps dust off their bikes.

Computer technology cannot render writing centers, WAC, or writing programs irrelevant however much it may appear to be doing so. To return to the application of the term *seductive* to technology, I believe that such technology is now more seductive than WAC, writing programs, or writing centers, which were once quite sexy themselves. Now they sometimes grow so comfortable in their marriage and so institutionalized as to become almost invisible. This is the risk that successful programs assume: to become successful to the degree that they disappear into the fabric of the academy. When their success causes them to disappear as cutting-edge programs, there exists the obvious urge to fill the vacuum—to move on toward other, more alluring investments. This movement is not an aberrance or error unless it supplants those other programs, and postsecondary administrators who surrender to it are doing so not perversely, but naturally following their predecessors in virtually every arena of endeavor. The steam locomotive was sexier than the horse-drawn coach (at least in a technological sense) and the tractor more productive than the plow. We cannot arrest this movement, and I have no desire to try. I agree with Moran (2001), who asserted that, on the one hand, we should not "all uncritically 'dive in' to the new technology," but, on the other hand, if we do not keep up with technology, we may end up as "roadkill on the information highway" (p. 203). Nonetheless, humans—with their tendency toward community and assimilation of language, culture, and values—will always prevail as speakers, thinkers, and representatives for their communities. Computer technology cannot replace this process. It can only, if understood wisely, enhance it. The discussion of WAC scenarios, consequently, remains relevant far beyond computer technology.

Writing-Intensive WAC Programs

The second WAC scenario reflects the first, lending itself to a central control or administration. It is the oldest and perhaps most pervasive approach to WAC depending on how that acronym is defined, and the one, ironically, most open to saving Wordsworth's Poet. Let us say that an upper administrator, aware of the publicity writing quality has been receiving, aware of the grumblings of faculty about the inadequacy of undergraduate and graduate student writing, aware of the faculty development potential of WAC and its consequent rewards to him or her, mandates that writing be included in some classes in all departments. This top–down approach can evidence immediate results, say even between the fall and spring semesters, but usually between summer and fall, as one or two classes in a department are designated as *writing-intensive*. These classes can be initiated quickly and without the costs of English departments bearing the burden. Administrators may readily insist, and have insisted to be sure, that teachers of writing-intensive classes come from within the institution, thus generating few new full-time faculty. Those usually given the charge to train the teachers of writing in other departments come from the English Department, which has the expertise to supervise teachers of writing in the disciplines.

The advantages of this writing-intensive scenario must be obvious. Such a program is cost-effective. It requires little hiring of new tenure-track faculty because professionals within departments are designated as their writing teachers; if no faculty can be found or coerced, many floating part-timers in English and other departments may be snared. This scenario operates out of a version of discipline-based theory, assuming that *teaching* writing within biology, history, nursing, engineering, and so on is more effective than teaching it merely in English. From the English Department perspective, the second model potentially offers many appeals.

It frees English from the onerous responsibility of teaching all students to write. English then maintains the department's literature programs without interference; it sustains English composition faculty in their discipline-based pursuits. At the same time, writing-intensive programs allow English to exercise control over writing across campus because experts in composition usually train and supervise the teachers of writing, thus supporting visions for WAC like those presented by Jones and Comprone. Intensive programs grant English the opportunity to avoid serious problems while freeing its writing experts to forward a value-based agenda, often involving writing to learn. The writing-intensive approach appears to satisfy many theoretical and practical demands at once.

Yet its disadvantages must be as obvious as its advantages. Perhaps its most obvious disadvantage shades itself under the umbrella of greatest advantage. Again writing-intensive programs teach writing within the disciplines—not one discipline becoming responsible for all students, but each discipline for its own. As such these programs accommodate the theory that students advance more readily as writers within their disciplines when they write within them. The writing-intensive approach, however, opens faculty to abdicating responsibility for using writing assignments in multiple classroom contexts in even more pronounced ways than the English-only WAC movement does. However much a faculty member in biology may want to believe that the writing needs of students are being met by a program based in an English department, it is a long, equivocating stretch to do so. When the designated writing course (or courses) is within the department, however, the instructor may rest easier that students are writing biology and not some other type of writing. Thus, under the umbrella of such in-house teaching, instructors give over writing to their colleagues within the department. Russell (1990) commented on writing-intensives:

> Writing-intensives, sometimes supported by a remedial lab, are perhaps the most common curricular model for WAC. But writing-intensive courses . . . concentrate responsibility for initiating students into the discourse community in a few professors or TAs, while freeing most faculty resources for activities which the community views as more important than initiating new members. As Brown's WAC director Tori Haring-Smith points out, when a few courses are labeled *writing-intensive*, students object when other courses require writing. (p. 297)

Few professors or TAs become responsible for teaching writing within departments under the writing-intensive model, and these are often people at the edge of departmental power and permanence. Because designated courses include writing, students expect it in no other courses. Further, writing-intensive programs disguise themselves as comprehensive to departmental faculty and inexpensive to upper administrators.

Although comparatively inexpensive, writing-intensive WAC programs are far from comprehensive. The writing courses are usually contextually located, often at the first term for juniors and the final term for seniors. There is rarely a sense of organic, developmentally progressive assignment making or grading in such programs beyond what supervisors from English or other supervisors encourage within the classes. The faculty talk, which occurs when everyone includes writing assignments, about which assignments succeed or fail, and which prepare students for the next level of learning, becomes obfuscated in this program by administrative matters: "Who's going to teach Engineering 301? None of us? Well, then, we'd better get some English Department lecturers to do it, or some competent TAs. Otherwise, we'll all be in the mix." I have heard these types of comments and questions from faculty within departments and by composition faculty who supervise the teaching of writing within departments. Who suffers? It is not the tenured faculty who probably will not teach the courses anyway; it is not the want-to-be tenured faculty, although these people are often called on to teach the writing-intensive courses, or are told, for their own professional well-being, not to; it is not English department supervisors, who can forward their agenda for writing under administrative mandate.

Who suffers, of course, are the students. They suffer because of the limited access to the language of their disciplines that one or two writing-intensive courses provide. Because of that limited access, they enter the workforce less able to solve problems specific to their disciplines and think critically or ethically about the work they do. We all suffer because of this situation—students leaving the academy underprepared. Potential stewards and agents, people with environmental imaginations, will find their ability to act constricted by their limited expertise, and this constriction disables all of us.

Discipline-Based Writing Across the Curriculum

Often accompanying both the English-only and writing-intensive administrative models for WAC is the attractive and frequently recommended method of team teaching. "In designing a writing course [in occupational therapy]," Detweiler and Peyton (2000) observed, "faculty members may also consider the following teaching" option: "a team-taught, writing-intensive course with an occupational therapist paired with a writing specialist" (p. 56). Within WAC, team teaching usually means that a content specialist works alongside a writing specialist, each collaborates with the other, but each also focuses on his or her own specialty. In this way, on the surface anyway, content and composition remain intact. Yet the team teaching model can be expensive because each faculty member often receives release from teaching another course within the home department. One might also ask, given the success of WAC at schools such as Montana State and UNR, "Why do it?" when faculty in the disciplines can teach writing themselves. Writing center statistics at Montana State show that the amount of writing assigned during a 6-year period increased by nearly three times. Center statistics evidence the same increase at UNR. Yet student exit interviews and phone surveys at UNR, as described in detail in chapter 7, present a more accurate picture of the increase and amount of writing being assigned there. Those instruments show that more than 90% of the undergraduate classes at UNR require writing assignments. Montana State and UNR operate almost exclusively from a discipline-based model for WAC. I remarked earlier that content and composition remain intact through team teaching, "on the surface anyway." The problem is the potential for conflict between the two instructors, which may emerge when content specialists insist that students learn to write in their classrooms and composition specialists insist that they write to learn about themselves and voices in relation to course material. One favors the content specialists' interests, classroom, and disciplinary culture, the other the compositionists'.

Many of these acute problems may be addressed by instituting a program based in the disciplines with faculty across a department sharing responsibility for teaching writing, the third model for writing across the curriculum. This model acknowledges as its theoretic foundation some combination of three principles: (a) each discipline has its own language and cognitive behaviors, and its own values, purposes, and forms for writing; (b) no one discipline's language or values are superior to those of another; and (c) WAC professionals must ground their activities in this sense of equality and difference, presenting workshops that avoid the extension of their own community's expertise to the members of another community. Instead, the interaction between the consultant and faculty member becomes dialogic, made up of questions and focused conversation between equals, as I explain. This activity and its theoretic underpinnings must at some point, from the beginning or during the process, become the subject of discussion so that all participants, the faculty first and then the students they teach, develop a critical consciousness about the impact of difference.

The advantages of this third approach may not be as readily obvious as those of the writing-intensive or English-only approaches. In the latter two, WAC may be instituted almost instantly, whereas in the third, it occurs over time (from my experience, visible results take 3–5 years). I argue here for a completely voluntary participation in WAC on the part of faculty. Although the program will saturate the campus with workshops on assignment design and evaluative techniques, WAC professionals must be comfortable with any attendance—even as few as one or two faculty volunteers. The program depends, at first, not on numbers, but on commitment—teachers seeing the value of writing assignments for their students and feeling enfranchised to make those assignments without the extended expertise of others. It relies for its growth on word of mouth, as those who experience success tell their colleagues about it and the program so that progress occurs from the bottom up rather than the top down. (Gere and Smith [1979] described the pyramidal change-agentry process—one person convinces two others who in turn convince two others, etc.—in *Attitudes, Language, and Change.*) The process of enfranchisement almost certainly will blossom, but it cannot be expected to do so immediately. Any WAC administrator inclined toward this model must recognize that immediate results sometimes drive the thinking of those who budget the money. Consequently, the time it may take to achieve results must clearly be part of the negotiating posture.

In addition to not offering immediate results, this third WAC model ignores and actively rejects the obvious: the English composition specialists' role, if that role includes imposing their values for writing across campus, no small point if we consider how ingrained those values have become and how active those specialists are in extending their position. There may be resistance from English.

Yet the advantages of a cross-curricular writing program devoted to faculty and students in the disciplines far outweigh its disadvantages. I admit it is expensive. As I argue, a center for the program must be established, a director, faculty consultants, and tutors hired. This costs money if done right—perhaps the equivalent of four or five faculty lines. Yet four or five faculty lines could not realistically hope to cover the cost of an English-only WAC program. It cannot realistically hope to cover the outsourcing of these services to private corporations. Writing-intensive programs, presumably, must also have a director, consultants, and perhaps even tutors. What benefits accrue for the institution from discipline-specific WAC? Ideally, all departments share responsibility for writing, not just in one or two courses, but dozens of courses and perhaps every course. All faculty members teach writing, and not just one or two designated instructors. These faculty members come from all ranks, not just the assistant professor, lecturer, graduate student, or part-time levels.

The activity takes place out of sound theory—that we grow in our academic languages in a way similar to how we grow in the languages of our family and culture, and that we think in the language of our discipline. Ideally, the process enfranchises students as it enfranchises faculty. Volunteers who come to workshops make good assignments because they want to, not because they are obliged to do so. They make assignments pertinent to their courses and disciplines, not to some other course or discipline. As the number of faculty using writing within a given department increases, and as their sophistication as writing instructors evolves, they begin to talk to each other about their assignments. They critique, sequence, and assess the quality of their students' writing across their department. All of this benefits students. It opens the gates of a discipline, where before they might be closed, because faculty begin to use writing with their students, courses, and disciplines in mind, and they think meta-consciously about its use in their own contexts, not some abstract, *from the other* context. Ideally, writing becomes a barometer for student success and progress, not a vehicle for failure and exclusion.

The ideal is not the real to be sure. Yet my own experience suggests that the ideal may nudge itself close to the real. At Montana State University (10,000 student full-time equivalent [FTE]), we followed (by necessity as much as intention) this third WAC approach. MSU's consultancy created an atmosphere in which faculty made their own decisions about the use of writing by helping them, through questions and focused conversation, to design assignments. The statistics for MSU's Writing Center, rising from 5,400 students in 200 different classes (recorded its first year in 1983/1984) to 9,000 students in 550 different classes (recorded during 1988/1989), suggest, although do not prove, a large increase in the amount of writing students did. More than twice the student writers and almost three times the number of courses are represented in 1988/1989 than in its inaugural year 1983/1984.

In the years between 1983 and 1989, Montana State experienced perpetual budget cuts so severe that a committee of active, widely respected faculty and administrators was called on to determine which programs and departments should be kept intact, which lessened, and which discontinued. The School of Architecture, to illustrate the seriousness of this process, was one of those decided on for discontinuance. After extensive investigation into each department and program, the committee judged departments, divisions, and programs as *not important, somewhat important, important,* or *critically important* to the mission of the university and the people of Montana.

Only one program received the judgment of *critically important*—MSU's Writing Center. Although almost all other departmental and programmatic budgets declined, its budget remained unaffected by the 20% budget cuts over a 3-year period. Given that writing centers were often the first to go when funds disappeared, the committee's endorsement was especially noteworthy.

Montana State's Writing Center became critically important to the university and its students, faculty, and administration perhaps because everyone there worked hard. Yet everyone in Architecture (which, in the end, survived) worked hard as well, and each of the courses in Architecture generated credit hours. Nothing that MSU's Center did produced funding, making it even more vulnerable. Everyone on the committee knew that. It was discussed openly. Hard work alone would not promote financial stability and critical importance in the face of so much decline of money and competition for it.

More important than hard work, it was the method that Center personnel used in working with both students and faculty, but particularly faculty. Although Montana State's Writing Center has lessened in importance during recent years, the use of writing institutionally has not. Montana State remains one of the most active, if unacknowledged, WAC schools in the country. The condition of remaining so substantially devoted to using writing in literally hundreds of classes, as the center for writing activity atrophies, suggests the power of discipline-based approaches to writing. When the faculty see the usefulness of writing to their students, courses, and disciplines, its use remains intact and viable regardless of the program or people who initially promoted it.

In the summer of 1989, four of us left Montana State to set up a writing center at the University of Nevada, Reno (13,000 student FTE), based on the same model as MSU's. We were committed to making nebulous features at MSU formally programmatic at UNR. Principal among those features was the use of inquiry and collaboration with faculty, establishing a discipline-based model for writing across the curriculum.

In its first year (1989/1990), UNR's Writing Center recorded 3,200 tutoring appointments from 200 different classes. In its most recent year (2000/2001), it recorded 7,000 appointments from 550 different classes. In other words, over the course of a 10-year period, the tutoring appointments and classes represented more than doubled. This increase does not exceed that at Montana State, although MSU's numbers are padded by the several required visits to the Center by first-year students. The increase demonstrates only one kind of success. Partly, the statistics reflect the increased visibility of the Writing Center as the years have passed. Nonetheless, UNR's other assessment instruments corroborate that center statistics include only one third to one half of the courses assigning writing during a given academic year. (In other words, the number of classes in which students write exceeds 1,100.) Not all students come to the Center for tutoring, and not all faculty urge that they should. Nonetheless, these are hard statistics demonstrating the minimum amount of writing required. We know that more than 500 courses in a given year at UNR use writing assignments, and that fact is cause to celebrate. These statistics, however, do not mean that teachers make better assignments or students grow as learners, but they are a start. When combined with the other assessment vehicles we have been using at UNR, two phone surveys of more than 400 randomly selected faculty from every department, in-person interviews with graduating seniors from widely represented disciplines, and the discipline-based writing assessment project, the evidence of comprehensive success begins to mount.

When considering writing across the curriculum, at first, I did not think of my beliefs about writing as values, but as the givens, which all English teachers and then everyone else would enthusiastically adopt after they saw the light. Yet what I discovered in the practice of my position countered and cooled these fires. A WAC writing center director's position exaggerates contradictions. Directors will certainly carry their own values for writing and its teaching into the arena. In their multiple roles, however, they will encounter students whose writing comes from dozens of different disciplines and hundreds of classes. They will encounter faculty members who have, perhaps for decades, written in the language and form of a particular academic community. If center directors press their own agenda for writing, if they insist that students be tutored out of their and their discipline's values for writing, if they consult with faculty urging their agenda, say, of process-expressivist (or cognitivist, socialist, feminist, postmodernist) principles for writing assignments, they will no doubt meet resistance.

The most significant teaching purpose faculty members have is to pass onto students the language of their academic community. Faculty initiate new community members, immersing them in a particular diction and syntax—a way of seeing and making meaning in the world. Few are fully conscious of how the process operates or even that it *is* operating, but the external, social language surrounding the new major becomes an increasingly important part of that person's speaking, writing, and then thinking, as the rich and complex surface language evolves into the abbreviated and individuated code Vygotsky (1962) described. People begin to think words instead of saying them, to think as biologists, sociologists, educationists, and historians would think. Even course sequencing is designed to encourage the linguistic development of students in a major, moving in nearly all disciplines from the introductory to the survey courses, and then to the more advanced specialized courses. Of course the usual justification for course sequencing is that it reflects progress from simpler content and critical thinking to more complex content and critical thinking. It must now be obvious that the sequencing, however faulty and seemingly exclusionary, is fundamentally linked to language acquisition.

Given the covert nature of that acquisition and acculturation into communities, faculty will not perceive their ensuing values for writing to be values, but givens. Thus, an obvious, potential crisis emerges in any WAC endeavor: "Whose givens prevail?" The conflict surfaces particularly between writing in English composition and writing in the disciplines, as well as between compositionists teaching writing and the same compositionists consulting colleagues in other departments. It is the crisis of multiple languages in the academy and the effort to bring the writing of those languages under one banner—to keep Wordsworth's Poet alive.

5

Still the Last Best Place for Writing Across the Curriculum: The Writing Center

I want to demonstrate how writing centers become intrinsically the best place to negotiate the *crisis* of difference. They can act out of a pedagogy that understands difference and create a forum where its impact might be openly discussed as part of their fundamental activity. As I observed at the end of the third chapter, writing centers align themselves within the academy in ways that no other department does. This position has been as much the source of their insecurity as their security. Aligned with no department, they risk amputation; aligned with a department, they risk dependency. Independent of any department, however, writing centers position themselves to work with all. WAC writing centers are potentially situated to aid both student writers and faculty assignment makers in generating writing that works for them both, and they are positioned to use writing technology in ways that benefit everyone.

The problem is, however, that few writing centers are situated in this way, and they are viewed by composition studies as Third World participants:

> Writing center staff are not seen as professionals, not even among compositionists. Consequently, we are not receiving support in terms of budgets, staffing, salaries, release time, recognition of our scholarship and teaching—in any of the considerations due academic faculty or programs. We are the third-class citizenry in English departments, and nothing is being done to rectify our situation. Rather than describing our place in the profession as a "niche," we might describe it as a "ghetto," mindful of the word's connotations of poverty, isolation, and low prestige. (Balester, 1992, p. 166)

Too often centers become sentence-level clinics, self-stroking technology palaces, or forums for passing competency tests. These may be worthy purposes for them, but they are distinctly limited in vision. Writing centers, however, sometimes make their own bed of abuse. They forward pronounced agendas. In some cases, paper ownership gains such precedence that tutors become mere sounding boards for student writers, asking questions that reach little beyond "How do you feel about your paper?" In other cases, the agenda becomes much more ideological (as I describe), where tutors challenge the fairness of the assignment and, by expressed extension, the fairness of the teacher making the assignment and of the institution to which the teacher belongs. These too may be worthy purposes, but given the environmental, social, and cultural conditions in which we find ourselves globally, they appear lamentably local, extending not far beyond writing to learn approaches. Like WAC programs, writing centers take many forms—perhaps as many forms as the institutions they serve. Nonetheless, it is possible to synthesize them.

A modestly growing effort to locate separate writing centers within departments, divisions, or colleges (of arts and science, business, education, etc.) is taking place. This movement has merit from a discipline-based, cross-curricular perspective because tutors hired from a given discipline work with students writing in that discipline. Under this model, faculty WAC consultants may also work with their colleagues from related disciplines. As a serious advantage, tutors and students share an understanding of content, and they often write papers on similar subjects. The development of these centers, variously decentered, reflects the increasing importance of writing centers to upper administrators. Along with the technology center, they may be the next phase in writing center evolution. Yet they do have their problems. First, to succeed, they will be expensive and perhaps not yet cost-effective as every department, division, or college would have the right to claim a need for such a center—in Nevada's situation, more than 10 colleges and divisions and more than 70 departments. Arguably, these centers might be dangled as a carrot to faculty for including writing assignments, but to dangle such a carrot means it must be supported financially. Even if this financial commitment could be attained and money given to a department for a satellite center, it would be difficult to track how the money was truly being spent (i.e., any money given to a department may find itself spent according to departmental needs regardless of the mandate to create a center). Second, if an abiding philosophy or theory for student tutoring and faculty consulting exists—say one of question asking and collaboration, which all tutors and consultants are expected to follow—then such decentering makes it more difficult to maintain the program's consistency. Certainly, satellite centers open themselves to a more directive or prescriptive approach to tutoring and consulting because they are decentered. Third, decentering may lessen the campuswide impact of WAC writing centers for curricular change. Writing centers must choose their arguments well; to argue every point of curricular disagreement would be suicidal. As a unit, however, centers can use the political power they have to forward well-chosen positions, shaping curricula and, if need be, assessment. Spread across the curriculum, they jeopardize that political power to affect resistance or reform; they become, in a real sense, service arms of the academy. Centers within departments, divisions, and colleges are not at present common: The University of Washington has attempted such centers as has Arizona State, and the results are not yet evident.

The most common writing center is appended to an English department. Many writing centers are funded within English and designated mainly to help students write within college composition courses. Their directors will often be English department members regardless of their tenure status. The tutors they train will mostly be English majors. Under these circumstances, the natural, organic approach to training students to tutor and consultants to work with faculty may be carved in the values of English composition, particularly in writing to learn, to train in voice, authenticity, originality, personal writing, writing as process, and so on. This model for writing centers also has merit, but it must be thought of as no more crossing the curriculum than the English composition program it supports. Yet many centers housed in English do cross the curriculum, tutoring student writers from every discipline because the administration says to do so or because students have no idea where else (the doors of their instructors being closed) to turn. Writing centers that follow a department's rhetorical agenda and promote a set of values for writing with students and faculty across campus locate themselves in unfortunate, sometimes comic, arenas for conflict.

UNR's Writing Center has no funding or physical connection to any department, and it hires graduate student tutors from a variety of disciplines. Few writing centers more consciously avoid departmental agendas for writing across the curriculum than does UNR's Center. We celebrate avoiding it, and we train to avoid it. Nonetheless, I can offer dozens of examples in which an agenda surfaces in both tutoring and consulting.

For example, I observed a tutor in Nevada's Writing Center—a graduate student in rhetoric and composition—tutoring a doctoral student writing a paper in educational administration. The assignment was to explain a pattern for bus routes in a rural Nevada county. It had an engaging context (all previous designs had failed) and a clear audience (school board members angry about the failures). Although the paper managed the assignment's requirements admirably, it was laden with the language of educational administration, without the accouterments of self that the tutor wanted to see. The tutor perceived this omission of self as the paper's principal area for improvement, and he peppered the tutoring session with questions concerning originality, the writer's personality and experience, creative imagery, and active voice. The student, however, resisted these questions, saying plainly, "I don't write in that way, and my professors don't want me to." This tutor could not seem to *hear* the writer's point, and the session, without intervention, would have been largely useless. It could have been worse than useless, being destructive both to the Center and to the writer. Center personnel worked with this tutor for many weeks after this session, hoping at once to point out the differences in writing between disciplines and the worth of helping students in disciplinary contexts. Yet so ingrained had his values for writing become, so unconscious was he of them as values, that he failed to see the point and continued to tutor as if all student writers were writing for his classes. I do not find much comic in this experience, but I do think of the next example as such.

In this case, an anthropology doctoral student tutored a second-semester composition student. The assignment asked writers to select a contemporary culture with which they had contact and about which they were interested enough to write. These cultures might be punk, mosh-pitting, skateboarding, snowboarding, or art; the list was extensive. The assignment required students to write an ethnography of the culture they had chosen, using outside reference sources, interviews, and personal experience. As a context, it described a situation about which they knew and their peers did not, although their peers wanted to know. The audience was their peers. Like the educational administration assignment, it had much to recommend it: goals, context, and audience. Our tutor, again a PhD student in anthropology, knew a great deal about ethnographies from an anthropological context. She had internalized the language, forms, and values for ethnography, and she saw none of them in this first-year student's paper.

In many ways, this tutor was/is one of our best, and her immersion in anthropology usually helped more than hurt. Anthropology graduate students combine qualities and backgrounds often essential to our work. They have extensive experience in the languages of the social sciences and ably tutor students from psychology, sociology, social work, educational psychology, history, and, of course, anthropology. In addition, they often bring training in the natural sciences to the tutoring table, being sometimes lapsed natural science students. Their hope consistently has been to do the job well, and we have had as many as four of them on our staff of 25.

It is pertinent to note, however, that anthropology has not recently been a friend to UNR's Writing Center, actually asking those tutors from their department to organize their own center for anthropology. The politics of this request mirror the politics of writing centers everywhere when they pay students from various departments and succeed in expanding significantly beyond their perceived home departments to enter successfully into the writing arena everywhere. Such a movement creates jealousy. In this case, jealousy certainly existed. UNR's Anthropology Department chair asked pointedly, for example, why the Writing Center is funded to hire anthropology's graduate students to tutor writing when the Anthropology Department is not.

Unfortunately, there was also a personal antagonism. One of the English graduate students whose committee I chaired selected an important anthropology faculty member as his outside reader. My student's topic for his MA thesis was the usurpation of Paiute Indian language and rhetoric by the language and rhetoric of the settling Whites. The anthropology faculty member's area of expertise was Paiute culture and language. She is acknowledged as, without much argument, the world's leading academic expert on the Paiutes. Clearly, my graduate student did not write as she wished. His thesis developed personal opinion. His references supported his voice. Unfortunately, his citations slid fluidly between MLA and APA, and sometimes items were not clearly referenced at all. She whispered ominously to me, before his defense began, that "this is not good, not good at all." Outside of the faulty citations, however, this graduate student had written an acceptable and, I think, admirable thesis about the disappearing language of the Paiutes, using Kenneth Burke's rhetoric of motive as an important part of his argument. In terms of an English master's thesis, it was convincing. In fact, it had all of the elements a compositionist would hope to find—a substantial body of research assimilated through the writer's self. The anthropology faculty member's arguments about what it lacked, however, were also convincing, although she agreed with the thesis' basic premise—that regardless of whether there was intent, White rhetoric did overcome that of the Paiutes. My student made it clear, further, that he did not approve of this usurpation. The clear statement of his position also bothered her.

The psychological and political tables spun during his defense. From her perspective, he should not pass under these circumstances unless he wrote as an anthropologist would. From my perspective as committee chair, the differences between writing in anthropology and writing in English were substantial, and I urged that he pass with the promise of revisions. To this, in the end, she agreed, but not happily. Without objective proof, I believe she remained unhappy—translating that specific unhappiness into a broader unhappiness with the Writing Center, so pronounced that some anthropology faculty began advising large classes against taking their papers to the Center for help.

This experience was an object lesson for me in how roles appear to blend, and how my defense of my graduate student's voice in his thesis extended beyond to writing center practice. If I defend voice and expression of opinion here, will it not be part of tutor training and practice there? The answer is that I would try to separate what my student was doing from what an anthropology student would do with the same topic consciously. All the rhetorical cards must be on the table, in a metaphor close to home, all the time. I believe she came into this thesis defense fully acculturated in the language, thinking, and forms for writing in anthropology. This acculturation generated a singular view of writing so that her values for it became givens. Her cards remained understandably off the table. If I had not been a tenured associate professor myself, with the ambiguous weight of the Writing Center supporting me, I am sure she would not have dislodged.

With this aside (aside), we return to our PhD student in anthropology. Tutoring this ethnography from first-year composition, our tutor simply lost perspective. She pressed the writer hard with questions about the proper form for ethnography, and she bristled at the writer's inclusion of personal voice and experience. "You can't," she argued with the student, "write ethnography in this way: It has no abstract, introduction, or conclusion. It has only body. And it sounds as if you care personally about these mosh-pitters. How can you be objective if you care about them? You have at least to sound as if you don't. You can't use all these personal anecdotes, and try to avoid the pronoun *I*." This, in its own way, is worse than the first example cited (the student writer was a freshman, not a doctoral candidate) and, if left unqualified, would have more severe consequences. I find it funny, not in itself, but in its ironic confirmation of individual growth within disciplinary contexts, and the cross-disciplinary failure to acknowledge difference.

As an example of rhetorical agendas nearly scuttling WAC writing center consulting work, I turn to the case of a graduate teaching assistant in English who found himself completely transformed by his coursework from an avid and vocal current-traditionalist to an evangelical process-expressivist. This transformation is astounding for most of us who have experienced it, affecting professional as well as personal fiber. Tobin (2001) described this change for him as producing "something of the convert's zeal" (p. 10). It was certainly profound for Skip, who went from fiery argument with his teachers and peers about their softness with regard to voice, process approaches, small-group work, and reader response to fiery argument with anyone who appeared to think current-traditionally. I sympathized strongly with his change in perspective and liked him very much. Thus, I selected him as the teaching fellow for the Writing Center's writing assessment project, which requires extensive work in small groups with faculty from a variety of disciplines. I spent many hours with Skip describing the nature and delicacy of the work, how our attitudes toward writing and its teaching mostly differ from those of the teachers with whom we work, and how we are looking for their attitudes, not imposing ours. He knew his character, his tendency toward fire, and he seemed to understand the notion of disciplines as language communities with their own values, purposes, and forms for writing, one not inherently better than another. He assured me that he would become and remain a gardener and not a bludgeoner, at least in this cross-curricular context.

Yet it was not beyond the third meeting with accounting faculty, after they had explained their values for writing (clarity in statement of purpose; demonstrated analytical ability; accurate use of numbers, statistics, and equations; objectivity; appropriate form; few or no sentence-level errors), that Skip basically exploded: "How can you teach writing in that way? Where is there anything about voice, commitment, authenticity, and revision? What you offer as values seems nothing but mechanical to me!" His outburst nearly scuttled the project or at least accounting's participation in it. To recover, I tried to turn what Skip said into a discussion of the differing values departments have for writing, how they submerge into givens, and how they might emerge as "How can you?" statements. Nevertheless, it took weeks to regain accounting's trust that our plan was to help them measure the success of their students' writing in their terms, not ours. Thus, the writing center becomes a house of values even when its architect hopes the determining value will be the differences between us—their implications for tutoring students and consulting with faculty.

Despite these admitted gaffes, I remain convinced that WAC writing centers are the best home for WAC because of their independence from disciplinary constraints. They provide the best forum for helping students write in multiple contexts and aiding faculty in designing assignments pertinent to their courses. The may also be the best environment for fruitful discussion of specialization and its impact on students and faculty. The incidents described earlier, and many others like them, have become the basis for several training sessions with tutors. They have even supplied the content for workshops with faculty who teach in UNR's Core Writing Program, Western Traditions sequence, and Capstone courses for seniors. These faculty teach writing to students from every department on campus, and they will, especially in the Western Traditions and Capstone courses, encounter students whose writing and values are distant from their own. Sometimes they interpret this distance as bad student writing. For example, I heard a political science professor who was teaching a capstone course for seniors in other disciplines say that criminal justice students "can't write." UNR's writing assessment project worked for 2 years with faculty in political science and criminal justice, evaluating the quality of writing their upper division students did. Minimally, that quality was equal between these two groups of student writers. Discussing these tutoring incidents suggests in a practical way how "can't write" may mean cannot write according to a teacher's discipline and values.

The issues suggested by an imposition of values for writing would not find much play within a department. Within a department, there would usually be a barricade of objections, qualifiers, and flat-out rejections; little or no acknowledgment of the differences implied by the incidents; and little acknowledgment of the impact of multiplicity, if any at all. Why? Because most of the issues related to teaching writing within departments have become submerged beneath the level of critical consciousness. Writing centers, in contrast, may make it an important part of their activity to use these examples to teach difference and then understand its implications.

Still the Last Best Place

In two important articles published in the April 1988 issue of *College English*, Catherine Blair and Louise Smith argued in favor of modified versions of two of the three WAC programs discussed in the last chapter. Each writer supported one program over the other. Blair argued that WAC programs "should be designed, administered, and taught equally by all departments. True writing across the curriculum should be based on dialogue among all the departments, and, in this dialogue, the English department should be only one of the voices" (p. 383). The approach she favored is discipline-based. Unlike Blair, Smith argued that cross-curricular programs should be located in English departments, "secular and process oriented," housing "WAC by keeping *open*-house, initiating and sustaining dialogue throughout the curriculum" (p. 391). She did not argue an English-only model as I describe it, but rather more a writing-intensive approach, with English department experts in charge. Each offered substantive reasons for her position, reasons I want to explore in some detail, but each ignored what I believe to be the most logical home for writing across the curriculum—the writing center.

North (1984) hinted at this role for writing centers in his *College English* piece, "The Idea of a Writing Center," where he observed, "[Centers] have played central roles in the creation of writing across the curriculum programs" (p. 445). For North, however, WAC in the writing center seems no more or less important than establishing "resource libraries for writing teachers" or "opening a 'Grammar Hotline' or 'Grammaphone.'" In 1984, North did not intend to show writing centers as potential homes for WAC; instead he wanted to ask colleagues for some respect and understanding—to dispel confusion about what writing center personnel do. It was important at that time to define a good center's characteristics and counter the persistent impression of centers as skills labs and grammar garages. As Balester (1992) clarified, that respect remained an important issue.

Balester was mostly right about the negative attitudes toward writing centers. So many of the nation's hundreds of centers and labs remained focused on remediation, testing, and worksheets. So many were (and remain) subsets of English departments, composition programs, and basic writing classes. So many were and are directed by untenured and untenurable faculty. Because of these features, too many could have been (and might still be) construed as "ghettos," their residents as "third-class citizenry" by compositionists and others across campus as well. My work has sometimes been viewed as divisive because I have held writing centers and their personnel largely responsible for their lessened position, blaming the oppressed rather than the oppressor. Even so I admire the professionals in writing center positions; I applaud all their efforts to make writing centers essential institutionally; I recognize that the history of writing centers has been one of adjusting to the needs of an academic population; I acknowledge that people want jobs, and they will do what it takes to keep them. I accept, too, that computer writing technology seemingly affords a way out of the writing ghetto. Yet I continue to think that if we commit to systems that render us inferior foundationally (and then "Surprise!" find ourselves so), if we continue to operate out of reactive rather than proactive positions, gathering grammar phone materials, computer-based worksheets, advanced writing technology of every kind in an effort to remain viable, and if we continue to ignore theory and its implications for practice, we undermine rather than enhance our security. We continue to make a bed in a box rather than a house. Hence, in 1993, I wrote that, "Far from writing across the curriculum, these places may barely touch writing at all, or may touch it only at the sentence level. It is not, however, the skills lab or fix it shop which I assert would be a good home for the cross curricular program."

What I argued then, and continue to argue now, is a new breed of writing center characterized by several qualities requiring serious institutional commitment: (a) independence from any department; (b) a tenured or tenurable director; (c) highly skilled tutors, themselves teachers and students from various departments; and (d) an ambitious writing across the curriculum consultancy, steeped in language and cognitive development, critical thinking, postmodern theory, assignment making, and writing assessment.

The literature of difference has expanded dramatically since I published this portion of my chapter as an article in 1993, and awareness of postmodern theory stimulated that expansion. It has reached a pivotal point for WAC writing centers with the publication of Grimm's (1999) *Good Intentions: Writing Center Work for Postmodern Times*. Grimm began with the claim that, "Writing centers are often places where people develop what scholars call postmodern *skills*: the ability to simultaneously maintain multiple viewpoints, to make quick shifts in discourse orientation, to handle rapid changes in information technology, . . . , and to regularly renegotiate issues of knowledge, power, and ownership" (p. 2). She continued with an important case for centers: "This ability to work the border between tradition and change, to simultaneously entertain multiple—often conflicting—perspectives is a valuable survival skill for the turn of the century. Writing center work cultivates this mental agility" (p. 2). Yet in the decades-old deflation of that claim for importance, she pointed out that, "few people outside the writing center recognize this. In fact, writing center work is still imagined as dull, sentence-level editing" (p. 2).

Applying postmodernism to tutoring, Grimm demonstrated how tutoring and tutors may draw from student writers the best writing they can do in the context of their disciplines while helping them question what they are doing: "From a postmodern perspective, writing centers are necessary spaces for the critical orientation and contextualization that fosters real learning" (p. 25). Her argument contained many elements consistent with my own theory and practice, but at the point where tutors encourage students to question what they are doing, we part company. "I believe," Grimm asserted in one passage among many equally telling, "that writing center workers need to pay much more attention to the way institutional habits, practices, assumptions, and perspectives inadvertently oppress some students . . ." (p. 108). Students must learn that, through writing center practice, these institutional habits and perspectives are unfair: "When I meet with groups of students from traditionally under-represented groups on my campus, I tell them that the most dangerous assumption they can make, the one that may lead to academic failure, is that the institution is fair" (p. 104). Her claims about the unfairness of the institution are not the givens her argument suggested, although I largely believe they are true. The problem I have with *Good Intentions* is that it makes such a strong case for multiplicity and difference in the academy, postmodern implications for tutoring student writers, and then asserts its case through an ideological agenda as singular as any modernist process-expressivist agenda. "Critical orientation and contextualization" are indeed important pedagogic possibilities for writing centers because centers are the only space on campus that does not share the academic agendas of departments. Dependent on none, they may be committed to all.

However right or wrong Grimm's proposal is for what writing centers should be doing in the face of postmodernism, her proposal will not cross the curriculum in any broadly inclusive sense. Many faculty members may share her concerns about the unfairness and oppression that students experience (I do), but few have the opportunity or inclination to expose and correct that condition as the focal point of their positions. It may be a *border* point for them, but not the focal point, which is to advance their own research, its importance to their discipline, and to guide students into their discipline's work. A writing center that devotes itself to exposing the unfairness of academic discourse activity, and to explaining, say, how the mechanical engineering teacher's assignment excludes the student writing it, must do little to help the student write the assignment or the faculty member improve it. Grimm's position alienates more than includes. Because she is so public about her agenda, in an openness that I find admirable, faculty in the disciplines might be wary of her intent and wonder about encouraging their students to visit the center.

The difficulty stems from three points: First, Grimm operates out of her own and (one voice of) her discipline's values for writing—an opposition to the use of writing for gatekeeping; second, her position assumes the worst about faculty assignment makers who, advertently or inadvertently, will produce assignments that oppress, exclude, or fail students. This does happen, of course. Yet my experience of working with thousands of faculty members from nearly every discipline suggests that faculty care about their assignment making. They want writing to advance critical thinking and learning in their classes, and they hope for student inclusion, engagement, and success. When they make a bad assignment and are alerted to the difficulties it creates for students, they usually revise it or drop it altogether. From my experience, it would be an exaggeration to say that even 1% actually intend to stifle student success for any reason. Third, using a writing center to point out the inequities of writing in the academy and, as a consequence, intervening with students during tutoring sessions, rather than with faculty during consulting, risks increasing antagonism between faculty and students. Such a practice may not misuse postmodernism, but it does not make the best pedagogical use out of difference that it could.

If writing assignments oppress, exclude, and fail students, if they reflect institutional prejudice and gatekeeping, then at the least the faculty making the assignments should be alerted to these problems, along with the students writing them. To leave the faculty out is to place the writing center in a limited and limiting position, not unlike, in its cross-curricular potential, the skills lab or fix-it shop, which is to say little cross-curricular potential. Yet postmodernism appears compatible with WAC writing centers because there is so much critical orientation and contextualization possible for students (and faculty) within them.

Absent a heavy-handed ideological agenda, centers provide a definable space for expertise—with identifiable goals and services—the campus will need to initiate and sustain the WAC of difference. Absent the agenda—through their varying services for faculty—centers encourage dialogue within and between diverse disciplinary communities. Postmodernist educators make strong cases for one of the fundamental purposes of postsecondary education: to provide students with "a single system of formation," "the appropriation of a discourse" with "the knowledge and powers it carries with it" (Foucault, 1972, p. 227). Writing centers are not disciplines yet, and again without a heavy-handed ideological agenda they can resist imposing what they value for writing on other departments. In that sense, they offer a rhetorically neutral ground on which to carry on the conversation, perhaps the only such ground on the academic side of campus. Rather than imposing values, they are well positioned to help students succeed as writers and faculty as assignment makers in any discourse endeavor or community. They are well placed to elevate the language differences between departments to the level of critical consciousness and make those differences and their consequences a part of the conversation.

In short, housing WAC in writing centers unites the best characteristics in the reasoning of Blair, Smith, and now Grimm while rejecting their less convincing arguments. Blair argued persuasively for removing WAC from English:

> Entrusting the writing program to the English department is based on the belief that the English department has a special relationship to language and is, therefore, the department that knows the most about writing—in fact, the department that *owns* writing. But what the basic theory behind writing across the curriculum tells us is that the English department owns only its particular brand of writing that carries its particular context. Each discipline has its own relationship to language; the English department context is not a privileged one. There is no way to decide the primacy of a particular context because no discipline is better than any other. (Blair, 1988, p. 384, her emphasis)

Now, of course, what she wrote in 1988 about each discipline having its own relationship to language is well established. Blair's position on English—that it "owns only its particular brand of writing that carries its particular context"—seemed then and remains largely accurate to me nonetheless. Writing in English courses is different from writing in other disciplines; it has its own purposes, forms, and values. Although not less than other contexts, it is not a privileged context either.

I want to observe, however, that Blair's position has found rough footing in English, which has become increasingly nervous about giving up ownership of composition. Think of the university-wide dependence the department loses when a broad range of faculty use writing successfully in their classes. Think, in a worst-case scenario, of the credit hours and full-time equivalences lost if the number of composition classes decreases significantly because of WAC. As expertise in rhetoric and composition studies has developed, the willingness to let go has lessened on not only the level of practice but theory, as specialists assume their thinking is (or should be) everyone's. Blair's remarks about the theory behind writing across the curriculum do little to lessen the anxiety not only about where English fits, but where the composition program fits. She stated plainly that, "the English department should have no special role in writing across the curriculum—no unique leadership role and no exclusive classes to teach—not even freshman composition" (p. 383). Thus, she lumped composition with English as owning "only its particular brand of writing that carries its particular context."

I do not fully agree with Blair on this point. It is true that English forwards its "particular brand of writing that carries its particular context." Yet that truth, from my perspective, becomes the heart of English's argument for teaching composition to every student: It offers a small, inclusive class, demographically essential at the first-year level. It is the only class that prefers student writing to reading published text. It is one of the few classes that allows continual rethinking of content through revision so that drafts become as significant as final copies. One of the few classes in which students find themselves, their personal experience, as the subject matter of their papers, it may be the only class in which real self and authentic voice are matters of discussion. If the composition course devotes itself to exposing students to inequities, as well as the environmental, social, political, and/or economic problems around them, and encourages their agency, it serves a worthy and singular purpose, shared perhaps with some sociology classes but few others. Any one of these points is enough to make an argument for the requirement of first-year English, but together I believe they make an insurmountable argument for its requirement. The whole of the first-year composition sequence, and advanced writing courses beyond it, may be defended on its and their own merits. The problem is that now, as it was in the late 1980s, no one is making such an argument, not at least in a coherent and purposeful manner.

Blair is right about English's perception of its special relationship to language—that it knows the most about writing, in fact owns writing; and others believe (or want to believe) it as well. English departments have a strong motivation to corner responsibility for teaching writing, whereas other departments bolster that conception. This inclination may appear to strengthen English's position, but it simultaneously weakens the position because the only way to defend English's version of writing when it crosses the curriculum is to defend one personality for the writing experience—a personality that does not fit across the curriculum. Almost any disciplinary approach to writing is defensible as long as it is understood as a contextualized part of the process of students growing as writers and thinkers. Blair's argument capitalizes on the lack of understanding. Why shouldn't it? The struggle remains in 2003 as it did in 1989: to understand English's writing pedagogy not as preeminent, but only one among many.

Cross-curricular programs, however, were not conceived to curtail the power of English departments or composition programs. Quite the contrary. They were designed to broaden responsibility for teaching writing and generate a larger environment for active learning. They were meant to help, not hurt, English departments, which cannot successfully bear sole responsibility for writing competence on any campus and cannot be expected to know, let alone teach, writing in disciplines outside their own. Blair (1988) replaced English department control with interdisciplinary dialogue: "Dialogue among equals is the way to make and maintain true writing across the curriculum by ensuring that all linguistic communities are heard from" (p. 386). On an intellectual level, most academics would agree with her, including those in English. Yet at some fundamental level, perhaps the level of survival, Blair's proposition becomes threatening: "[The dialogic approach] could irritate the English department and make others on the faculty feel rudderless without English department control" (p. 388). "Could irritate English departments" is probably, as I argue, a politic understatement on her part.

Nonetheless, Blair's proposal and Bucknell University's practice of decentering the cross-curricular writing program has appealed to me primarily because it lands the purposes for writing in the hands of the various disciplines. For example, it is sound policy to have faculty in the Economics Department helping their students develop writing competence instead of complaining in *Newsweek* that English is failing to do its job ("Why Johnny Can't Write"). That economics professor must assume a modernist, universal view of writing: Learn it in one place and you have learned it in all. As WAC participants, we must work to explode that myth. A broad sharing of responsibility for writing lessens chances for ghettoizing composition, sometimes the consequence of designating one or two classes within a department as writing classes. Such writing-intensive programs make more possible the dumping of writing on junior faculty and more likely the view of writing as isolated punishment. In principle, at least, the dialogic approach supports a wide sharing of responsibility for using writing assignments in classes, contradicting the writing-intensive model. At Bucknell, Blair remarked, the majority of faculty volunteer to teach writing courses.

Blair's proposal, therefore, has many attractive features. One of its most positive qualities, however, is also potentially one of its most negative: Being housed everywhere, writing across the curriculum runs the risk of being housed nowhere. There seems to me a danger that such dispersion might lead to diffusion of focus, confusion of purpose, and a threat to funding. Blair did not set out to address this issue in her article, yet I believe it deserves to be addressed because it suggests the need to house writing across the curriculum somewhere—that a purely dialogic cross-curricular program may be impractical and "probably does not exist" (p. 388).

Is the English Department, then, the best place for WAC? Smith (1988) offered two reasons favoring English. The first is "our expertise in the study of the construction and reception of texts." Second, she suggested that because we are the experts, we want to house WAC "so that we can invite—and keep on inviting—the historians and sociologists, the chemists and biologists to join with us in dialogue" (p. 392). I do not deny the expertise in composition theory and pedagogy that often exists in English departments. English departments use that expert knowledge to develop composition programs and train teachers; their faculty should have much to share in the cross-curricular dialogue from their discipline's perspective.

I note, nonetheless, the sense of control English has in a relationship like the one described by Smith. She argued that English faculty, at least the non-hermetic members, understand and care about the writing process more than do other faculty: "To the extent that they have informed themselves in composition theory, English faculty are more likely to [apply similar assumptions and questions to both professionals' and students' processes of composing] than are faculty in other departments who, however well-intentioned, may see composition theory and pedagogy as even more peripheral to their professional interests than do the English department's most 'hermetic' members" (pp. 392–393). Smith was probably right about the deeper concern for process, but her attitude toward process is ironically elitist. She could not have known the recently developing literature, which, from its postmodernist perspective, challenges the "one process theory and practice" for writing. Composition theory and pedagogy as we knew them, clearly important to her, *were* and *remain* peripheral to the professional interests of most faculty in the disciplines. Does this mean that these faculty cannot use writing to positive effect in their classes? Absolutely not. If they use writing to advance the critical consciousness of their students, within and about their disciplines, they put it to good use indeed. The English Department may attempt to make English teachers out of their colleagues, but to do so is unnecessary to the success of WAC and will work to its detriment.

Smith (1988) attacked the two notions she assumes keep English from its cross-curricular calling: (a) its "supposed devotion to the traditional canon," and (b) the claim that " 'literary texts are metaphorical and non-literary texts are literal.' " English departments, she asserted, can show other departments how their writing is "contextualized—though not constrained—by the knowledge of canonical and non-canonical 'intertexts' " (p. 392). "English faculty can share with other departments' experts in textual theory their mutual insights on how to carry textual studies over into pedagogy" (p. 393). Finally, English faculty can share their "relatively expert knowledge of such matters as reader-response theory, error analysis, writing-to-learn, and collaborative composition pedagogies" (p. 394).

There is refreshing optimism in the idea that our expertise will make our colleagues eager to converse with us, and there is good-natured generosity in "knowing we're equally interested in their expertise . . ." (p. 391). As positive in tone as her reasoning is, however, Smith did not show us why writing across the curriculum belongs in the English Department. In fact, her comments show us more why English should not house WAC than why it should. Her observations remain, however they are couched, based mostly in her own discipline, in writing to learn, and in process-expressivist pedagogies. Her insular view and claim that faculty will blunder as they attempt to teach writing without expertise in composition studies suggest the real reasons that English should be kept from its cross-curricular calling. Imposing its expertise on others may and does have a stunting effect on the growth of WAC. "English faculty," Smith wrote, "can show colleagues that errors provide windows into writers' minds as they acquire new modes of discourse." Maybe they can, but why would they want to? Making error a focal point of the cross-curricular program has always been a serious mistake. On the one hand, some content teachers avoid using writing assignments in class because they fear they cannot correct the errors; on the other hand, some focus almost exclusively on the errors. In either case, the student loses.

I realize Smith said repeatedly that "our colleagues have a lot to show us, too." English departments, she told us, can resist ownership of writing, avoid colonization of other departments, and initiate and sustain the dialogue; yet her argument shows us something different—an agenda that places English in control. More exactly, her position implies, imposes, a linguistic control, by making the English Department's relationship to language a privileged one. Smith's argument is, for me, theoretically less attractive than Blair's because it contradicts Blair's most important premise: "There is no way to decide the primacy of a particular context because no discipline is better than any other." Smith's proposal openly states a preferable context: English.

The positions of Blair and Smith are essentially incompatible despite Smith's apology to the contrary. Blair's program encourages the view that all academic discourses are equal, that students will learn the language of a major by writing in that major, and that faculty should carry on dialogue about writing. Blair would share responsibility for using writing among all the disciplines. The problem posed by her argument is a practical one: If writing across the curriculum is wholly dialogic, where do faculty and students turn for help? Also urging equality and dialogue, Smith's proposal argues the need for expertise—a place where faculty and students can turn for help. Yet she blankets the cross-curricular program with English department values, making English primarily responsible for teaching writing. The problem posed by her argument is theoretic: If we believe that disciplines have different discourses and values for discourse, each equal, what gives English primacy?

WAC writing centers bridge the gap between these two positions—Blair's homelessness and Smith's cloister. Potentially, centers are in the best position to offer the expert services the WAC program needs while preserving the rhetorical integrity of the disciplines. They do this by acknowledging differences between campus language communities purposefully, making it a matter of talk with faculty and tutor training. They focus on goals that join us: to advance critical thinking and ethical consciousness, increase a student's ability to analyze and synthesize material, see opposing points of view, make arguments, solve problems, develop hypotheses, and reflect on consequences. This focus may be an agenda, but it is one we at least claim to share across disciplines.

As homes for WAC, writing centers combine two features that become vital to the campus: consulting for faculty and tutoring for students. The writing center's consultants can nourish openness and respect for disciplinary boundaries by focusing on such areas as assignment design, evaluative techniques, and the cognitive behaviors which assignment design and evaluation are meant to stimulate in students—all within a voluntary context. Consultants will ask a faculty member questions, not give directives; carry on conversations, not deliver lectures. Aware that different writing assignments encourage different types of learning (Applebee & Langer, 1987, pp. 130–131), consultants ask questions that reveal what faculty want to accomplish with their assignments and what they most value in grading. They will help faculty to clarify every aspect of their assignment, given the class in which an assignment is used, and sponsor "norming" sessions, turning goals into criteria for grading. Although not rejecting process-expressivist, feminist, Marxist, postmodernist, multicultural, or any other set of values for writing, this consultancy would not insist on any one of them. It is open to all the values faculty may express or imply in assignment making and grading with the provision that faculty consider the following: How are writing and learning connected in my assignment? Is this connection consistent with my goals for learning in my class? Does the assignment stretch, without breaking my students, just beyond their cognitive development and language assimilation? Can that gap be closed at Vygotsky's zone of proximal development, where my help and the help of their peers will produce success? Does the assignment include clear goals, an engaging context, and an identifiable audience consistent with my class, a combination that fosters real learning? When I grade my assignment, do I know what I am looking for? Do I grade based on the goals, context, and audience embedded in my assignment?

After these questions are answered "yes" (or perhaps "mostly yes" because we are not dealing with absolutes here), other more abstract questions may come into play, ordinarily after trust between the consultants and faculty has been established: In what ways does my assignment include some students while excluding others? If the assignment works well for my students in my class, how are its results consistent with the next class at the next level and with assimilation into my community overall? How might this success be compared to faculty within my department and student success campuswide? Does my assignment support a healthy stewardship and agency given global conditions? (This last question, which touches on consequences, becomes part of the concluding chapter's discussion.) Again, my WAC experience in my home institutions and across the country tells me that faculty care about these questions.

The writing center's tutoring program will complement the consultancy by developing appropriate question asking and collaborative strategies for drawing students to make improvements on their papers. Why is a tutoring program essential? Hillocks (1986) argued that teacher feedback during the process of writing a paper is much more effective than teachers writing comments on final drafts. It makes sense then that tutoring intervention during the process also helps improve writing. My own experimental research supports this conclusion. Students write better across the curriculum if they receive good tutoring. Blair's dialogic model probably produces much student writing, but I object to the model's homelessness mainly because it offers little indication of where students turn for help.

Students might turn to their professors. Many times I have heard the argument that professors must be willing to conference with students about writing. "It's part of their job," people say. I would agree with this position if the academy were perfect, but professors resist using writing, especially in large classes, if they perceive conferencing as an overwhelming consequence. Further, few professors outside of composition collect, write comments on, and return student drafts before the paper is due. They do not have the time. Therefore, it is crucial to WAC's success to offer the university a strong tutoring program—one to which faculty and students can turn with confidence.

This confidence comes from having a tutoring staff experienced and versatile enough to work with students from any class at any level. On the surface, this may seem so much common sense it does not bear comment. Yet the depth of experience and versatility highlighted here actually contradicts typical approaches in writing centers. That is, if the center is to house writing across the curriculum, it should be staffed primarily with professional tutors whose minimal qualifications include BA degrees from various disciplines, broad experience with academic writing, and prior teaching or tutoring experience. Writing centers typically include a few tutors who have these qualifications, but often this group is a small minority—the majority being undergraduate student tutors.

Undergraduates can, of course, be good tutors. They might even be more comfortable with question asking and collaboration than some teacher/tutors who may tend toward the prescriptive in their tutoring. Problems arise, however, from the student tutor's lack of experience with upper division and graduate student writing—problems that become more glaring as tutoring sessions with this population increase. Other difficulties stem from having too many student tutors from one department (English). Students choose a discipline, consciously or not, in large part because they are attracted to its language and culture. Just becoming immersed in the language, they are likely to adopt the rhetorical values of their teachers. Because these values are not necessarily shared across the curriculum, effort should be made to counter them or any other pervasive influence from any one discourse community. The best way to counter this influence is to employ a highly experienced and eclectic staff and fewer undergraduates.

Second and perhaps more practical, however, is to focus tutor training and philosophy on the values shared between disciplines. Training should show tutors how to advance critical thinking by creating an atmosphere in which students re-see their papers with regard to the assignment and their response to it. "So this a problem-solving assignment? A data/analysis assignment? An opposing viewpoints assignment? An argument?" "Re-explain your description of the problem. Talk through your solutions." "Explain the context for the data, why you analyzed it in the way you did." "Re-describe what's most important in each of these opposing viewpoints." "Talk about your argument, who disagrees and why; re-explain your own position." These types of inquiries initiate a tutoring process committed to the instructor's assignment and the student's writing. They encourage the values we share and discourage imposition of values. They are only a beginning, after the assignment and the student's concerns have been discussed and the paper read (aloud) by the tutor, but they will eventually lead to obvious strengths and fruitful areas for improvement. I recognize that not all assignments will include goals, contexts, or audiences. Some may be as open ended as "write on a topic of interest to you," making tutoring (and grading) a trying task. Even so, it is not the tutor's responsibility to determine the instructor's values or assert his or her own. In this situation, the tutor needs to understand the student's interpretation of the assignment, send the student back to the instructor for clarification if that understanding is demonstrably unclear, or work with him or her on purpose, context, and audience if the writer displays a confidence in his or her approach.

As a home for consulting and tutoring, the writing center must be its own program, not a subset of English or any other department. Independence, desirable in itself, is critical in this case because of the varying disciplines with which the center will work. Physics, for example, usually has a different purpose for using writing and measuring its effectiveness than composition. In a composition course, students may learn to write by writing. In a physics course, they learn to solve problems and pass those solutions on to others by writing. The writing center needs to be versatile enough in its practice to handle these differences and broad enough in its theory to bridge them.

The center needs a theoretical frame independent of discipline for its practice—a frame that gives its tutoring, workshop, and consulting activities research legitimacy. Fulwiler and Young (1990) concluded that most institutions base their WAC programs "on a common core of language theorists, most often including some mix of James Britton, Donald Murray, Janet Emig, and Peter Elbow" (p. 2). I know that Fulwiler and Young meant this as quite a positive feature of WAC, but it is hardly neutral. To base WAC programs on this core of language theorists would not pass the Blair neutrality test. It lodges WAC in English. It makes more sense to go to a less discipline-controlled theoretical base, evolved from the research in language and cognition by developmental psychologists, linguists, and composition scholars; studies in question asking and collaboration from speech communication experts, therapists, and writing center professionals; the brain/language relationships explored by biologists, anthropologists, and linguists; ethnographies of modern knowledge and writing communities from anthropologists and compositionists; thinking in modernism and postmodernism discussed by scholars in philosophy, sociology, and psychology; research in the development of critical consciousness and findings on critical thinking in college-age students; and research into the relationship of writing, thinking, and specialization. Just one of many possible theoretical frames, this one has an important advantage: It is bound not by what one discipline values about writing, but by insights into human development and learning, especially with regard to language and thinking.

When the type of writing center described here houses WAC, the number of classes using writing across campus will increase substantially. This increase results from the expertise offered to students and faculty through the center's programs. More abstractly, it grows out of the center's rhetorically neutral focus on the relationship between writing and learning. That is, owing allegiance to no one department's linguistic context, and providing a forum for the discussion of difference, writing centers position themselves to work with all. At bottom, systems of higher education are designed to create specialists. Their classrooms, labs, and lecture halls are largely forums for distributing and appropriating disciplinarity, and they measure success by the effectiveness of faculty distribution and student appropriation. No wonder friction is generated by one discipline when it attempts to impose its discourse on another discipline. Little wonder, too, why writing centers have an advantage in housing WAC. They can build on what we share about language and thinking while helping students gain the authority needed to succeed in their discourse community.

6

Workshops for Designing Assignments and Grading Writing Across the Curriculum: A Difference-Based Approach

How could English departments and the compositionists within them have developed such an edge of superiority about the teaching of writing; and why, when that superiority is challenged by a WAC process that gives responsibility for teaching writing to the disciplines, could English become vindictive and hostile?

For an explanation, I turn to Karen Horney (1970), therapist and researcher into the neurotic condition, whose chapter "Neurotic Pride" is particularly applicable. I have changed Horney's referents from the *neurotic*, the *person, he, his,* and *himself* to the *English department, English, it, its,* and *itself.* Given that (and the fact that I am not taking myself too seriously), here is the Third Force explanation of the phenomenon:

> Even though god-like in [its] imagination, [the English department] still lacks the earthy self-confidence of the simple shepherd.... [English] still feels at bottom unwanted, is easily hurt, and needs incessant confirmation of its value. (p. 86)

> Neurotic pride ... rests on the attributes which [English] arrogates to itself in [its] imagination, on all those belonging to [its] particular idealized image. Here the peculiar nature of neurotic pride comes into clear relief. [English] is not proud of [the department it] actually is. Knowing [its] wrong perspective on [itself], we are not surprised that [its] pride blots out difficulties and limitations. (p. 90)

> The idealized image is a product of [English's] imagination. But this is not something which is created overnight. Incessant work of intellect and imagina-

95

tion, most of it unconscious, goes into maintaining the private fictitious world
. . . through finding ways to make things appear different from what they are.
(p. 91)

In terms of subjective experience [neurotic pride] makes [English] vulnerable,
and does so exactly to the extent that [it] is obsessed by pride. It can be hurt as
easily from within as from without. The two typical reactions to hurt pride are
shame and humiliation. [English] will feel ashamed if [it does, thinks, or feels]
something that violates [its] pride. And [English] will feel humiliated if others
do something that hurts [its] pride, or fail[s] to do what [its] pride requires of
them. (p. 95)

That any hurt to [English's] pride may provoke vindictive hostility is well known.
It goes all the way from dislike to hate, from irritability to anger to a blind mur-
derous rage. . . . What operates here is the straight law of retaliation. (p. 99)

The quotes I remade are hyperbole, meant, when applied to English departments, to amuse and stimulate thinking about a problem and strategies
for solving it. Although it is hyperbole, there are many scholars within English whose publications tend to substantiate the points about English's uncer-
tain history, insecurity, idealized image making, and sense of vulnerability
(see e.g., Graff, 1992; Eagleton, 1996; Ohmann, 1974; Parker, 1967).

In an effort to define the problem, I want to isolate three phrases—*needs
incessant confirmation of its value* and *blots out difficulties and limitations*—to
make things appear different from what they are and then place them in context.
English departments have long been unsure of their value to the academy.
Beyond many other disciplines, their work appears disconnected from that of
others on campus and that needed by society. An exception to this claim is
the teaching of writing, which the campus and society value highly.
Although teaching composition has, ironically, been thought odious by literature faculty (Hirsch, 1982), it provides a sustaining confirmation of value.
As Blair (1988) explained, English certainly imagines itself to have a special
relationship with writing, know the most about writing, and produce the best
writing and writers.

This impression of itself often leads English to blot out difficulties and limitations—two of which become most striking. First, English cannot teach
writing by itself. A few (at most) composition, technical writing, and team-
taught courses over 4 or 5 years will not produce the better writers for which
the institution and the public long. The effort must be much more broad
based and inclusive to achieve that result. Perhaps the degree to which English knows this is the degree to which writing across the curriculum succeeds.
Even as English does not want to bear sole responsibility for writing, however,

it does not want to lose its most public confirmation of value and its belief in its heart that it can teach the best writing courses. Thus, it may ignore or even resist the obvious need to change and share, unnecessarily damaging itself and others in the process.

Second, what may have been vague and controversial a decade ago has now become widely accepted—that postsecondary institutions are in David Russell's terms loose affiliations of separate disciplines, with specialized languages and frames for thinking, and their own values, purposes, and forms for writing. Given that a large part of a teacher's job depends on how well he or she teaches students the language, thinking habits, and culture of a discipline, and given that the work of a discipline could not be done without its language, it is hard to understand why English would want to make things appear different from what they are—to appear, that is, as if English composition and its values for writing fit every discipline. This situation becomes clearer, however, when we realize that English (as with most disciplines) rarely recognizes its own values for writing as values at all, perceiving them to be everyone's values. To continue with the Horney schema, English thus fosters an idealized image, not proud of the department that it actually is, but of a department it has created in its imagination (i.e., English imagines itself to teach a plural, transcendent model of writing when in reality the writing it teaches is singular, contextualized by its classes and specializations). The difference between English and other disciplines lies in English's pride of ownership of writing and its position to act on that pride (to extend expertise in composition to novice faculty and students, teach writing in other disciplines, and urge values for writing on cultures to which those values are alien) and the endorsement of that pride and those practices by other disciplines ("Teaching writing is English's job," "they're the experts," and when their own students are not writing so well, "why isn't English doing its job?"). Given this context, the problem becomes formidable especially if hostility or retaliation are the consequences to the WAC professional, who urges that responsibility for teaching writing be taken out of English's hands. Horney has a response even to this situation.

Horney (1970) remarked of dealing with those afflicted with neurotic pride:

> Thus, when a friend or relative [an English department] behaves in an obnoxious fashion after we have liberally helped [it], we should not be upset over [its] ingratitude but consider how badly [its] pride may have been hurt by accepting help. And, according to circumstances, we might either talk to [English] about it or try ourselves to help [English] in a way that saves [its] face. (p. 100)

Does a WAC program and/or WAC writing center liberally help English? Yes, in most cases, it does. If it stimulates pertinent writing experiences in a broad range of disciplinary contexts, it relieves English of a responsibility it cannot hope to bear effectively: to teach all writing to all students. Such programs open doors to English to be the department it actually is—in Third Force terms, its *real self*, to pursue its own purposes in teaching and research—as important as any on campus, but not more important. On a reflective level, everyone acknowledges this fact, including English. Yet on the level of pride of ownership, an affective condition, reflection may disappear in favor of idealized image making. Does English react to WAC/writing center efforts with ingratitude? Sometimes. Is its pride hurt by accepting help? Arguably, yes. Does it need occasional help saving its face? Well, who does not? Does this context mean that WAC personnel and writing center directors have to become Third Force therapists, placing English on the couch? In a way, yes. Horney's advice, translated, encourages conciliation and compromise between the WAC program and English—and mostly, so do I. How might conciliation and compromise manifest themselves? A good way to start might be to ask colleagues in English about what they would like the WAC/writing center program to do for them and their students. Asking the questions of faculty one on one would uncover common ground, areas of difference, and concerns on which to act.

Whether this process would help English let go of ownership of writing is debatable. Perhaps it would. Perhaps not. Letting go of ownership, however, is critical to the success of WAC. Ownership of writing belongs to those communities in which writing occurs for teachers making assignments and students writing them. If WAC is to be cross-curricular, then that truth, and not neurotic pride, must be recognized and sustained.

Nonetheless, without accounting for an English department's attitude toward its own composition sequence, the nature of the composition curriculum, the disposition of its faculty toward WAC and writing centers, and then further adjusting to these variables, WAC consultancy with faculty in the disciplines may be unfruitful and even mute. None of us can see to its end a program from which we have been removed.

Freire Conducts WAC Workshops

I have talked to many faculty in disciplines other than English who have attended assignment design workshops given by composition experts. These faculty have often described those workshops as "better for English teachers than for me," voicing the kinds of reservations our hypothetical biology teacher (from chap. 1) felt—that composition's values for writing supersede their own.

WAC presentation has been largely deductive, proceeding from experts to initiates. As a developing discipline with its own undergraduate and graduate training, its own nomenclature, conference presentations, and publications, composition studies has become at once increasingly insular and superior in its attitude toward writing. Its insular character, like that of any discipline, stems from its maturing expertise and sprouting subspecializations—where people, say, with expertise in and commitment to social construction have trouble communicating with process-expressivists. There is some communicative trouble between subspecialists in composition studies, but as the discipline as a whole has evolved, it has become more isolated from the university community's other members. It teaches writing theory and practice to its own members and publishes most of its scholarship for them as well. This isolation is a natural consequence of the emergence of a discipline, but it becomes more problematic when the discipline makes some claim of expertise outside itself, as composition studies does. In a self-importance stimulated in part by neurotic pride and public affirmation, composition studies has generated a body of knowledge about writing and its teaching, and from that body fundamental principles have emerged. It is the fundamental principles that often guide WAC workshops: what composition specialists have found to be good for writing in their own field translating to what is good for those in other fields. In Freire's (1990) terms, this act of translation amounts to *extension*, which "means that those carrying it out need to go to 'another part of the world' to 'normalize it,' according to their way of viewing reality: to make it resemble their world" (p. 95). His chart defining *extension* clarifies this experience:

extension . . . . transmission

extension . . . . active Subject (who transmits)

extension . . . . content (chosen by the transmitter)

extension . . . . recipient (of the content)

extension . . . . delivering (e.g., in extramural activities— something brought by a Subject who is "within the wall" to those who are "beyond the wall" or "outside the wall")

extension . . . . messianism (of the extension agent)

extension . . . . superiority (of the thing given away by the person giving away)

extension . . . . inferiority (of those who receive)

extension . . . . mechanical transfer (the action of the extension agent)

extension . . . . cultural invasion (through what is brought, which reflects the
bringers' vision of the world, and is imposed on those who passively receive). (p. 95)

This chart accurately represents much that has been WAC practice, especially in its representation of delivering—from those with expertise in composition to those who have little expertise; in its representation of *messianism*,
the evangelical character of the presenter(s) and of the superiority of those
principles and values for composition given away by the experts; in its representation of inferiority, as those in the disciplines who do not know are
graced with the information provided by those who do; and in its representation of *cultural invasion*, with the term's implications for one academic culture
(composition) imposing its enlightened vision of the world of writing pedagogy on another, which passively receives that vision. I have been criticized
for using Freire's notions of extension in discussions of WAC practice. The
context for Freire's remarks is the South American peasantry and the pronounced interference of agricultural experts on their farming practice. I admit that, in the face of the historical viciousness of colonization and cultural
invasion, whatever English may do to control writing pales.

Nonetheless, Freire made his specific observations in support of a more
universal pedagogic point. His work is rightly quoted in a variety of composition studies, literacy position papers, and WAC texts. My use of Freire's work
here describes a real condition—composition specialists imposing their values for writing on others. Yet that warrant is less significant than what I support as his ultimate points: that education "to be authentic must be liberat-
ing," and as the "practice of freedom," it must enfranchise both educator and
educatee alike; it is not "the transfer, or transmission of knowledge or cultures." Nor is it the extension of technical knowledge, the act of depositing
reports or facts in the educatee. It is not the "perpetuation of the values of a
given culture" nor "an attempt to adapt the educatee to the milieu" (p. 149).

For Freire (1990), the process of knowing is mutual, and education is defined by communication—Hegelian dialogue between the educator and
educatee in which both are participants in an atmosphere where "knowledge
is sought and not where it is transmitted" (p. 150). Together the educator and
educatee begin with a problem and reach a consensus in solving it, which involves no imposition of values or options. ("In the conscientization process
the educator has the right, as a person, to have options. What s/he does not
have is the right to impose them" [p. 150]). Instead, options and values become part of a mix of active dialogue in which both educator and educatee
have equal status, and the surfacing solutions are created by and enfranchise
both. This process is inductive. It proceeds from the roots up—a seed sprout-

ing and growing into a plant (in an organic metaphor) rather than from the branches down, in an impossible metaphor, the tree somehow through manipulation, being grown from its parts. WAC consultancy will have difficulty succeeding if it proceeds from the assumptions of the latter metaphor, somehow hoping the tree will grow from its branches.

The problem Freire articulated about education, the difference between seeking and transmitting knowledge, is compellingly the problem WAC consultants face. It is no longer difficult to find WAC consultancy acknowledging and encouraging "learning to write in the disciplines." After all, how could much of anything happen without such acknowledgment and encouragement? It is almost equally difficult to find WAC consultancy that does not include in its practice the process-expressivist components of writing to learn—a seemingly innocuous phrase with its attributes of personal response to material, free writing, writing as process, sustaining authentic voice, and so on. Most compositionists would say, "of course, writing to learn must be a part of WAC." Almost anyone would say so in the abstract. "Writing to learn" is not wrong in itself. Its values have been foundational to the discipline of composition studies and made the writing experience more enjoyable for many students.

The problem is, as I have remarked repeatedly, that what are values (*options* in Freire's terms) too often become givens (*extension* in Freire's terms) in WAC practice. When writing to learn is imposed on the faculty at large, and I think it has been and continues to be, it undermines learning to write in the disciplines. It does so because faculty members in the disciplines recognize the difference between hearing pronouncements about what they should be doing with writing and questions about what they want to do. It does so because the two, although compatible, are hardly complementary in terms of the cognitive and affective behaviors engaged. One process leads to quite different learning than the other. Learning to write depends on the disciplines, whereas writing to learn often has to be inserted into them. Some good WAC material has been generated for writing to learn, especially in Bean's (1996) *Engaging Ideas*. However, even this material strikes me as belonging in a second or even third workshop, after assignment-design and paper grading workshops take place. This is why I would argue that writing to learn should become an option rather than a requirement in WAC consultancy, and that, as consultants, we adopt an inductive rather than deductive approach with our cross-curricular constituents. Writing pedagogy in the inductive approach is acknowledged at the beginning as different for different disciplines, rather than being the same for all—bodies of knowledge about writing pedagogy begin with the educatees, rather than the educators.

Assignment-Design Workshops

Constructing a discipline-based model for WAC workshops at Montana State University in 1984, we centered our assignment-design workshops on five requests: We asked faculty to (a) choose a class in which they would like to require writing, perhaps a class they had not required writing in before; (b) offer one or two goals they have for learning in that class; (c) describe two or three critical thinking behaviors in which they would like their students to engage through writing, perhaps behaviors that have given students trouble in the past; (d) choose between an assignment forwarding a goal for learning or one enhancing a particular thinking behavior, distinguishing between the two mainly by the length of the papers; and (e) after examining successful and not so successful models, write a preliminary draft of their assignment to be shared in a small-group format. This process succeeded even early on (in 1984); and these questions still constitute the fifth step in our assignment-design workshops.

Now, at the University of Nevada–Reno, we envelop our workshops with materials focused on developing critical thinking skills. We follow the process mapped out next, and I have made available in the text or as appendixes many of the best materials we have collected for use in the workshops. The faculty demography for our most recent two assignment-design workshops breaks down in this way: 26 faculty participants from 20 different disciplines.

We start with this question: How would you characterize students as thinkers when they come to your lower division classes? Faculty response to this question is almost uniformly that freshman/sophomore student thinking tends to be narrative, chronological, dualistic, and dependent on external authority. Our consultants use Perry's (1981) "Cognitive and Ethical Growth," which summarized Perry's findings about freshman males at Harvard, and the Belenky et al. (1986) *Women's Ways of Knowing*, which built on Perry's scheme by grouping women's perspectives on knowing into five categories, to substantiate faculty impressions of the freshman student's level of cognitive development (Appendix B). We also allude to Vygotsky's (1962) observations of language growth and its relations to thinking to open the discussion of how different majors expect assimilation of different languages and how difference is the foundation for values, purposes, and forms for writing.

We ask faculty to identify the critical thinking behaviors they want their students to use as they progress from the lower to the upper division. The behaviors they describe include some form of the ability to analyze, synthesize, critique, summarize, persuade, problem solve, and examine complex issues from multiple points of view. What faculty members identify as critical thinking behaviors is consistent with the way in which experts identify it as well, as demonstrated by the nine definitions provided in the "Toward Identifying Critical Thinking" handout (Appendix C). We treat this handout in two ways principally—first, to find the characteristics common to many definitions (e.g., problem solving is the most frequently listed, appearing in six of the definitions; and second, examining complex issues from multiple points of view appearing in four).

The second way in which we treat the definitions is to choose two or three that express singular ideas and then talk about those ideas. For example, Bean (1996) asserted that "these mental habits are discipline specific . . . ," reinforcing the premise that differing languages generate differing thinking patterns, the patterns of no two disciplines necessarily being the same—an idea essential to the way in which WAC encounters faculty. As another example, Belenky et al. (1986) powerfully applied the metaphor *the new poem* inside her/their observation that constructivists imagine "themselves inside the new poem or person or idea that they want to come to know and understand." This new poem, from our reading of it, constitutes as much learning to read mountain sheep excrement in the Montana wilderness as it does to read Shakespeare's Sonnets in the classroom. In the activity of doing either, "constructivists become passionate knowers. . . ." Because this metaphor of the new poem is so unusual when applied to critical thinking within disciplinary communities, the notion of passionately knowing in any disciplinary text, mountain sheep excrement or Shakespeare's Sonnets, we spend much time trying to link it to our audience's interests.

From the discussion of developmental levels and critical thinking behaviors comes the question of how writing is linked to critical thinking—first from the workshop participants' points of view (i.e., what can they tell us about their own experiences of thinking through writing, both personally and professionally?) and then from our perspective, in which students develop particular thinking skills by responding to assignments asking for those skills:

- writing analyses of data develops analytical results and behaviors,
- writing about problems and their solutions develops problem-solving results and behaviors,
- writing about complex issues from multiple or opposing perspectives counters dualistic thinking while promoting dialogical thinking, and
- writing arguments helps writers examine multiple points of view, gather evidence, organize it effectively, and present their own positions persuasively.

The act of writing evolves these skills, and the product of writing demonstrates them. We offer support for our own claims for writing from the conclusions of Applebee and Langer's (1987) study of *How Writing Shapes Thinking* and Bean's (1996) *Engaging Ideas* (Appendix D).

We next begin to discuss assignment making. Yet before asking the questions of faculty already described, or producing assignments that encourage particular thinking skills, we describe central features of our assignment-design package—that assignments succeed best when they include clear goals, engaging contexts, and specific audiences, and when they challenge students at Vygotsky's zone of proximal development, where they are stretched without breaking. This discussion counters the assignment making that thwarts students when they are asked, say, to "write an essay of seven to ten pages on a topic of interest to you" or write assignments that rank and sort.

This section depends for its persuasiveness on readers accepting two related propositions. First, if instructors design their assignments with goals, contexts, and audiences, students will write better papers and instructors will have better grading experiences. Second, students need to know, as they read the assignment even for the first time, that they can succeed at writing it because it is relevant to the material they have been studying and discussing. The assignment challenges them to be sure, but with drafting and thinking on their parts, and with collaborative help, they know they can write it successfully. These two propositions are true for any class—from those in physics to those on diversity issues.

Research supports these claims drawn from our experience and the experience of others. Before offering it, I want to explain what I mean by clear goals, engaging contexts, and identifiable audiences. I also want to assert that conferencing with students as they write, when time allows, markedly improves student performance.

Clear goals are the most important quality that writing assignments can have to enhance the writing and grading experience. All writing assignments have goals, whether explicitly stated or not. Some assignments ask students to write on topics of interest to them discovered during the course of the term. Others are much more specific in their expectations. To illustrate, imagine a composition instructor assigning one of the following two assignments in her course, "English 102: Issues in Cultural Diversity": "Write a paper (4–5 pages) on a topic in cultural diversity (on race, gender, culture, or life style choices) which interested you during the term." Or from the alternative assignment, "write a paper (4–5 pages) examining the three most significant opposing viewpoints generated by the issue of providing health insurance to permanent partners in gay relationships. The paper must be balanced and well developed without taking a position on the issue. It must also include a minimum of five reference sources, two of which may be from class readings."

The first assignment offers no clear goal at all (except to write four to five pages on a cultural diversity issue). It could develop into an argument, analysis, synthesis, or examination of opposing points of view; it could develop into any expository task, but probably ends up being a general treatment of a topic or topics composed largely of quotes and paraphrasing. When students do not know what the instructor expects from the assignment, their first thinking strategy is trying to figure out what he or she wants. As a second strategy, they "cover all the bases," writing about everything in an effort to hit on something acceptable. The third is to rely too much on their sources, too little on themselves, because sources seem safer than the expression and support of their own ideas. None of these strategies is usually what instructors want. Instructors view these open-ended assignments as an opportunity for students to choose topics about which they can write the best papers, use sources of their choice, and organize according to a pattern they determine—all admirable goals.

Unfortunately, these admirable motivations too often lead to poor results because open-ended assignments, without instructor intervention in topic selection or essay revision, omit the essential information most lower and upper division students need to write successfully. Writing on the open-ended assignment, most students do not know what they are supposed to be writing about; they struggle with selecting a topic, often choosing topics too broad to be covered within page limitations; they write in unsupported generalizations and overuse sources (or plagiarize); and they grapple with organizational patterns dictated by the broadness of the topic or the research sources they have selected. Unless required to do so, they often refuse to ask questions in class or go in for conferences with the instructor because of ennui, fear, or embarrassment.

I also note that such assignments reflect almost nothing in the real world of writing, either inside or outside of the academy. How many faculty write much of anything without a sense of goals (and context and audience) or without the help of colleagues, journal or book editors, or both? There sometimes exists a pronounced disconnect between what faculty expect from their students and what they acknowledge as a writing reality. Electrical engineering (EE) faculty members participating in UNR's writing assessment project, for example, initially told WAC/writing center personnel that "our students can't write. We're interested in this project to help them write better, or even to help them write coherently at all." Yet during the 2-year period of reading their students' writing, the EE assessment committee members usually found individual papers *good* or *excellent*, and in some cases publishable—an assessment with which we agreed. How could this disparity in initial opinion and outcome exist? It existed because the "writing was not perfect," as one of the

EE committee members observed, including some sentence-level problems (*their* for *there*, *its* for *it's*, etc.). This specific lack of perfection, he regretted, led to a much larger impression that students could not write, although under this banner of perfection he acknowledged that faculty could not write either nor could anyone. The problem here, which the electrical engineering faculty appear to have solved after 2 years, stems from a lack of critical consciousness about what they expected of students versus the reality of what they do themselves. The gap is often wide, as Geisler (1994) noted, and its closure requires months (even years) of interaction. Requiring students to write in environments in which those inside and outside the academy almost never write is destructive and hypocritical. Yet so many of us seem oddly unconscious of the difference and its consequences.

Open-ended assignments present other difficulties. Ironically, they often lack the information teachers need to grade fairly and efficiently. Grading becomes an arbitrary and time-consuming activity, which requires the grader to interpret each paper's goals, decide how well the goals are met, and then justify the decision by explaining, usually in the end comment, the grade for the paper. Under these conditions, teachers may slip into biased assessment. In contrast, writing on assignments with clear goals, students begin by knowing what the teacher wants. They think critically about the quandary the assignment poses, not the assignment itself. They organize according to specific parameters. If they have questions of the instructor, they know which ones to ask. The design of the assignment helps instructors create criteria for grading, increasing fairness and efficiency. In other words, specifying goals presents advantages not only for students as writers, but for teachers as graders.

Designing another kind of faulty assignment—one that has clear goals, but those goals beyond the cognitive and linguistic grasp of the students writing them—is usually (as I have remarked before) an accident. Almost all faculty wish for students to succeed at writing the assignments they require and will change or abandon those assignments that block success.

In addition to clear goals, effective assignments provide students with an engaging context. In the case of health insurance for partners in gay relationships, for example, student writers may be placed in the position of arbitrator between management and those seeking such insurance, as siblings to a gay employee who simply cannot accept the issue from management's or their sibling's points of view, or as consultants to a legislative body that may be considering action on the issue. They may merely be given the context of the classroom: "assume a division in thinking about the issue in your class; help those on each side understand the issue's complexity and implications." Each one of these situations will affect how writers think about the paper—its content, organization, and pertinent sources. As an important qualifier about context, it should engage students at their levels of interest and preparation.

Assignments should also offer an identifiable audience for writing, clearly related to the assignment's context. Again in the case of insurance for partners in gay relationships, students might write to employees and management explaining the merits and demerits of both sides—to gay siblings, legislative bodies, each other, or their teachers. Writing to specific audiences helps students develop a sense of the shape and tone for their essays. To illustrate, writers adopting a neutral, examine-both-sides point of view have severe limitations conditioning their tone—limitations reflecting knowledge without bias, enthusiasm without advocacy. However, if they write to persuade an ambivalent audience, those who have not formed an opinion about the issue, they have a chance to convince this audience because of its ambivalence. Under conditions of persuasion, writers' tones should reflect moderation, their arguments a charitable representation of those of their opponents, followed by a focused refutation of those arguments, and then a complete explanation of their own position. Audience and context are obviously closely related, and each should be consistent with an assignment's goals.

I have been using this hypothetical assignment from a second-semester composition course emphasizing diversity issues to substantiate the value of goals, context, and audience for assignment making. I want now to offer three sample assignments outside the arena of cultural diversity to assert that the principles for assigning and grading writing remain the same in all classes. These samples are presented out of order with regard to our own workshop sequence: We offer the first four questions about assignment design before presenting the samples to establish our audience's ownership of the process. After asking participants to "Decide between goals or concepts, or some other cognitive or affective task, in designing the assignment," we discuss the models and then ask them to "Write a preliminary description of the assignment. (Consider defining a specific audience, an engaging context, and a pertinent format)." I want now to contextualize what may have been a somewhat abstract discussion through the use of specific and highly successful assignments. Certainly, faculty participants in workshops find the use of model assignments clarifying.

Goals, Context, Audience Across the Curriculum

The advantages to the students assigned (and the faculty grading) papers with the features I have described become evident through looking at an assignment written by Larry Kirkpatrick, a physics professor at Montana State University, for an introductory physics course:

You go out to the mailbox one day, where you receive the following letter from your younger brother:

Dear Pat: You sent your younger brother a bum recipe. Either you Bozeman people don't know what a good soft boiled egg is, or you made a mistake in your last letter to me. In New York a three minute egg is cooked for three minutes. So how come you cook your three minute eggs for a longer time? Come on, is the boiling water colder in Bozeman? (Ha, ha—that's a joke!) Please explain to me what is going on.

Write a letter to your brother (one page single spaced) explaining why you have to cook three minute eggs for longer than three minutes in Bozeman. He's a bright kid but he hasn't had a college physics course. Don't try to smoke him with textbook jargon. Just explain to him in clear language what is going on. In your letter discuss such features as 1) the relationship of atmospheric pressure to altitude; 2) the effect of pressure on boiling point; 3) the relationship of the heat content of water to boiling point; and 4) the transfer of heat from the water to the egg.

Because the following criteria are included as part of the assignment, students know they will be graded on (a) the accuracy of their explanations; (b) the clarity, development, and completeness of their explanations; (c) the appropriateness of their explanations for their brother; and (d) the overall effectiveness of their writing style. This assignment poses an interesting (and cognitively challenging) problem for students in an introductory physics class. It gives them an engaging context: Nearly a mile above sea level, the eggs *would* take longer to boil. It supplies an audience: a bright but uninformed brother to whom textbook jargon would be abhorrent. These qualities make possible the best writing experience for students.

Even a first reading of the assignment would demonstrate to students who have been responsibly immersed in the course that they can succeed at writing it. They may need the help of their instructor and peers in the process of drafting a successful essay, but again who writes without some help? Students will not have to guess at the goals for the assignment (to explain the four features), context (it takes longer than 3 minutes to boil 3-minute eggs in Bozeman), and audience (a sibling) as they do with an open-ended assignment. If they have questions, they know which ones to ask (about the dilemma the assignment poses and not about the assignment).

Although a few faculty have argued that assignments such as this one guide the students too much, the largest majority recognizes the physics assignment to be challenging, especially for the student population (freshmen/sophomores) for which it is intended. However well explained, the assignment is not easy. Its goals make it cognitively demanding because they combine problem solving with analysis and persuasion, its context implies a place-oriented and playful response, and its audience requires an accessible and personable tone. These characteristics unite in complex ways to generate a formidable writing experience.

For example, student writers cannot address the goals for this assignment without its context because each locale's altitude plays a critical role. They may ignore specific locales, recognizing altitude in its relation to the four questions without any specific reference to the remainder of the assignment, but doing so could omit context and audience, opening the door to textbook jargon. They may attend too much to locale and audience, failing to answer one or more of the four questions. For the physics professor, answering his questions constitutes the central requirement: His goals for learning and reflecting learning are paramount. Even with this emphasis on answering the questions (on understanding the physics), context and audience play critical roles. They each become part of the grading. Thus, the assignment creates a complicated writing situation specific to his course and discipline while accessible to freshmen and sophomores.

The second assignment, written by Ken Peak, a criminal justice professor at the University of Nevada–Reno, is designed for an upper division course in criminal justice administration.

THE PRINCE ASSIGNMENT

Criminal Justice 312: Administration

General Situation: You are employed in a criminal justice agency where you have provided competent, faithful service for 3.5 years. A supervisory opening has been announced recently, for which you meet the minimum qualifications (a bachelor's and three years experience). After careful consideration, you decide to apply for the promotion; you are informed by the jurisdiction's personnel office that, instead of an objective (multiple-choice, true–false) examination for the candidates, the agency's tough chief, I. B. Ruff, is emphasizing writing and cognitive ability. You also learn through the agency "grapevine" that Ruff's master's thesis was an analytical treatise on Machiavelli's *The Prince*.

Personnel further informs you that Ms. Ruff is requiring all promotional candidates to prepare a position paper, wherein they must elaborate on their administrative views. Specifically, they must present their philosophies in three general areas: 1) the assumption of authority, 2) personnel administration, and 3) financial administration (which by sheer coincidence, could be construed as the three primary subject areas of The Prince).

Your mission: to develop a position paper setting forth your views as they pertain to those three areas. (You may wish to utilize the outcome of your "T-P Leadership" exercise done in class early this semester to assist in "staking out" your position.) You must inject as many "pearls" of Machiavelli's wisdom as necessary. However, remember that Ruff did a critical analysis of The Prince, so you need not be totally positive and should feel free to disagree with Machiavelli where necessary. Remember, this is a position paper, so your views are important to this assignment.

You are to prepare and submit a cogent position paper of 5–7 double-spaced pages, with pagination and a cover page (no "showy" cover), and stapled in the upper-left corner. Compare and contrast your views with those of Machiavelli so as to explain your philosophy in the above three areas and show how you would perform as a supervisor. Machiavelli's quotes should be intermingled throughout the paper. The following criteria will be employed:

1. How well you set forth your administrative position (while adhering to the above scenario).
2. The extent to which you have "woven in" (pro and con) Machiavelli's views, thereby demonstrating that you have read and understand the book.
3. Your ability to *communicate* the above information, being clear, concise, and accurate. Papers will therefore be evaluated on content, grammar, spelling, punctuation, and appearance. The timeliness of the paper will also be a factor. The due date will be provided in class.

This paper will be worth 75 points maximum

This assignment is appropriately more complicated and challenging than the physics assignment. Embedded in the context of applying for a promotion is the requirement that students write a pro and con treatment of Machiavelli's The Prince, and not just generally, but in three specific areas, requiring close reading of the text. This assignment has many positive qualities: It places criminal justice students in a position they may well find themselves, applying for promotion; it presents an obvious and real-world audience, the savvy I. B. Ruff; its goals are consistent with the course and discipline; but perhaps most important, it turns a potentially flat book report into a genuine thinking exercise, necessitating serious analysis of text and then persuasive application of that analysis driven by context and audience. The assignment is cognitively challenging, but aptly so, because it is designed for juniors and seniors in criminal justice.

The third assignment returns to a freshmen and sophomore audience. It was written by Gary Hausladen, a geography professor at the University of Nevada–Reno.

GEOG 106 CULTURAL GEOGRAPHY

Exercise #3 30 points

At a recent conference, a round-table discussion of leading world economists came to the consensus that Gross National Product (GNP) per capita was the single most important indicator (useful measure) of the standard of living/quality of life for individual countries. During the discussion period, you rose to take exception—not with the fact that GNP per capita may be the best indicator, but with the use of only a single indicator to assess and/or compare standards of living throughout the world. You eloquently defended the position that it is better to use a range of variables that are demographic and social, as well as economic to more accurately depict the quality of life in some areas of the world.

The chair of the discussion was impressed by your argument and requested that you write a brief defense of your position for the possible publication in the proceedings of the conference. The chair strongly encouraged you to use a single country as an example and to compare its standard of living with that of the United States.

To defend your position, you will write a three-page (maximum), typed, double-spaced paper on the standard of living in a single country based on at least three variables, one demographic, one social, and one economic. You will compare these to the same variables for the United States. Your particular country and the kinds of variables that fit each of these categories will be discussed in class.

Your paper will contain (1) a description of the three variables and a brief discussion about what each one tells us the standard of living in your selected country, (2) a brief comparison of these same variables with the United States and what this says about similarities and/or differences in the standards of living between these two countries, and (3) a concluding paragraph about why it is better to use a range of variables, as opposed to using a single variable, when describing and/or comparing standards of living throughout the world. You must cite the source(s) of your data using footnotes in the text and a bibliography at the end of the paper. Refer to the handout from exercise #2 for the correct form for bibliographic citations ("B"). For footnotes in the text, employ a simple scientific notation method, using, in parentheses, last name(s) of the author(s), date of publication, and pages only, eg. (Smith, 1988, pp. 45–67).

You will be graded on (1) the accuracy of your data, (2) the clarity and completeness of your explanations and comparisons, (3) the persuasiveness of your argument, (4) the quality of your writing, and (5) your ability to use citations correctly.

Papers will be graded on a 30-point scale. A top grade (30) will clearly demonstrate how your variables measure standards of living and will strongly support the importance of using a range of variables. A middle grade (15–20) will demonstrate that you are able to gather data and make comparisons; however, your audience would still be unconvinced about the need to replace GNP per capita with a range of variables. A low grade (10 and below) will either demonstrate a lack of understanding on your part or be so poorly written that it makes little sense.

Gary begins this assignment with an engaging event that I have witnessed. He passes through the class of more than 100 students with the names of 140 countries on individual slips of paper contained in a hat. Each student draws one country to which he or she must compare/contrast the standard of living with that in the United States using the three variables. The buzz of talk emerging between students as this process occurs is astonishing. Also astonishing is the enthusiastic convergence on the library, evidenced by reference personnel, of students seeking the information and data they need to make the three comparisons. Writing Center personnel do a draft workshop in the class before students submit their papers; as a whole, we have never experienced a student group more eager to discuss their drafts or more committed to write successfully than this group.

Much of the student enthusiasm and commitment is generated by Gary, who hurries through his class with hat in hand, working it as the smartest game-show host might work his or her own audience. Yet this simile is in no way meant as disparaging; when we teach classes as large as Hausladen regularly does, we find ourselves under some burden to entertain as well as educate. When we require writing in such courses as he regularly does, we do well to make that writing experience interesting and pertinent. Yet the main reason for the assignment's success stems from its design: its goals (to compare/contrast standards of living from three perspectives), context (publication in conference proceedings), and audience (academic colleagues). This assignment, as engaging as it is challenging, requires data/information analysis and then persuasive application of analysis. Its outcome is revelatory to students who in a sense rediscover the United States in the face of living conditions, which they ably and energetically discuss, in the country they have drawn. (Other assignments offered in Appendix E: These models link themselves, although not exclusively, to various other cognitive behaviors: the ornithology assignment [how birds fly] to process analysis and the environmental science assignment [analyzing two professional articles on one pertinent issue] to opposing points of view, critique, and synthesis.)

Kirkpatrick, Peak, and Hausladen offer these assignments in courses that usually enroll more than 100 students—yes, even the upper division criminal justice assignment. They have committed themselves to the value of writing despite course size, and so the time involved grading papers becomes critical. Sometimes they have a graduate student's help with grading the papers, but more often they do not; and as I understand the situation, Ken Peak from criminal justice never has graders. Over the many years of my relationship with these teachers, representing a tiny portion of MSU's and UNR's teachers who require writing, they have not abandoned their writing assignments based on whether they have graders. They assign writing.

The design of a writing assignment is critically linked to ease and fairness in grading, and the prior assignments present obvious advantages to the grader over any form of open-ended assignment making. In them, grading criteria can be readily identified and rubrics developed out of the goals, context, and audience. In fact, each of these assignments includes criteria and rubrics as part of its presentation. Graders know what to expect. They evaluate papers according to the degree they find the features required. In a sense, their grading and student response to it remains controlled by a contract.

Personnel from UNR's Writing Center have conducted more than 60 paper grading sessions with five randomly selected papers written from the physics assignment (Appendix F). During these sessions (involving several hundred participants), instructors read the papers and rank them from *most successful* to *least successful*, offer reasons for their ranking, and share their rankings and reasons with their colleagues. Faculty almost uniformly agree on which papers constitute top, middle, and bottom papers. (See explanation of "criteria-based scoring" for further detail.)

Common sense supports the notion that the more care teachers take in designing their assignments, the better for students writing them and teachers grading them. However, does this mean that open-ended assignments (write on a topic of interest to you) should be eliminated? Yes, I think, mostly. They fail in the fundamental ways already described and especially in a singular way: teacher/researchers, people deep into their postsecondary positions (even teacher/researchers with the most radical of process–expressivist inclinations), do not write anything resembling these assignments, not for publication or presentation at least, (almost) never write without goals, context, and audience in mind. Significantly, the professional positions into which they place their students rarely, if ever, require such writing. Nonetheless, it is hard to close the door on student-driven topics and papers, feeling as if doing so may close the door to student ownership, creativity, and independence. Thus, I endorse a strictly limited and heavily ministered form of open-ended assignment design.

Teacher intervention with students as they write can make an unclear assignment better and a clear assignment truly superior. This intervention may take the form of conferences between student and instructor, focused small-group work with peers, or comments on drafts followed by revision. It may occur after students have completed a draft of their papers or before they begin the first draft. If the purpose of the intervention is to help students limit and shape topics, obviously it is most effective at the beginning as students are considering their topics. They can do so with their instructor's guidance. This activity also has obvious advantages for grading because the instructor will know, even with assignments as open-ended as those described earlier, the goals the student has for writing. He or she can then base grading on how well students have met the goals outlined in the conference and paper.

Intervening after students draft their papers, but before they turn them in for grading, also has a positive impact because students can make changes between rough draft and final copy. As I discuss in more detail in chapter 7, commenting on written drafts of papers and then allowing students to rewrite with the comments in mind dramatically improves final copies. If faculty take the time to put comments on the papers they receive from students, and most do, our own research and that of others firmly support the idea of doing so on rough drafts and not on final copies so that students have time to make changes. Clearly, however, conferencing with students about their topics or writing comments on rough drafts requires a significant commitment of time. No one should expect, and as a WAC consultant I do not, faculty members teaching large classes to conference with each student. I would expect them instead to abandon the notion of requiring writing.

For this reason and many others, a conscientization of writing across the curriculum is necessary. The consequences (potential and actual) to students and faculty of requiring writing must be discussed openly and fully with faculty workshop participants. Under the banner of discipline-based writing activity, the program begins with volunteers, not draftees. Thus, it becomes easier to convince teachers to use writing assignments in their classes. Mostly they are already there to do so. However, even these volunteers want an understanding of how writing will help their students improve their courses, not curtail their positive student evaluations and not bury them in immense amounts of work.

During the workshops, we examine at least one assignment in detail (half-day workshops allow for more time to stretch out than 90-minute workshops) for its goal(s), audience, and context and for the critical thinking behavior(s) it promotes. Presenting effective models supplies hands-on text to which participants may refer as they construct their own assignments. The activity of sharing models with faculty is part of Stage 5 in our assignment design workshop. Again I presented the models out of sequence here to illustrate the value of goals, context, and audience to both the student writers and teacher graders of such assignments. The placement of these models in this text is appropriate given my goals in this text, but such discussion during the workshop should be shorter. As part of the effort to ensure faculty ownership of the process, we proceed with the following questions:

1. "Choose a class in which you would like to try using a writing assignment, perhaps a class in which you have not required writing before." This request requires little explanation and takes little time to complete. Workshop participants—volunteers—are there to design assignments, and they immediately list their class or classes. The second question, however, requires deeper reflection.

2. "Isolate one or two goals for learning in the class (i.e., if students were to take away a core theory, argument, or principle from the term's work, what might that be? In an upper division biology course in genetics, for example, a goal for learning might be for students to understand the biological basis for heredity: a writing assignment might certainly be developed to help achieve that goal)." However obvious this question may appear, it will take a bit more time than the first question. (I encourage readers to answer it now for one of their classes.) We all have goals for learning in our courses, but we may have never been asked to articulate them in any formal way. Workshop coordinators should pause for a few minutes here, perhaps enhancing thinking about the issue by providing further examples consistent with the genetics example. My own experience of asking faculty to list one or two goals for learning suggests some discomfort, uneasy shifting, and then a settling down to the task. It is not, largely, that as teachers we do not know what we are doing in our classes, but that we are rarely asked what we want to do. Even so, listing a goal or goals does not take much time. The third question jars somewhat, moving from larger goals to more local thinking tasks.

3. "List concepts, problems, or processes important to understanding course material—those which perhaps have given students trouble in the

past. (In a course in museum training for biologists, an assignment might ask students to explain how to collect sagebrush specimens for display, say, in the Nevada State Museum.)" These thinking tasks link themselves to smaller venues than goals for learning in the course; they include problem solving, information/process analysis, examining multiple points of view, making arguments, and so on, and they come from more contextualized pieces of the course. If teachers have taught the course in the past and required any form of evaluative device, they often know the problem areas that the course presents for students. Short, focused writing assignments can help students negotiate a path through these areas. The contextualized nature of these assignments, however, needs to be discussed. Explaining how to collect sagebrush specimens for display in a museum will help students understand that process and articulate it, but that understanding remains local: It will not necessarily translate to understanding the life cycle of sagebrush.

4. "Decide between goals or concepts, or some other cognitive or affective task, in designing the assignment. Assignments connected to goals often involve longer projects than those associated with concepts, processes, or problems." (A practical way to distinguish between assignments linked to goals for learning or specific thinking tasks is through the assignment's length.)

At this point we present the model assignments.

Presenting models is fundamental to workshop success. They supply hands-on text to which participants may refer as they construct their own assignments; they demonstrate goals, context, and audience; they show how grading is linked to design; they evidence writing across the disciplines in ways based in the disciplines, and writing required in heavily enrolled classes; and they represent themselves as rationally demanding—encouraging relevant writing, talking, and thinking behaviors in students. They open rather than close the gates. These are all important reasons to provide models, and I promise that after one assignment-design workshop (and follow-through), presenters will have at least a few assignments from their own faculty to use in future workshops. Yet another advantage to including such models is that they open a discussion of sequencing, moving from less complex writing and thinking behaviors to more complex writing and thinking behaviors. They show, in a limited way, how Perry's and Belenky's theory of cognitive development—that we move from dualistic thinking to relativism with commitment, and we move from received knowledge to constructed knowledge—can be reflected in assignment making.

5. "Write a preliminary description of the assignment. Share the drafts with other workshop participants." The promise at the beginning, even in the fliers advertising the workshop, is that faculty will leave with a draft of an

assignment that, with refinement, they can use in the class. They almost always draft an assignment, not only because they want to, but because of the request that they share their drafts with other workshop participants. Sharing text is a hidden motivator to draft text even if the draft is merely notes that participants have jotted down because they might have to share their assignment with others. This is the final point in the assignment-design workshop, but not in the process. The consultant, of course, should further collaborate with faculty participants on their assignments.

The second most common workshop we offer to faculty concerns evaluating student writing and is often presented in sequence with the assignment-design workshop. However, it is more straightforward and less labor-intensive. It begins with a discussion of several options for grading and providing feedback on papers and ends with what we term *criteria-based scoring: grading papers based on the design of the assignment.* This section provides the form our consultants use with faculty, along with some of our observations under each heading. As faculty participants often fill in the blanks, these observations are not part of the form we distribute. I include them here as aids.

EVALUATING STUDENT WRITING: LESSENING THE PAPERWEIGHT OF GRADING

Options for Providing Feedback and Grading Papers

Writing End Comments on the Final Copies of Student Papers

• Although end comments demonstrate to students that their teachers have read their papers and have reasons for the grades they give, there is *no* evidence that future student writing is improved by the effort. Nonetheless, teachers often want to write end comments on final drafts as a matter of tradition and commitment. They received such comments on their own papers and claim that they benefited from them. At the same time, they often express doubt about whether their students read their comments or benefit from them in any observable way. (In fact, a few have noted to us that their students "glanced at the grade and tossed the paper.")

- In situations where assignments include no criteria for grading (e.g., open-ended assignments), a closing comment may be essential for explaining the basis for grading individual papers. Of course it is easy to see how time-consuming this practice would become if one is grading 30 papers.

- Sometimes end comments are too extensive, covering whole pages and overwhelming student writers. We recommend that if teachers insist on writing end comments on final drafts, they remark briefly on the paper's greatest strength and its one area for improvement. This way they provide support and critique simultaneously, they connect with their students, and they can write the comments with comparative quickness. Similarly, correcting all sentence-level errors in a piece of writing sometimes tends to blur these problems for student writers. We recommend isolating repeated errors, correcting them, and explaining how they interrupt the piece's communication.

Commenting on Rough Drafts

- Common sense suggests that if a teacher is going to take time to write substantive comments on student writing, doing so on rough drafts rather than final copies is more effective. This technique yields superior results because students have the opportunity to make changes before submitting the paper for grading. Hillocks found that students who received comments and then did revisions generated nearly twice the gain in quality of writing over receiving comments but doing no revision. Hillocks' findings are confirmed anecdotally by our writing assessment project findings with papers from electrical engineering students. Assessment committee members, including two faculty members from the Electrical Engineering Department and two from the Writing Center, found six of seven group papers, representing all of the students in a 400-level course in digital systems, to be of *publishable* (their term, not ours, although we agreed) quality. The instructor, as the committee discovered after its evaluation, had regularly read and written focused comments on drafts. In another example, 8 of 10 lab reports (representing a random selection of over one third of students in the class) for a 400-level course in integrated circuit engineering were judged by the committee to be at the A or B letter-grade levels. The instructor had intervened once with commentary on the drafts before the reports were submitted.

- Telling students what to do through comments on drafts may be a teacher's natural inclination. Student writers will do what the instructor tells them to do, especially if doing so is required and improvement will result, at least within the context of instructor demands. This process may limit revision to an exercise in pleasing the instructor, not necessarily bad in itself (editors often take this approach as do supervisors), but it does confine student writers to the instructor's editorial mandates. More important, it limits learning to write and think within disciplinary parameters by making revision too easy and the student writer too dependent on external authority. Under this condition, student writers do not learn much about how to become the best writers and revisors of their prose. We recommend, instead, question-asking and collaborative comments. In an obvious example of the contrast between the two approaches, instructors may point out that some elements of the assignment are missing, explain what they are, and indicate where they belong. As an alternative, they might ask what the missing elements are and how and where the writer might fill the gaps. I recognize the line between these two approaches may appear nearly invisible because both are directive. However, one thinks for student writers, whereas the other asks them to think.

Conferencing With Students as They Write

• When teachers conference with students as they write, they produce a situation similar to writing comments on their drafts. That is, they increase the possibility for students to respond to their assignment with success because students will have time to make changes before submitting their final copies. Like writing comments on rough drafts, however, conferencing is labor-intensive, and instructors may not, and probably will not, wish to invest the time. For example, it is unimaginable to me that faculty teaching classes of more than 100 students would open their doors to conferencing students on their writing. Such a scenario is anti-WAC because it denies what postsecondary institutions have become, at least those in which I have worked. Reality in these institutions means large student enrollments in many classes. The first-year writing sequence has politically positioned itself to counter large class sizes because of its writing intensity and expertise, and the success of this positioning on campus is another reason to support its requirement. Yet most undergraduate classes enroll many students, and even those at the upper division level often include 40 or more students—a number considered intimate in some administrative quarters. At UNR, we target such courses for the use of writing, and we know that labor-intensive approaches, although attractive and perhaps even the most beneficial, will discourage faculty participation in the writing enterprise. Labor-intensive approaches ignore institutional reality, and they ignore faculty interests, disciplines, and cultures. These instructors want to teach their students the language, cognitive behaviors, and culture of their disciplines, but not at the sacrifice of their own careers. To sustain WAC under the conditions in which it finds itself, consequently, other alternatives should be presented for improving student writing.

Students Evaluating Each Other's Writing

• Faculty have probably heard of, and perhaps have even tried, dividing students into small groups to exchange and review drafts with each other. Faculty worry seriously about how this activity might take away from their teaching time, and they also worry that it may be ineffective. They have reason to worry. Teachers of first-year composition have long complained that small-group work on drafts often degenerates into talk of school, relationships, sports, movies, and music. I have never thought of this degeneration as particularly bad in my own writing classes; after all, it is communication. Yet to those outside my realm, it seems pointless. To those outside my realm, it *is* pointless. Nonetheless, draft workshops can be effective in any class when guidance and support are provided by the teacher who circulates to ensure that students are on task. At the beginning of draft workshops in my classes, I reread the assignment sheet to my students, isolate the two or three questions I want them to answer in writing about each other's papers, and walk from group to group, veiling my policing by trying to be helpful. At UNR, draft workshops are common in classes outside the English Department. These classes are often large (e.g., Geography 106, which typically enrolls more than 100 students), and their teachers call on the Writing Center for help. Center personnel discuss the goals for the assignment with the entire class and clarify with the teacher any points about which students express confusion. Then the students are asked to read their colleagues' papers with two or three issues in mind—those most important to writing the assignment successfully. The class then breaks up into groups of three or four, and Center personnel circulate among the groups answering questions, reading sections of papers, and providing guidance. Even without a writing center in support, however, having students give feedback to each other lifts some of the burden from the teacher and is an effective technique if it is focused on two or three issues related to the assignment. (Open-ended directions such as "read each other's papers and tell the writers what you think" are not as effective because they allow for unreflective responses—"Hey, I like this; it's good.") In some situations, UNR students have been charged with applying letter grades to each other's papers—a process to which many other instructors object. Less objectionable, senior majors who have taken the class previously are paid to grade papers.

Writing Center Feedback

• If the institution has a WAC writing center staffed with graduate student tutors from various disciplines, it will no doubt provide students with critiques that help them improve their papers. Studies conducted on the relationship of tutoring to improved student writing at Montana State and UNR (see Johnson, 1996; Waldo, 1988) demonstrate that tutoring focused on instructor goals for an assignment increases the student's chances for writing successfully.

• Tutoring in writing centers often occurs through inquiry and collaboration, helping students solve writing problems on their own without prescribing solutions for them. As with writing inquiry-based comments on rough drafts or asking questions during conferences, this technique generates thinking about writing and revising, making student writers more independent and, as one of my colleagues once said to me, "perpetually putting the writing center out of business" (Jeannie Anderson). Writing centers want to put themselves perpetually out of business because they do not want dependent student writers. Scott Johnson's dissertation, already cited, shows that student writers internalize the question-asking process they hear in writing center tutorials. They take it home and, when they write, use it themselves. Sending students to WAC writing centers must be understood as a viable alternative to faculty comments or conferences on drafts of student papers. As such, a writing center becomes greatly supportive of the WAC endeavor and, under the conditions described here, essential to it. Faculty across campus who wish to include writing assignments in their classes, but fear, rightly, the amount of time the whole process will require, must feel confident that their students will receive valuable help elsewhere.

Models Feedback

• During any assignment-design workshop I have conducted, the moment of most significance is when the sample assignments appear—mostly effective assignments, but one or two problematic ones as well. After all of the abstractions we have discussed about first-year student thinking, cognitive behaviors, student development in writing and thinking abilities in the disciplines, and goals, context, and audience, I present model assignments. My audience sighs in relief. Here, they are probably thinking, is what he means. They see examples of successful assignments and those not so successful, and they begin to formulate their own assignments with the models in mind. Of course, students are much the same. They appreciate reviewing student papers that have succeeded on a given assignment in the past, and they learn from papers that have not. Models feedback accomplishes many useful tasks simultaneously. It familiarizes students with the goals for the assignment and the criteria by which they will be graded. Such feedback gives them a sense of how past students have written and how the instructor responded to their papers. If there is no time for writing comments on drafts or conferencing with students, models feedback presents an efficient and effective technique for talking about student writing.

No Evaluation

• In some instances, writing may be assigned that will not be graded or commented on by the instructor. In fact, it may not even be read, but merely noted as completed. This writing often takes the form of journal responses to questions posed during class or about reading the students are doing. Suggesting that faculty assign writing they will not have to evaluate may be the only way to convince some to include writing in large classes. Of course many students will not take such writing too seriously, and faculty often resist the notion of assigning, but not responding.

Criteria-Based Scoring: Providing Feedback and Grading Papers Based on the Design of the Assignment

• When UNR's Writing Center personnel come to this point in the evaluation workshop, they distribute the physics assignment on the impact of altitude on boiling eggs. They discuss the assignment with participants, particularly its goals, context, and audience and then the criteria the instructor offers for grading. After they finish talking about the assignment, they distribute five student papers written in response (Appendix F). Workshop participants read the papers and rank them from *most successful* to *least successful*, write down reasons for their rankings, and then share the rankings and reasons with their colleagues.

I have conducted this workshop myself more than 30 times—not only with faculty at UNR, but with faculties from other institutions across the country. My audiences have totaled more than 300 faculty members representing nearly every discipline. I mention this because of the remarkable agreement faculty demonstrate after reading the papers, particularly with the highest and lowest ranked papers (conservatively 90%), but also with the second highest (conservatively 80%). There is less agreement about the order of the middle two papers, although the same two papers are almost always in the middle, and there are disputes between science faculty in the audience about the science in the papers. The defining characteristic is agreement, and participants acknowledge the ease with which the papers could be read and evaluated.

Further evidence supporting the merits of focused assignment making comes from comparing evaluations of 10 papers on each of two different assignments in upper division criminal justice classes. The first, assigned in a junior-level course on juvenile justice, required students to write "on a topic of interest to you discovered during the semester, five to seven pages, due at term's end. It may be written about the juvenile court system, crime, detention, etc." The second, also assigned in a junior-level course—criminal justice administration, is Ken Peak's "Prince" assignment (included in this chapter).

Because there are no stated expectations for the first assignment (beyond writing five to seven pages on topics of interest in juvenile justice), the readers reviewing these papers (the Criminal Justice Department Writing Assessment Committee: four criminal justice faculty and two consultants from the Writing Center) had a difficult time evaluating them. Goals for each of the papers, and the degree to which the writer met the goals, were matters of reader interpretation and preference, creating jumbled rankings and pronounced disagreements. Reaching consensus on what constituted top, middle, and bottom papers did not occur because readers could not establish uniform criteria by which to judge them. Reading each of the papers took committee members, by their report, 20 to 30 minutes; presumably the instructor took longer because the time required for writing notes in text and closing comments would presumably be greater. (As part of the criteria for our study of papers, we never read papers with teacher commentary or grades written on them.) Characterized by topics too broad and complex for the length required, the majority of papers were flaccid and unfocused, overused outside sources, and included many sentence-level problems. The readers agreed that only four of the papers would succeed in any minimal sense of the word, and 6 of the 10 would receive a letter grade of D or F.

In contrast, the assignment using *The Prince* produced papers that nearly uniformly succeeded, 9 out of 10 receiving the equivalent letter grade of A or B. Each of these papers took the six readers under 10 minutes to read and evaluate. The instructor confirmed this assessment, claiming that approximately 90 out of 100 students did receive A or B grades and that each paper took under 10 minutes to read, comment on, and grade. The difference in success rates between these sets of papers supports the findings of Hillocks (1986), whose research in composition determined that paper assignments with clear and specific objectives—those that he termed *environmental*—produce markedly better writing than paper assignments without those objectives.

• The physics assignment, the papers it generates, and the agreement about their levels of quality present a convincing case that grading should be based on the design of the assignment and that assignments should be clear in their goals, context, and audience. When criteria for grading are linked to how well students address goals, context, and audience, grading becomes comparatively easy to explain to students and fairer and more efficient. The instructor's principal effort is front loaded into the design of the assignment and not into evaluating and grading it. Efficiency is an especially vital feature if WAC consultants want faculty teaching large classes to require writing; fairness is vital to students in classes of any size.

Wanting faculty to require writing assignments at mid-sized research/ teaching institutions, WAC professionals need to be dialogic with their constituents, seeking knowledge much more than transmitting it. Their goal is not to mold little English teachers, attempting to "adapt the educatee to the milieu." Instead, they need to connect their assignment-design workshops to the primary interests of their colleagues, making them relevant to their students, classes, and disciplines. If forwarding the development of critical thinking through WAC is an agenda, it is at least, unlike many others, an agenda we share across disciplines. The type of assignment making described here helps produce an effective pedagogy of writing and critical thinking. The evaluation workshops lessen the paperweight of grading by linking the design of the assignment to the creation of grading criteria. WAC evaluation workshops need to present faculty constituents with many options for giving feedback on and grading papers. Yet given the class sizes and teaching loads at most public institutions, it is vital for the health of WAC to provide options that are efficient for graders and fair to students. Certainly criteria-based scoring is both efficient and fair. When workshop techniques such as these are offered, UNR's assessment instruments suggest that, over the years, the use of writing will grow steadily.

7

Assessing Student Writing Within the Disciplines

I start from our dilemma. On the one hand, we know too much about reading and writing to trust the quantitative scores on large-scale writing assessments: about reading, we know the immense contribution of the reader to the meaning and value of the text; about writing, we know the immense influence of audience, situation, and the writer's mood or even health on the quality of the text. On the other hand, we probably cannot forgo all large-scale writing assessment.

—Peter Elbow (1996)

The UNR Writing Center has existed for 13 years. During that time, its personnel saturated the campus with workshops in assignment design and paper grading, much along the lines described in chapter 6. As demonstrated by a phone survey of 400 UNR faculty members, the workshops helped generate an impressive increase in the amount of writing students were doing. The workshops also produced an abundance of student writers for the Center to tutor. A typical representation of students tutored for a given semester appears in the following table—in this case, for the spring semester 2002. For this semester, the Center tutored 3,222 students from 257 different classes and 47 different departments. More than 1,500 students were turned away.

Since 1997, a typical year means tutoring 7,000 students from 550 different classes taught in more than 70 departments. Certainly these statistics are a partial demonstration of the success of the Center and its various WAC enterprises, but that is not why I begin the assessment chapter with them. These

Course	Total	Course	Total	Course	Total	Course	Total	Course	Total	Course	Total
ACC 410	4	CI 620	1	ENGL 470	1	HIST 411	12	NURS 453	12	SOC 470	2
ACC 754	3	CI 726	6	ENGL 618	5	HIST 482	2	NURS 497	1	SPAN 101	1
ANTH 101	34	CI 744	5	ENGL 666	8	HIST 490	9	NUTR 113	2	SPAN 222	4
ANTH 102	6	CI 771	2	ENGL 711	5	HIST 681	10	NUTR 121	20	SPCM 113	5
ANTH 190	1	CI 784	11	ENGL 725	22	HP 403	2	NUTR 440	4	SPCM 480	1
ANTH 281	1	CI 789	12	ENGL 789	1	IAFF 300	22	*Personal*	6	SW 207	1
ANTH 350	1	CI 795	4	ENGR 301	18	INTD 451	2	PHIL 101	5	SW 220	5
ANTH 468	3	CI 799	4	ENGR 700	5	INTD 452	5	PHIL 113	1	SW 230	3
ANTH 470	2	CIS 360	1	ENV 100	3	INTD 456	6	PHIL 210	8	SW 330	15
APEC 332	3	CJ 201	1	ENV 300	2	JOURN 101	4	PHIL 212	1	SW 404	19
ART 112	3	CJ 211	3	ENV 301	4	JOURN 201	7	PHIL 213	1	SW 453	1
ART 116	2	CJ 289	1	ENV 415	2	JOURN 205	1	PHIL 244	6	SW 467	8
ART 117	6	CJ 320	2	ERS 210	3	JOURN 241	1	PHIL 255	1	SW 474	1
ART 170	2	CJ 420	5	ERS 440	2	JOURN 320	2	PHIL 314	5	THTR 118	1
ART 257	5	CJ 463	9	ES 100	1	JOURN 331	16	PHIL 481	7	THTR 471	2
Application	15	CS 634	1	GEOG 103	3	JOURN 343	3	PHIL 494	3	*Thesis*	11
BCH 406	3	EC 301	4	GEOG 106	4	JOURN 353	4	PHYS 110	1	*Misc*	55
BIOL 100	36	EC 321	1	GEOG 305	14	JOURN 421	1	PHYS 151	1	WS 101	4
BIOL 101	1	EC 332	1	GEOG 325	15	JOURN 453	8	PSC 102	1	WS 345	3
BIOL 110	2	EC 457	6	GEOG 456	2	ME 452	1	PSC 211	2	WS 433	1
BIOL 190	3	EC 459	5	GEOG 460	2	MGRS 210	3	PSC 231	12	WS 450	1
BIOL 192	41	EC 462	2	GEOG 476	5	MGRS 321	26	PSC 309	1	WT 201	44
BIOL 315	3	EC 464	27	GEOG 485	3	MGRS 324	2	PSC 410	2	WT 202	74
BIOL 316	6	EC 650	1	*Grad Sch*	26	MGRS 365	2	PSC 411	2	WT 203	48
BIOL 330	2	EC 765	2	HDFS 132	20	MGRS 367	1	PSC 413	7		
BIOL 360	2	*EC 797*	7	HDFS 232	2	MGRS 423	1	PSC 417	10		
BIOL 395	8	EE 101	5	HDFS 390	5	MGRS 455	2	PSC 430	7		
BIOL 415	12	EL 700	4	HDFS 400	5	MGRS 462	18	PSC 701	2		
BIOL 491	2	ENGL 80D	25	HDFS 432	5	MGRS 470	2	PSY 101	12		
CE 411	2	ENGL 1	68	HDFS 435	21	MGRS 471	3	PSY 102	1		
CE 771	1	ENGL 101	556	HDFS 436	14	MGRS 475	1	PSY 233	6		
CEP 154	2	ENGL 102	643	HDFS 438	26	MGRS 484	6	PSY 261	4		
CEP 354	4	ENGL 104	7	HDFS 470	2	MGRS 488	2	PSY 408	4		
CEP 454	1	ENGL 113	44	HDFS 472	10	MGRS 493	2	PSY 431	14		
CEP 705	2	ENGL 114	93	HDFS 636	4	MINE 321	2	PSY 433	19		
CEP 754	2	ENGL 223	4	HE 100	1	MINE 700	2	PSY 441	2		
CEP 760	4	ENGL 282	2	HE 310	2	MUS 101	1	PSY 446	5		
CEP 780	2	ENGL 297	2	HE 314	8	MUS 109	4	*Resume*	7		
CEP 790	5	ENGL 321	1	HE 340	2	MUS 121	17	RST 101	3		
CHEM 100	2	ENGL 345	1	HE 345	5	MUS 190	1	SOC 101	4		
CHEM 634	1	ENGL 400	3	HIST 101	4	MUS 321	2	SOC 207	4		
CI 160	5	ENGL 421	3	HIST 200	1	MUS 730	4	SOC 209	2		
CI 350	16	ENGL 427	1	HIST 102	2	NURS 100	15	SOC 210	2		
CI 358	1	ENGL 433	6	HIST 106	1	NURS 305	5	SOC 393	1		
CI 410	6	ENGL 438	2	HIST 202	3	NURS 343	2	SOC 395	2		
CI 453	4	ENGL 448	4	HIST 217	5	NURS 346	3	SOC 425	5		
CI 498	2	ENGL 454	1	HIST 408	1	NURS 435	4	SOC 453	11		

Totals:

Depts.	47
Courses*	257
Sessions	3222

*Excludes

Appl., Grad Schl,

Pers., Resume,

Thesis, and Misc.

126

statistics show the myriad writing communities that exist on our campus, each with a specialized discourse or discourses it passes on to its students. Basing our WAC interaction with faculty and tutoring interaction with students on acknowledgment of difference—not only in the languages of various disciplines, but also in the values, purposes, and forms they have for writing— had a large impact on the way in which we viewed writing assessment. More than 90% of UNR's teachers now require writing of their undergraduate students. Sixty-one percent require more writing of their lower division students than they did 3 to 5 years before, and 54% require more of their upper division students.

In 1994, five years after the Center opened, significant pressure began to build to institute a schoolwide writing assessment program. Fortunately, the administrator who brought the request for assessment to me was quite open-minded and agreed to a multilayered program, which, in theoretical and practical terms, stemmed most closely from our model for helping faculty to assign writing in their courses and majors: a discipline-based approach. This assessment project has involved four elements, principally, and each has been very labor-intensive. First, we have used Writing Center student-visit statistics. Second, as part of a larger exit interaction with students graduating from the university, we have interviewed graduating seniors about their experiences with writing in their classes and disciplines. Third, we have called approximately 400 full-time faculty (not graduate student teaching fellows or letters of appointment) to ask them multiple questions from a two-page survey (our questionnaire is available as Appendix G). Finally, we have engaged in a unique assessment relationship with selected departments. With members of the faculty from the department, we review and judge the quality of written work their junior and then senior majors are doing, ending with the assessment of a portfolio of 6 to 10 pieces of writing from each student.

Writing Center Statistics

WAC/writing center statistics can present compelling evidence of the growth in the number of students being tutored and, sometimes more important, in the amount of writing being assigned on a campus. At UNR, for the fall semester 1989 (its inaugural semester), the Writing Center recorded visits from 1,678 students coming from 77 different classes. A year later, fall 1990, the Center recorded visits from 2,682 students from 155 different classes. The percentage of increase in students is notable (63%), but the increase in classes is remarkable (100%). Extend this examination to fall 1991, when the Center tutored 3,256 students from 205 different classes, and one begins to see a powerful pattern emerging—a pattern demonstrat-

ing increased tutoring to be sure, but also increasing amounts of writing being required. Statistics for the fall semester 2000, a decade after the Center's
founding, indicate that there were 3,489 tutoring sessions with students
from 271 different classes. As mentioned, steady yearly traffic at UNR's
Center now amounts to over 7,000 students from 550 classes. This figure is
impressive, and it evidences a university far more active in having its students write than one, say, that requires writing in one or two writing-
intensive courses per department. Yet the figure is deceptive. Our Center
does not tutor student writers from every class in which writing is required.
More than 50% of our faculty respondents answered "no" to the question,
"Do you encourage your students to use the Writing Center?" This fact
demonstrates that at least 1,000 classes require some form of writing assignment per year. The statistics I am about to offer indicate a much larger figure, reflecting that we are tutoring students from no more than one third of
the classes that actually require writing.

Nonetheless, writing center statistics provide hard numerical evidence of a
program's single-year traffic and growth in traffic over multiple years. They
imply that the program is successful because more students want to use the facility year by year. (In the case of UNR's Writing Center, student visitation
figures have flattened to around 7,000 since 1997. That is not, however, because increasing numbers of students do not want to use the facility. They do.
The Center turned away more than 3,000 students during 2001. The problem
is that the tutoring budget has flattened.) The statistics also show an increase
in the amount of writing being assigned, suggesting that the program's WAC
workshops are succeeding in drawing faculty into the campuswide writing enterprise. Despite the limitation that statistics do not/cannot prove that the
quality of student writing or the climate for assigning it is improving, keeping
these statistics is essential, and sending them with interpretive comments to
all upper administrators is crucial, certainly year by year, but even semester by
semester during the early years. The singular advantage of these types of statistics is that they represent the only irrefutable evidence of a WAC writing
center's success at least in terms of its growth.

For additional statistical data, we regularly ask student visitors to the Center to fill out a response sheet (Appendix H) that includes several questions
regarding the quality of the tutoring session. We also ask teachers who require that their students be tutored to do blanket evaluations of Center tutoring. These two sources have generated thousands of tutoring reviews by students and an accumulated approval rating of more than 90% for the
effectiveness of the tutor and the tutoring process. (This figure contrasts with
the approval rating for tutoring at Montana State University's Writing Center, which was just above 70%. I attribute the difference to the experience

levels of the staff. At Montana State, Center tutors were almost exclusively undergraduate English majors; at UNR, they are graduate students from a wide variety of disciplines.) We have also kept records of the number of UNR faculty participating in WAC workshops (approximately 600 during 13 years of presentations) and their responses to the quality of the workshops (approval rating of 96%).

Student Interviews

Also useful to us has been participation in a larger program of exit interviews with 300 randomly selected (graduating) senior majors from a variety of disciplines. Taking place during the past 6 years, these interviews fall under the headings "College Student Experiences Questionnaire" and "Senior Exit Interview Report." They suggest that UNR's graduating seniors perceive themselves to have made noteworthy improvement as writers and thinkers during their tenure as students. When seniors are asked about "understanding and abilities" with regard to writing in their classes and disciplines, 97% report making gains in "effective and clear" writing, and 68% of the students characterize the gains as "substantial." In related areas, students report significant gains in "learning on one's own" (97%), "integration of ideas" (96%), and "analytical and logical thinking" (95%). That students say they have increased their abilities as writers and thinkers does not prove it so, I acknowledge. Yet the figure of 68% who characterize their improvement as "substantial" certainly suggests that something favorable is happening. I attribute these figures, which again are drawn from students across the entire curriculum, not only to an increase in the amount of writing assigned, but also to a substantial improvement in the quality of assignments that teachers are making.

Phone Survey of 400 Faculty

Calling 400 faculty to ask for answers to questions on a two-page questionnaire (Appendix G) is not an easy task. Completing it took Writing Center assessment personnel 1 month for each of two separate calling sequences—200 contacts per sequence. The first sequence of calls occurred during 1995 and the second during 2000. Different faculty members from every department were contacted during each sequence. We chose this survey method over the less expensive, less labor-intensive surveys, such as the blanket mail-out because of the dismal return elicited from blanket mail-outs—usually from 10% to 20%. Calling individual faculty members ensured that we would have a sample of

30%, producing statistically reliable figures. Calling also allowed for personal contact with teachers and an opportunity for them to talk to Center professionals about the survey questions and to qualify their responses. Their responses to five of the questions concern me particularly here:

Question 3: In how many of your lower division classes do you require at least one of those types of writing [nine different types of writing tasks are listed in Question 2]?

ALL   MORE THAN HALF   LESS THAN HALF

Question 4: In how many of your upper division classes do you require at least one of those types of writing?

ALL   MORE THAN HALF   LESS THAN HALF

Question 5: Over the last 3 years, have you required more writing from lower division students, less writing, or the same?

Question 6: Over the last 3 years, have you required more writing from your upper division students, less writing, or the same?

Question 7: Do you perceive that upper division students in general are better writers than lower division students?

In response to Question 3, 84% of the faculty respondents said they required at least one type of writing task in all of their lower division courses. Six percent required writing in less than half, and 10% in more than half of these courses. To Question 4, 85% said they required writing in all of their upper division courses, 3% required it in less than half of their courses, and 12% in more than half. The only significant difference between the 1995 and 2000 samples appears in response to Questions 5 and 6. In 1995, 61% of the faculty reported that they required more writing of their lower division students than they did 3 years before. In 2000, 23% reported that they required more. (Seventy-five percent required the same amount.) In 1995, 54% required more writing of their upper division students than they did 3 years before. In 2000, 33% of the faculty required more of their upper division students. (Fifty-eight percent required the same amount.) I was pleased to learn that such large percentages of faculty required more writing of undergraduates in 1995. The Writing Center had been operating for roughly 6 years at that time. In addition to offering many thousands of tutoring sessions to students, it presented to and consulted with several hundred faculty members. If the Center could not claim singular responsibility for this movement toward the use of writing assignments in class, it could at least assert significant responsibility. The lower figures for the year 2000 do not suggest a loss in the momentum of the WAC program (although a survey of this sort can certainly demonstrate that). Lower than they were in 1995, the 2000 figures still represent increases. The amount of writing required of undergraduates continues to rise at UNR, but at a slower pace than in 1995. The large percentages of faculty who require the same amount of writing as they did 3 to 5 years ago suggest that writing has reached something akin to saturation levels. In answer to Question 7 about whether students improve as writers between the lower and upper division, the responses also differ slightly between the 1995 and 2000 surveys. In 1995, just over 80% perceived improvement in undergraduate writing; in 2000, 87% perceived improvement. Either one of these figures is definitely an endorsement of institutional efforts and student achievement, but of course 87% is a stronger endorsement than 80%. I attribute the increase to a better writing pedagogy within disciplines and a more supportive atmosphere across campus for student writers.

The survey follows Question 7 about improvement in writing abilities between lower and upper division students with a question about improvement in eight more specific writing abilities, including ability to problem solve, reflect an assignment's requirements, assert an argument, support an argument, achieve sentence-level correctness, reflect complex thought, and so on. Faculty are asked to characterize the degree of improvement in each ability by labeling it *great, moderate, small,* or *none. Small* and *none* were indicated few times by respondents, falling into the 2% to 3% range for each ability (except in ability to assert an argument, where 7% said there was no improvement, and in sentence-level correctness, where 7% said there was small or no improvement). This means that the vast majority of faculty respondents, in the 91% to 99% range, perceive great to moderate student improvement in a variety of writing abilities. According to our survey, by the time they are seniors, students have more trouble eliminating sentence-level problems (23% of faculty respondents indicate *great* improvement) than they do reflecting complex thought in writing (43% of faculty indicate great improvement). Senior students have more trouble synthesizing information in writing (30% of faculty respondents indicate great improvement) than they do the ability to problem solve (39% claim great improvement). The survey also asks faculty whether they design their assignments to help students develop critical thinking behaviors, and in large numbers they reported doing so.

What makes this survey particularly noteworthy is its size (400 faculty respondents) and scope (from every academic department on campus). Given a sample of this size, representing roughly one third of UNR's full-time faculty, I think it is justifiable to conclude that 80% to 90% of all undergraduate courses offered at UNR require some form of writing task (excluding note taking); the amount of writing assigned to undergraduates continues to increase (although at a pace somewhat slower than 5 years ago); large percent-

Percentage of Faculty Whose Writing Assignments
Require the Following Elements

Category	Percentage
Analysis and critique	89
Synthesis	89
Problem solving	80
Review and summary	68
Examining multiple points of view	66
Arguing issues	65

ages of faculty link their assignments to the development of cognitive behaviors; and in numbers exceeding 80% faculty perceive students to improve in writing abilities between the lower and upper divisions. These figures evidence an institution active in the WAC endeavor and successful at it. Combine them with writing center statistics and senior exit interviews and the case becomes stronger.

Nonetheless, I recognize a few potential problems with this process of assessment, and particularly with assessment through the phone interviews. The first problem is a practical one. WAC and WAC writing center programs may not have the personnel and financial resources to conduct such labor-intensive surveys. UNR's program did and does. In addition to tutoring and office and operating budgets, the Writing Center is funded to include three professional positions: two graduate student teaching fellowships (one in tutor training and the other in writing assessment) and a full-time faculty member released from teaching a course to work with me on WAC projects. The faculty member and assessment coordinator have been principally involved in writing assessment within disciplines, as I am slowly coming to, but they were also involved in the design and conduct of the senior exit interviews and interviews with faculty. They trained other tutors to conduct the interviews during periods of nontutoring. The Center's office manager also engaged in the interview process occasionally, and I did as well. This formidable staff made it possible to interview so many and at such length.

Minimally, however, any writing center engaged in WAC activities must keep complete and accurate student visitation statistics (including student name, class, department, and further data if possible) and can do so out of its appointment sheets. Data from appointment sheets can readily be transferred to spread sheets. Why must WAC writing centers keep these statistics? There are at least a dozen good reasons to do so, but my response immediately concerns offering an answer to the administrator's question, "Why should we spend the money on your program?" "Because," you respond with the confidence that proof provides, "we tutored 2,600 students from 200 different classes last semester." Even without the staff UNR has to conduct interviews, others (office personnel, tutors) can be trained to do so. Although the scale may be more limited, such surveys can provide useful, compelling data.

The following potential problems with the survey are bonded together by similar, if more abstract sources than the problem of limited resources. Hence, I wish to explain them together here and then use them to transition into the last assessment device we employ: departmentally based assessment of student writing. While conducting the faculty surveys, I worried that some of the responses may have been shaped by paranoia. Perhaps a few teachers held the view that the Writing Center Police ("We know where you live") were calling to find out whether they assigned writing, and thus they may have exaggerated or even lied about their requirements. After all a telephone call is more immediate and personal than a blanket mail-out. We did what we could to mitigate this worry. From the beginning of the conversation, center interviewers opened the door to faculty refusal to respond, and for various reasons, roughly 5% did refuse. Interviewers also assured their faculty respondents that they would remain anonymous, and anonymity has been emphatically maintained. No one respondent has been identified by more than a number and a department; none was ever identified by name to me or anyone else except the interviewer, and no one faculty member can any longer be identified. Any kind of large-scale surveying depends on faith in the honesty of those doing the surveying and those taking the survey, just as it depends for its accuracy on asking large numbers of people the same questions. We have kept faith. Nonetheless, I acknowledge the possibility that a few teachers may have felt coerced.

As another potential problem, experts and interested parties outside the institution (say, writing assessment professionals, testing agencies, and legislatures) might challenge the results of internal interviewing. Will teachers within departments, they might wonder, want to appear to be increasing the amount of writing they assign? Will they want their students to appear as if they are improving as writers? Is it not in their interest to indicate increase and improvement, and will that *interest* bias their assessment? Let me acknowledge, as I did in qualifying the student response to improvement during the exit interviews, that faculty *claims* of increases and improvement do not *prove* they have occurred. Hard statistical evidence from the Writing Center supports, as I have shown, dramatic increases in the amount of writing being assigned at UNR, with impressive minimums in the number of classes requiring writing per year (approximately 550). Because of this and accruing anecdotal evidence, I accept as accurate the figures about increased numbers of assignments. About faculty claims of improvement, however, hard statistical evidence is more difficult to gather. Students claim that they improve, and faculty say so as well. I think the combination of students and faculty, and in such large percentages, strengthens the case. Yet the case for improvement basically rests on perception: student and teacher perception. *In fact, all writing assessment is a matter of perception and of whose perceptions prevail.*

Administrators within the institutions may also question the survey results because they might not trust their faculty to assess the quality of writing that students are doing. Faculty within departments may, in these administrators' view, be biased in favor of their students—a problem seemingly solved by assessing writing through a one-test-measures-all writing exam delivered by teams of outside experts. These experts have already determined the values, purposes, and forms for good writing, the pertinent rubrics for measuring the quality of writing, and they have developed topics applicable to all students. They can enter the institution and administer the test, taking thousands of student exams away to committees of language arts graders who score them. Then the resulting 4 or 8 out of 10, the pass or failure on the essay, can be reported back to the institution and student. Such a process seems so comparatively clean, objective, and cost-effective. Student or faculty bias appears to be eliminated. However, if faculty and student bias is eliminated, a much more pervasive and insidious bias is introduced. *All writing assessment is a matter of bias and of whose biases prevail.*

In addressing the question of faculty bias in the survey responses, that they have a local interest in endorsing improvement, I respond with this question: Who is better equipped to assess the quality of writing students are doing than the teachers for whom they are doing it? If readers understand the argument I have been developing, the answer is "no one." I ask my readers to consider this question in the context of the professions into which we (hope to) send our students. Will these fledgling professionals be fired if a committee of external experts determine that they do not write well, or will they be fired because experts within the profession, department, or company determine that they do not write well? The question is rhetorical because the answer is obvious. *All writing assessment is a matter of opinion and interpretation, community-based; there is no objectivity, no one standard.*

Ed White (1990) made this point about writing assessment being a matter of the opinions, interpretations, and biases of particular communities in a powerful and revealingly ironic way in his CCC's article "Language and Reality in Writing Assessment." Trying to develop the case about community bias in assessment, he first had to establish the different languages we use as academics. "We are caught," he observed, "in the languages we speak and in the discourse communities of our disciplines." Sharing a compositionist perspective and evangelizing a bit, he does not approve of this condition of being caught in these communities: ". . . the language specializations that largely define our disciplines and allow us to work as 'professionals' also cut us off from other important communities," causing us not to "see or read or value these other communities . . ." (p. 191). He supported the notion of not valuing the discourse of other communities by poking confessional fun at himself: "I often work professionally with those in other disciplines, but I confess that my PhD in English literature has so confirmed a particular discourse community that I routinely . . . find it hard to respect the scholarship of nonliterary communities" (p. 191). Finding it hard to respect the writing done by other communities can have serious implications for writing assessment.

White exposed a serious problem with the one-test-fits-all writing exam. "The choice of an evaluator," he argued compellingly, "often means the selection of a unique set of assumptions and definitions that emerge out of the language of the evaluator's world; the implications of such a choice . . . can be profound, affecting funding or even the survival of the program" (p. 191). The implications White offered here are less profound than the implications suggested by his argument. With the choice of an evaluator, schools also select values for and assumptions about what makes writing good. What impact will the evaluator's assumptions have on the scoring of the essays? Will the evaluator's immersion in one language community, in a slight revision of White's confession about himself, cause him or her to lack respect for the writing of students from another community? Will students fail or pass because of the biases of the evaluator's community? White prepared us for these powerful questions, exposing a problem with blanket assessment: Who is to do it? From what set of assumptions? How can those assumptions cross disciplines? He then turned, with unconscious irony, to a narrower target—linguistic/conceptual differences between the measurement community in education and the composition community.

There is no doubt he was right as far as the micropicture goes. The College of Education's value-added and value-free assessment, particularly if it is (as he remarked) "amateurish, filled with another discipline's jargon, expressing ambiguities and untested assumptions" (p. 197), is going to be dismissed as "inappropriate measurement; not data, but data misused" (p. 198) by the assessment community in composition studies. The irony occurs not so much because he limits his attention to two comparatively small communities after suggesting such large questions about bias and assessment. The irony surfaces more because of his emphatic support for the composition community. Every one of the problems he exposed and the questions he implied or asked is consistent with housing writing assessment in composition studies. Composition studies, too, is a discipline, with its own language, and values, purposes, and forms for writing. Evaluators from composition would enter the process with a unique set of "assumptions and definitions that emerge out of the language of [their] world." White actually demonstrated how blinding immersion in a community can be. Despite its limited vision for writing, in White's world, composition becomes the natural inheritor of writing assessment across a campus. On the point that asks how the electrical engineering student can be measured as a writer by an evaluator from education or composition studies, White missed the mark or ignored it. Nonetheless, his comments have significant implications for assessment of student writing competence. They suggest the potential and actual difficulties with the one-test-fits-all approach to writing assessment because of the community-based perceptions, biases, opinions, and interpretations of the persons designing and/or grading the test. If separate language specializations define our disciplines and students assimilate one or two of those languages as the principal process of being a major, how can we confidently expect any one measurement instrument to determine student writing competence? Wouldn't many separate instruments be necessary? Wouldn't the instrument and evaluator have to come from the student writer's community?

Blanket Writing Assessment

If I thought it would do any good, I would argue that large-scale assessment of student writing mostly wastes time and resources. Too often assessment processes make students write in contrived situations and under unnatural time constraints. These processes oblige students to write on topics that are alien to them or their academic majors. Despite their often startling inadequacies, such writing assessment processes can result in dire consequences for students—in the worst case, blocking them from graduation. Take, for example, the Graduation Writing Assessment Requirement (GWAR) used by the California State University System. Its various models employ one or more than one of the following instruments: at two California State University campuses, a designated course; at five campuses, a timed exam; at eight campuses, an exam or a course; and at four campuses, an exam and a course.

Typically, the timed exam lasts 60 minutes to 3 hours, and students write essays from one or two questions or prompts. The exam sometimes includes an objective portion: students identifying subjects, verbs, or objects; correcting fragments, comma splices, or pronoun antecedent disagreements; and placing semicolons, commas, or periods. The writing portion for one of the exams is described this way: "Within the one hour time frame, students are required to plan their work for five minutes, write for 40, and review and edit for 15." In an effort to encompass the widest student population, a model essay prompt may sound as if it came from a course in first-year composition:

> In an essay, write your own or your family's five (instead of Ten) commandments. (That is, explain several of the precepts and rules you or your family abides by, whether these rules are openly stated or not.) What value, if any, did these commandments have for you? Do you consider them meaningful only to your family or for others as well? Try to write your essay in a tone which is at once inviting to a large audience and very personable.

A problem with such topics, or any that call on personal experience as their foundation, is that they favor one set of values for what makes writing good over other sets of values. The writing in these exams is then usually evaluated by literacy professionals trained as trait scorers. What do these types of prompts ignore? They ignore the community within which many students have been writing, speaking, and thinking for an extended and focused period of time. The problem here, as I have argued throughout this text, is the urge to generalize from the particular. That is, these exams pretend to certify the macroquality of writing based on an extraordinarily microsample. They privilege one kind of writing over others and one set of values for writing over others, thereby favoring one group of student writers over others. Of course the time limits are also a difficulty. The 5 (to plan)/ 40 (to write)/15 (to review)-minute sequence did or does exist at a reputable university. I quoted it directly from a document describing the GWAR, but it is an extreme example and easy to discredit. How can any binding claims (e.g., the blocking of students from proceeding into their senior years or graduating) be made based on an essay written in an hour? Such claims cannot be made in any research-based, legal, or ethical sense. Yet what about essays for which students are given 3 hours or even 3 days to write? Lengthening the amount of time that students have to plan, write, review, and edit helps, but what does it omit? If the exam remains designed by the testing industry or English departments, it omits the contexts in which students mostly write—their majors. It generalizes a writing experience in which all of us engage contextually. Yet even if the timed writing exam is local, designed, that is, for the majors and graded by faculty within the discipline (a developing trend and a notable improvement over campuswide writing exams), it remains disconnected from the real world of writing, where the time that people have to write varies, they collaborate with colleagues, and they understand the relevance of goals, context, and audience. It continues to make macroclaims from microperspectives.

Discipline-Based Writing Assessment

However flawed the process and its results may be, I recognize assessing student writing as a reality that will not soon disappear. Therefore, I place myself in Elbow's (1996) camp with regard to writing assessment: "we probably cannot forgo all large-scale writing assessment" (p. 120). Even in 1993, there was no doubt that writing assessment was coming to the University of Nevada–Reno. I had been invited out to lunch by the Director of the Core Curriculum to discuss how it might be accomplished; and, horrified at the prospect of having one of those timed writing exams forced on UNR's students, I presented a plan that would reflect the nature of our WAC program, have no negative impact on students, and provide useful data. Because all writing assessment is a matter of community-based *perception, bias, opinion and interpretation*, our assessment program would acknowledge these conditions up front. It would consciously choose to make faculty within the disciplines the prevailing determiners of the quality of writing students were doing within their departments and disciplines. It would use (in judging the portfolios at least) "minimal holistic scoring" (Elbow, 1996, p. 123). What are the program's features? First, we choose departments with which to work and then ask their department chairs whether the department might be interested. This contact has usually resulted in our attending a departmental meeting to explain the program and its potential benefits to faculty and students. After that we invite faculty members to serve on their Departmental Writing Assessment Committee. Although serving requires a 2-year commitment and much extra reading and grading of papers, we have not yet had a problem with gathering committee members. Of course the stipend might have helped: $750 per year. However, in 2000, that stipend was taken away; nursing faculty were still eager to participate (2000–2001), and geography faculty also readily volunteered (2002–).

Since 1993, our assessment personnel have worked with criminal justice, electrical engineering, political science, accounting/computing, biology, English, curriculum and instruction, nursing, and (currently) geography. These choices were based on developing an eclectic sample: so far three social science disciplines, two professional disciplines, and one discipline each in the sciences, humanities, business, and education. Once a department agrees to collaborate, our personnel randomly select junior majors (every second, third, or fourth major depending on the size of the junior class) from computer lists. Our hope has been to get a student sample size large enough to provide statistically reliable data, but small enough for the papers to be manageable for the faculty committees. (Nursing, for example, had 34 junior majors during 2000–2001; we selected 14 of their majors for a sample size of just over 40%. We believed this would provide a reliable picture of the writing quality of this particular nursing class. Of course the number of papers and portfolios we and the nursing faculty had to read was quite large.) Having selected the students, our assessment personnel anonymously collect and photocopy (preferably before papers are graded or after all comments are whited out) every paper they write from their junior through their senior years. Each student becomes a number, and no student can fail or be delayed in graduation as a result of this examination of his or her writing. (In an ironic twist, UNR's Human Subjects Committee mandated that students could not be delayed or failed as a result of our project; how did California bypass this requirement in establishing the GWAR? I guess because the GWAR was state endorsed and not experimental.) If a faculty member objected to his or her students' anonymous participation in the project, we open the door to telling the students about the project and asking for their permission to participate. Students have chosen not to participate, of course, though not often.

Again this process begins during the fall semester of a given year; during that semester, faculty committee members meet only three or four times: The first session explains the project in greater detail, the second session asks faculty to share the values that they and their discipline have for writing, and the last two meetings begin the norming sessions that will be continued through the next two semesters. For each of these norming sessions, committee members read, evaluate, rank, and grade 4 to 10 pieces (the number of pieces depends on their length) of writing on a single assignment produced by students in the sample. During the meetings, committee members (which have always included me and at least one other center professional) share their findings and attempt to reach evaluative consensus about papers.

Consider the effort involved here: With the two norming sessions during the fall semester and then seven sessions for each of the next two semesters, the committee members will have evaluated from 64 to 100 pieces of student writing before they reach the portfolio stage during the last semester. At that stage, they will read from 7 (political science) to 14 (nursing) portfolios, each of which includes as many as 10 papers. In addition to their other full-time work, this activity amounts to a substantial commitment.

These efforts of the first three semesters, however, provide singular advantages:

- They present a context in which faculty can determine and discuss their own and their discipline's values for academic writing. In a sense they can norm values, deciding which take precedence and which do not. (The values for writing held by English and Biology faculty referred to so often in the first chapter were determined in this way.)

• They give faculty opportunities to work together in focused ways—opportunities that are lamentably rare in departmental contexts, but especially so when it comes to dealing with student writing. "I think most of us want our students to be very well prepared for graduate and professional study," a member of one assessment committee remarked, "but we probably need a little more clarity about what we are trying to develop in our junior and seniors in order to prepare them, rather than just have 10 or 12 of us have our own sense of that. Maybe the nature of the modern university doesn't make that possible, but maybe more conversation like we are having in this room might make that a little more possible." (The quotes I include come from transcriptions of tapes made of the assessment meetings with eight of the nine departments. We took extensive notes of the meetings with electrical engineering faculty, but they would not allow us to tape the meetings. I do not include the sources of the transcript quotes because the quotes are meant to be descriptive and representative, and not "who said what about whom and what," although such comments were a significant part of the discussion with faculty from every department.)

• They initiate a serious, informed discussion about assignment making. Not only is the quality of individual assignments heavily scrutinized, but spirited discussion persists about linking assignments between classes and throughout a department's curriculum. Our "courses are too randomly connected to each other," observed one committee member, "and I think someone coming out from another place, looking at what we are doing, would probably suggest to us that we should set goals in terms of what we want a senior to be able to do." Another committee member lamented, "Patterns seen in these students involved in the assessment program show a randomness in our curriculum." Nearly all of this talk keeps the success (and lack of success) of students in mind, perhaps with some naivete during the early sessions, but then with increasing sophistication as the sessions progress. Success generally relates to how assignment making can enhance a student's cognitive performance in a given course and then in the major, and failure relates to the variety of ways in which success is countered. Thinking critically about course material and disciplinary concepts becomes an essential goal that almost all of the assessment committees held for students, and one committee member made the wrenching discovery that "the assignment sheets we saw asked [students] not to deal with theory or to any way think about it. [These assignments] simply asked for them to spit back what they have been told. It is the same kind of shit they got when they were in school." A member of a second committee observed that, "The writing was acceptable. The level of analytical ability was not. It was interesting," she continued, "because that is what we are getting criticized about. We are not teaching them to think. If these people were evidence of the writing skills of the average student, then they would be acceptable. Clearly we need to work on analytical capabilities." The meetings during the first three semesters of the 2-year period have created a situation in which faculty can discuss, probably at unprecedented lengths, the conditions under which they and their colleagues assign writing, the conditions under which students write those assignments, and the conditions under which assignments are graded. I think these sessions produced the best kind of faculty development, in which faculty examine the assignments, read the papers, evaluate them, and then discuss conclusions with abundant evidence in support.

• These efforts produce experts at writing assessment within the context of their disciplines. Faculty come into the norming sessions doubting their ability to assess the quality of their own students' writing. They fear that they do not know the technical terminology of composition teaching or writing assessment. They may not know this terminology, but they do know the values, purposes, and forms for the writing in their disciplines. They do know the language of their discipline, teaching and writing it themselves, and the longer they talk about the papers, the more evolved becomes their assessment expertise. "As the project matured," wrote Peak (1997) of Criminal Justice,

> the faculty participants became very well qualified to engage in the writing evaluation process. In our view, this process could be replicated by any group of faculty members who wished to become qualified to evaluate papers in their discipline. . . . Faculty members became much more competent to develop and explain assignments created for their students.

• The most significant discovery of the first three semesters of norming papers has been that open-ended assignments, muddled assignments, or assignments that exceed the cognitive and linguistic development of student writers do not produce writing as high in quality as assignments with clear goals, engaging contexts, and specific audiences. Peak and Waldo (1997) reported on the difference in scores between an open-ended assignment—"write a paper on a topic of interest in the area of juvenile justice": "The writing group's assessment of papers resulting from this assignment revealed that about 60 percent of the students failed to meet minimal criteria for success; that is, they would have received a grade of D or F" (p. 77). "Consistently, more than 90% of the papers on *The Prince* successfully fulfilled the assignment" (p. 77). From the member of another committee, "even with my assignment making in the future I will make mine more like _____'s [more cognizant of goals, context, and audience] to yield the type of writing I would like to see. The worst type of assignments are the type that ask simply, Tell me what you know about Ireland, like _____'s."

The norming of more than 900 papers by faculty in the listed disciplines provides an 88% success rate for junior/senior student writers when success is measured by the letter grades A, B, and C. Yet differences exist between faculty with regard to level of success (several people's A might be one person's C; less often, several people's D might be one person's B). The purpose of a norming session, however, is to bring a minority point of view into line with the majority, without forcing the issue, and this most often happened. Arguments center on the goals for the assignments and the demonstrated ability of student writers to meet those goals. Regardless of whether the portfolio phase is included, this process suggests that ongoing norming sessions within departments would be useful.

I should explain that the portfolios are compiled of substantial and shorter essays, book reviews, lab reports, letters, journal entries, diagnostic evaluations, team writing, and so on—any type of writing beside note taking done by students selected for the study. By the fourth semester, when portfolios are evaluated, there were many new pieces collected that committee members had not read, but there were also many that they had. Familiarity with the work often existed and, along with it, some ability to cross-check findings. The more general questions we ask of faculty in response to reading the portfolios follow, "Is the writing in this student's portfolio of acceptable quality for a student receiving a bachelor's degree in your program? If it is, then why? If it is not, then why not?" More specifically, we also want to have a sense of how assignments promote critical thinking and how assignments seem to promote different types of critical thinking in these disciplines. We also hoped to determine, as a cross-check of the student exit interviews and faculty phone surveys, whether the portfolio writers advance as writers and thinkers between their junior and senior years. Faculty responses to these questions are admirably, remarkably detailed as transcripts of the sessions show. The detailed responses are part of a problem Center personnel experienced especially in the early years of the project. It is difficult, without exercising nearly severe (and with colleagues, laughable) coercion, to get the faculty to stop talking about a given portfolio within the time allotted (e.g., we collected 10 portfolios for the criminal justice study, roughly a quarter of the graduating class, but we only had time to discuss 7). To be sure, there are varying levels of acceptability in the responses. Yet of the 62 portfolios judged so far (we should have 30 more by the end of next year), 58 were deemed acceptable and 4 were not. This amounts to a 93% acceptability, which is consistent with most of the other figures presented.

The two departments chosen for the pilot years (1993–1994) were Criminal Justice and Electrical Engineering. We selected criminal justice because it represents a growing number of departments nationwide in which small faculties deal with large numbers of students. Because of the obvious obstacles, writing is often not assigned in classes offered by these departments. The Criminal Justice Department at UNR has a large number of majors and only 5.5 faculty members to teach classes, and upper division classes often have over 100 students. Criminal Justice 326, Juvenile Justice, averages over 85 students. Two Criminal Justice 320 classes, Courts in Criminal Justice, have had 103 and 104 students in them, respectively, and the numbers continue to increase. Nonetheless, in the face of such discouraging figures, Criminal Justice faculty manage to incorporate writing into every class. Here are their stated values for writing.

Criminal Justice: Values for Writing

Criminal Justice faculty want their upper division students to

- Address what the assignment asks;
- Show a clear conceptual understanding of underlying issues, often demonstrated through examining all sides. Also their understanding can be demonstrated through efficient and effective use of secondary sources, not simply listing them throughout a paper, but incorporating them;
- Show strong organizational skills by logically presenting arguments. One faculty member noted that matching introductions and conclusions greatly benefits this cause;
- Write in a direct manner, addressing the main point early in the text and avoiding long anecdotal introductions;
- Display factual correctness, and write with minimal sentence-level errors;
- Write clearly, demonstrating an understanding of the material included and her ability to incorporate it into her own thinking; and
- Be creative; creativity shows students' ability to view problems in ways that may help them find solutions. Creativity can manifest itself in many ways, like finding solutions to problems with the law or submitting video papers for one of _____'s classes.

Writing within the portfolios included some lengthy papers (although rarely exceeding eight pages), essay exams, short essays, and book reports. Committee members determined the seven portfolios to be acceptable in quality for graduates of their program, with varying degrees of acceptability. The portfolios were judged largely successful in some of the areas the criminal justice faculty most value—demonstrating a clear conceptual understanding of underlying issues (although the committee emphasized that some assignments produced far better writing and thinking than others) and logically developing and organizing papers. The committee found student writers to be less successful in following the assignment, integrating outside sources, and writing with minimal sentence-level errors. The four Criminal Justice committee members all perceived student advances as writers and thinkers between the junior and senior years.

We chose electrical engineering (EE) for assessment for two reasons: It is a preprofessional discipline that focuses on science and engineering curricula and requires assimilation of a complex language of problem solving and persuasion. As another incentive, a few engineering faculty had told us that their students' writing was decidedly weak, and we were interested to see what sort of writing they did. We planned to track 10 entering juniors through their remaining 2 years—about half of 1995's graduating class in EE. We also decided to collect all of the papers written in five lab classes ranging from the 300 to 400 level, some of which, we learned later, included 10 to 12 lab reports per semester.

Electrical Engineering: Values for Writing

Electrical Engineering faculty want their upper division students to

- Demonstrate clean engineering by properly framing problems;
- Use appropriate formulae and write in appropriate forms;
- Abide by the prior precepts, as well as produce writing that contains creative ideas;
- Produce writing that is always purposeful, clear, organized, and appropriate for its audience (when papers lacked proper organization, in an interesting appropriation from his own discipline's discourse, one EE committee member said that the papers "demonstrate a flat feature space"); and
- Write perfectly with no sentence or citation errors.

The use of the term *perfectly* is not my embellishment. One of the committee members actually said it. As the weeks and months of EE writing assessment passed, it became clear to all that the writing of this sample of students was very good. After reading and evaluating one set of team-written papers from a course in digital systems (a 400- to 600-level course), for example, the committee determined six of the seven to be of *publishable* quality. Some explanation had to be found for the impression that EE students could not write. That explanation has something to do with the fact that the student writers did not write *perfectly* at the sentence level. The faculty shared their own experience with publishing in professional journals and confessed their feelings of shame as editors red penciled them. They were expected to write perfectly and, through some process of transference, expected their students to write perfectly as well. This unreasonable situation was mitigated (somewhat) by their eventual acknowledgment that they could not write perfectly either, not at least before they had the help of an editor's corrections.

The most surprising discovery in our work with the EE Department is that the students we reviewed generally wrote so well. No faculty expressed with more certainty that its students couldn't write; no faculty entered the project more predisposed to find fault with their students' writing than did the EE faculty. Yet as it read and evaluated that writing, lab reports (initially hidden writing because EE committee members did not include it as one of the types of writing their students did), precis, proposals, letters, individual projects, and group projects, the committee determined it all to be almost uniformly successful. All 10 of the portfolios were judged to have been written at a level acceptable for a graduate in the EE major. In addition to underestimating their students' abilities, the faculty seemed unaware, as was I, of the inherent rightness of EE assignment making. That is, we never saw an assignment without a clear goal, an engaging context, and a specific audience.

When writing is used in EE classes, more often than anyone realized, it tends to be integrally linked to the teaching and learning. Students recognize that writing lab reports and team projects has value for their work at school and their jobs beyond. Understanding why they are writing and doing the large amounts of hidden writing that they do lead EE students to become surprisingly able writers and thinkers, at least when perfection is not the ultimate standard for assessment.

Political Science: Values for Writing (1995/1996)

Political Science faculty want their upper division students to

- Explain opposing or multiple points of view on complex issues relevant to political science and international studies (one committee member observed that this is a cognitive behavior you have to require students to do; they do not do it "naturally and spontaneously");
- Provide in-depth analysis of conceptual and theoretical material;
- Sustain a thesis-based argument throughout a paper; do not drift off topic, digress, equivocate, argue the person, and so on ("I want a thesis

statement," one PS committee member said, "development in a logical fashion, and justification");

- Earn the right to state an opinion, to make a paper one's own, by dealing effectively with outside sources; and
- Write well-organized papers with minimal sentence-level errors.

The committee was able to read and discuss seven portfolios. Of the seven, it found six acceptable in quality for a political science graduate. One was not. When I pointed out that six out of seven amounted to an 85% success rate and asked, "Does that seem representative to you as far as your graduates go?", two thought that the figure was "a little high," and one thought it was representative. Although all of us perceived improvement in the writing and thinking between the junior and senior year, the political science faculty members did not see the amount of improvement they had hoped for or expected; one even remarked that he did not see many students break through to the "top-quartile." Like the criminal justice faculty, the political science faculty clearly saw the relationship between the quality of the assignment and the quality of student writing.

Accounting/Computer Information Systems: Values for Writing

Accounting/Computer Information Systems faculty want their upper division students to

- Use numbers, formulae, statistics, equations, graphs, charts, and other data accurately;
- Analyze and synthesize data objectively and ethically;
- Offer clear statements of purpose and follow appropriate form; and
- Write coherent, well-organized papers with few or no sentence-level problems.

Accounting/Computer Information Systems faculty read and assessed 12 portfolios. Eleven were judged to be at an acceptable level of quality for students earning bachelor's degrees in the Accounting/Computer Information Systems Department. When I asked the committee members if 11 out of 12 (91% acceptability) seemed a little high to them, one responded, "No, I don't think so because if they can't write at an acceptable level they end up getting out because they cannot pass the exam." To the question, did anything surprise you about what we "discovered or uncovered during the last couple of years," one observed "that the level of writing tends to exceed what I expected. My prior experience has been with sophomores primarily but their writing leaves a lot to be desired." Another faculty member summarized the efforts of 2 years: "Based on what we have seen, the department can say that we are producing graduates who have an acceptable level of communication skills and that they are all improving throughout the program." The writing assignments in Accounting/Computer Information Systems, like those in Electrical Engineering, were much more often than not professionally contextualized ("You are a junior accountant in a large nonprofit organization ...") and had obvious goals and audiences. I assert that these conditions helped generate students' success as writers. Nonetheless, I must also say that Accounting/Computer Information Systems faculty perceived the writing to be better than the thinking in some of the portfolios. "Clearly," one committee member remarked, "we need to work on analytical capabilities."

English: Values for Writing (1997/1998)

Faculty in the English Department want their upper division students to

- Express voice—show the writer's self in the piece of writing;
- Demonstrate independence—thinking that distinguishes the paper from the writing of others (students "take their own stand," one faculty member said, "articulate their own view of things");
- Show meta-consciousness of language (intentional use of diction, syntax, rhetorical figures, etc.);
- Write with vividness of detail and originality;
- Show awareness of rhetorical purpose and audience;
- Evidence critical thinking (effective summary, interpretation, analysis, argumentation); and
- Write with few or no sentence-level problems.

Biology: Values for Writing

Faculty in the Biology Department want their upper division students to

- Be clear in their statement of purpose (the paper's abstract includes a clearly stated hypothesis);
- Adhere to appropriate form (report writing contains the following sections: abstract, introduction, methods and materials, discussion, and conclusion) and placement of correct material in pertinent sections;
- Integrate secondary sources coherently;

- Cite secondary sources accurately;
- Depict graphs and tables accurately;
- Evidence critical thinking (problem solving, data analysis and interpretation, argumentation);
- Demonstrate commitment to experiment; and
- Include few or no sentence-level errors.

In a disabling turn of events, the box containing the portfolios, including all of the individual papers the committee had read in both the English and Biology Departments, was lost during the Writing Center's move from one side of campus to the other. We were ready to enter the fourth semester, had already read approximately 50 papers from students in each discipline, and had recorded committee responses to those papers. We decided, with regret, to continue reading individual papers and abandon the portfolios we had ordinarily assessed during the last semester. This event lessened the total number of portfolios by 28—a significant blow to the project.

Nonetheless, on both committees, we were able to read a large number of papers and get some sense of the quality of writing and assignment making occurring in each discipline. If no other department than Electrical Engineering was more convinced that its students could not write well, no other department than English was more convinced that its students could. As far as the English Department assessment committee (four faculty members and two Writing Center personnel—also Department members) was concerned, none of the more than 50 papers read was unacceptable. In a situation similar to Electrical Engineering, the biologists believed that no more than 20% of their students could write *well*, but they discovered that roughly 90% could write *acceptably*.

Curriculum and Instruction: Values for Writing

Curriculum and Instruction faculty want their upper division students to

- Define complex issues, controversies, programs, pedagogies in elementary, middle, and secondary education; examine opposing viewpoints concerning issues, controversies, etc.;
- Be reflective and take informed positions;
- Demonstrate passionate commitment to positions; and
- Examine educational theory, and develop theoretical justifications for what students propose to do as classroom teachers.

The committee examined 12 portfolios from curriculum and instruction seniors, and all of them were found to be acceptable in terms of writing quality. Few of the portfolios, however, were found acceptable in terms of the level of critical thinking demonstrated. Regardless of whether students could do it, the Curriculum and Instruction committee found little examining of opposing viewpoints or making and supporting of critical judgments, little reflection, little passionate commitment, and little examination of theory and justification of practice. They found many competently, even splendidly, written papers describing unit and lesson plans, summarizing texts, and regurgitating lectures and course material. Having this general impression of the portfolio pieces, it became important for us to remember, as one committee member remarked, "they take these courses and this is acceptable stuff and we have looked at some of the assignment sheets, remember, and what we were seeing was that [instructors] didn't ask for much more than this." The committee concluded that the writing was competent stylistically and contained few sentence-level errors, but it was usually superficial and general, with little support provided for assertions. This condition was at least partly the result of listless assignment making, which too often asked students to repeat information from the text or class notes. Few of the assignments could be called *intellectually challenging*. At the close of the 2-year period, the committee discussed causes of the problem ("It's been around for a long time in teacher training" observed one committee member) and procedures for countering it, including bringing the Dean of Education into the process. Everyone agreed that change would require commitment from more than just two or three faculty.

Nursing Faculty: Values for Writing (1999/2000)

Nursing faculty want their upper division students to

- Write correctly at the sentence level ("Basic grammar. How to write a complete sentence. How to make your subject and verb agree and . . . basic writing skill"). There is a compelling reason for nursing to place correctness at the sentence level first, the only committee to do so: "Imagine a legal problem comes up and you're brought to court. An attorney will take your chart and blow it up and put it on the overhead in front of the jury and they will highlight every one of your misspellings and they question your credibility and your ability and competence";
- Write coherently at the paragraph level ("How to separate paragraphs. When you're into a new thought you create a new paragraph . . .");

- Organize entire papers effectively ("Tell me what you're going to say, say it, and then tell me what you said" or "give me your hypothesis, give me your arguments, reach a conclusion and then summarize");
- Follow APA format; and
- Follow the assignment.

Committee members from the Nursing Department demonstrated one of the differences between assessing several pieces of writing in a portfolio and assessing one piece of writing, as might be produced in a timed writing exam. These faculty found a substantial portion of the individual papers they read for norming sessions—say 30% of those papers—to be *horrendous* and *appalling* at the sentence and paragraph levels. Yet when they read the 14 portfolios, many of which included the same papers, they judged 12 of 14 acceptable (86%) in quality for graduates of their program. The difference can be accounted for, I think, by the broader, more inclusive basis for judgment of student writing afforded by portfolios.

Conclusions

The sample size, at least the number of portfolios, is regrettably small. Because of that, I make observations more than draw conclusions. First, out of 62 portfolios, 58 from students in 6 departments were found to be acceptable in quality of writing for the given years in which the departments participated. This acceptability rate amounts to 93%. In more than one department, in Accounting, and Curriculum and Instruction, for example, faculty separated quality of writing from quality of thinking and determined that the writing was better than the thinking. This separation is reflected in the acceptability rate. In other words, if my question about portfolio acceptability had combined writing *and* thinking, the percentage would have been lower. All of the departmental committees, however, perceived at least some degree of cognitive and intellectual growth in their students between the junior and senior years.

There is a 5% difference between acceptance rates for portfolios (93%) and the acceptance rates for individual papers (88%). Although the difference is quite small, I believe it may be accounted for by the tendency to perceive more merit in a body of work than in single pieces of writing. The condition of perceiving less merit in individual pieces was most pronounced in the Political Science (many of the assignments were vague and open ended) and Nursing (many of the papers were faulted severely for their sentence-level problems) Departments, which, combined, found 85% of their portfolios acceptable (18 of 21), but approximately 30% of the individual papers unacceptable (C– or lower). This difference may suggest another reason that the blanket writing exam is unfair to students as a one-time, one-paper affair.

The quality of committee experience reading and grading student papers depended heavily on the design of assignments, with the standard open-ended assignment ("Write on a topic of interest to you" or "Write about the politics of Ireland") falling far short of focused assignments in generating readable and effective papers. Certainly, the committees' reading and grading experience reflects the students' writing experience. The more clearly and carefully the assignment is designed, the better the writing experience is for students. It also became clear that certain types of writing assignments promote specific kinds of thinking skills—another advantage of focused assignment design.

Faculty in each of these departments had trouble reading and evaluating the writing of English as a Second Language students. Tending to acknowledge the immense difficulties of writing specialized discourses in a non-native tongue, they grade English as a Second Language students less stringently than native speakers. Faculty, nonetheless, express concern about the ethics of applying different standards to different groups of students.

For writing center personnel, the listing of values for writing by discipline was intriguing. A few values are shared by almost every discipline. Thinking critically appears directly on six of the lists, writing with few or no sentence-level errors appears on seven, with that value becoming most important to Nursing. Writing *clearly* appears on five lists, although as abstract as that term is, it is implied by all of the lists. Being creative is present on three lists, and creativity seems to be contextualized by discipline and related to critical thinking, as in Criminal Justice's comments: "Be creative; creativity shows the students' ability to view problems in ways that may help them to find solutions," or in Electrical Engineering's: "Abide by the prior precepts, as well as produce writing that contains creative ideas," or English's: "Demonstrate independence—thinking that distinguishes the paper from the writing of others." "Addressing what the assignment asks" appears on two lists (three if Geography is included). Curriculum and Instruction's admonition to "demonstrate 'passionate' commitment to positions" seems the closest to English's admonition to "express voice—show the writer's self in a piece of writing." Perhaps not surprisingly, English and Curriculum and Instruction faculty regard writing and thinking in similar ways.

We wanted these lists to be created during the second meetings with assessment committees. Although committee members were not required to have the lists completed before that meeting (I worried, wrongly, about alienating by overburdening them), I hoped that they would think about their values for writing during the 2-week period between the first and second meeting. Many did so, whereas many did not. In other words, we have had much spontaneous value making. (Faculty often, like students, operate according to calendars, which require them to do something; and faculty, like students, will not do the thing until it is required, suggesting to me more reason to empathize with students.) During the second meeting, we asked faculty to develop and share their values; after that sharing, they were to norm or prioritize them from *most important* to *least important*. These lists are the product of that process. I acknowledge that spontaneous value making may not produce concrete values (as if any approach could). I acknowledge that the same group of faculty might decide on a different list and ranking another day. Nonetheless, I believe these lists are unique in that they have never been solicited before, they are important, and, in qualified ways, they are representative.

The values that faculty and their disciplines hold for writing differ, often in discipline-specific ways. This finding may have been predictable, but it does have implications for the discipline that often teaches writing to every student: composition studies. In a telling irony, English's list is the most distant from any of the others. None of the other disciplines privileged voice as a value for writing, let alone the most important value. No other list values meta-consciousness of language, originality, and vividness of detail. This distance may explain why some teachers in the disciplines observe that first-year writing does not teach their students to write or others who argue that composition should be discontinued as a requirement. The differences between English's and the other disciplines' lists also suggest why writing to learn cannot complement learning to write in WAC practice: The values inherent to writing to learn belong to one discipline, whereas learning to write belongs to all. If composition studies is to teach writing to everyone, then it *must* acknowledge that it has values for writing, and that those values may not, and probably do not, cross the curriculum. The course(s), as I have argued repeatedly, however, are important for what they teach and how they teach it, and they are defensible on their own terms. If composition studies is to supply the bulk of WAC consultants, they should be trained to recognize differences in disciplinary languages and values. They do not need to know the languages or even the values held by their constituents, but they do need to develop dialogic methods for interacting with them.

8

Specialization, Stewardship, and WAC: An Essential Partnership

**KEY NATIONAL FINDINGS ADAPTED
FROM THE U.S. NATIONAL ASSESSMENT
(All quotes from U.S. Environmental
Protection Agency Web site, p. 89)**

Increased warming is projected for the 21st century—Assuming continued growth in world greenhouse gas emissions, the primary climate models drawn upon for the analyses carried out in the U.S. National Assessment projected that temperatures in the contiguous United States will rise 3–5°C (5–9°F) on average during the 21st century. A wider range of outcomes, including a smaller warming, is also possible.

Throughout this chapter, I have placed the quotes summarizing the Impacts chapter of the EPA's (2002) *U.S. Climate Action Report*, which describes the consequences of global warming to the United States. Under Republican political pressures, the term *global warming* has been changed to *climate change*, but the document describes with surprising, if not complete, frankness the process of planet heating and its impacts. That it attributes global warming to human activities, even that it admits to the existence of global warming at all, might be considered a major coup. Less than a year before, President Bush had said that global warming did not exist or claimed instead that whatever the phenomenon was it probably had natural causes, such as gas vents percolating thousands of feet below the surface of Earth's oceans. This document attributes global warming mostly to the emission of greenhouse gasses into the earth's atmosphere—gasses that come from the multitude of fossil fuel burning machines. These gasses have thinned the protective ozone layer above the earth, allowing a flood of less filtered sunlight to heat the atmosphere and the earth's surface with a speed and in ways that people are having a hard time ignoring. The report limits itself to the United States, although its writers point out that few countries have the resources and technology to face the problem with an adaptive capability equal to the United States. Almost every other country will fare worse. Two distinctive qualities underlie the document. First, global warming is already having an impact, and that impact will soon accelerate (although the document describes consequences over the 21st century, its focus seems to be on the next three decades—within most of our lifetimes); second, the way in which people adapt will determine the degree to which the heating becomes catastrophic. That is, catastrophic consequences are probable; how large or small they are depends on human behavior in response: "Because of the momentum in the climate system and natural climate variability, adapting to a climate change is inevitable. The question is whether we adapt poorly or well" (p. 82).

Using the document is pertinent to this book's conclusion mainly because of the currency and immense complexity of the problems presented by climate change. We face many hundreds, perhaps thousands, of serious problems as local and global citizens—problems hinted at throughout this text; each of them requires specialists doing their best work individually and collaboratively to solve. Yet climate change rivals population growth, its likely cause, as a process that is broadly threatening, immediately visible to all, and calling for the largest number of specialists to counter. I think it could be demonstrated that the expertise of nearly every discipline might be called on to address the process of climate change. To adapt to the process well, to become the most effective stewards in a time of crisis, experts need to be capable problem solvers, completely native in the languages and cognitive behaviors of their specialties.

> *Impacts will differ across regions*—Climate change and its potential impacts are likely to vary widely across the country. Temperature increases are likely to vary somewhat among regions. Heavy precipitation events are projected to become more frequent, yet some regions are likely to become drier.

Certainly the study and language of *climatology*, the "physical characteristics of the atmosphere," "world climatic classification," and "local atmospheric field study" (as UNR's catalogue describes it), are essential. This appears to be as much a matter for *geography* as any other specialization because of its further attention to the study of regions, past physical environments, and conservation of natural resources. It is also, and with equal weight, the purview of *atmospheric science*, which teaches courses in atmospheric physics, air pollution, chemistry, radiation, and weather modification, to name only a few relevant courses. These may be added to courses in *physics*, *environmental science*, and *meteorology* among others.

> *Ecosystems are especially vulnerable*—many ecosystems are highly sensitive to the projected rate and magnitude of climate change, although more efficient water use will help some ecosystems. A few ecosystems, such as alpine meadows in the Rocky Mountains and some barrier islands, are likely to disappear entirely in some areas. Other ecosystems, such as southeastern forests, are likely to experience major species shifts or break up into a mosaic of grasslands, woodlands, and forests. Some of the goods and services lost through the disappearance or fragmentation of natural ecosystems are likely to be costly or impossible to replace.

It is hard for me to hear, as it must be to many readers, that "a few ecosystems, such as alpine meadows in the Rocky Mountains and some barrier islands, are likely to disappear in some areas." Nonetheless, I am sure that the observation is true. As our environment heats, dries, and burns, it loses previously identifiable characteristics. I have seen the process of disappearance as I hike in the Sierra mountains. Yet the EPA statement is saturated with inevitability—as if we are too late to do anything about it. Perhaps we are, but addressing ecosystem vulnerability must be central on the agenda of specialists in the disciplines and the WAC consultants who help them create assignments. The languages of *ecology*, *evolution*, and *conservation biology* are critical here as are those of *environmental and natural resource science*, *environmental engineering*, *environmental policy analysis*, *environmental sciences and health*, and *marketing* to name only a few. Is marketing an aberrance on this list? No. Marketing specialists, if knowledgeable about climate change, must be engaged to sell it as unattractive to a population that largely ignores or denies it. Sooner rather than later, the reluctant population will have to be convinced to make major sacrifices. Many other disciplines may enter into this arena as well: *philosophy* with its science and ethics courses, *history* with its courses on paradises lost, *journalism* with its reports of those losses, and *English* with its university-wide writing courses. I envision at least some semester-long writing courses at the first year defining the problem, its potential and ongoing solutions; the specializations charged to solve it; and techniques for collaboration.

Widespread water concerns arise—Water is an issue in every region, but the nature of the vulnerabilities varies. Drought is an important concern virtually everywhere. Floods and water quality are concerns in many regions. Snowpack changes are likely to be especially important in the West, Pacific Northwest, and Alaska.

In other parts of the document, *snowpack changes* are characterized by snowpack declines, which certainly suggests consequences for drought in the "West, Pacific Northwest, and Alaska." In Reno, recent summer walks along the Truckee River, as it declines to a trickle and then to a river bed, demonstrate the lessening snowpack in the Sierras. The Truckee River begins at Lake Tahoe and drains into Pyramid Lake. Along its course, it provides drinking water for a burgeoning population and water for thousands of lawns, crop fields, and endangered trout at Pyramid. Like so many rivers and river systems in the United States, the Truckee is the principal source for water in an entire region, and a splendid book has been written about it—aptly entitled *A Doubtful River* (Dawson, Goin, & Webb, 2000). Unlike many other regions, Reno and its region are in high desert country, deep beneath the rain shadow of the Sierras, and rarely get more than 8 inches of precipitation per year. During recent years, even those 8 inches have lessened. There is no doubt that climate change will have, and has been having, a most severe impact on the Truckee River and the people who depend on it. Thus, in Reno, but also everywhere else in the United States, understanding water and its sources, distribution, and politics becomes extremely important. Actually provided by coursework in a variety of disciplines, expertise in *hydrology* and *hydrogeology* becomes essential as do courses in *political science*, such as those in global environmental policy, U.S. environmental policy, and land and water resource policy.

Food supply is secure—At the national level, the agriculture sector is likely to be able to adapt to climate change. Mainly because of the beneficial effects of the rising carbon dioxide levels on crops, overall U.S. crop productivity, relative to what is projected in the absence of climate change, is very likely to increase over the next few decades. However, the gains are not likely to be uniform across the nation. Falling prices are likely to cause difficulty for some farmers, while benefitting consumers.

Scattered within the document are at least a couple of instances in which readers are invited to take some comfort from the probable consequences of global warming. The security of the food supply is definitely one of them. Increasing carbon dioxide levels are likely to increase agricultural productivity, the document claims, over the next few decades. Of course this consequence is dependent on regional precipitation and specialists in *agriculture, biotechnology,* and *natural resources.*

> *Near-term forest growth increases*—Forest productivity is likely to increase over the next several decades in some areas as trees respond to higher carbon dioxide levels by increasing water-use efficiency. Such changes could result in ecological benefits and additional storage of carbon. Over the longer term, changes in larger-scale processes, such as fire, insects, droughts, and disease, could decrease forest productivity. In addition, climate change is likely to cause long-term shifts in forest species, such as sugar maples moving north out of the country.

Forest growth is another arena in which readers may experience some small feeling of comfort as "forest productivity is likely to increase over the next few decades in some areas," although some tree species will be migrating north. This increase also results from carbon increases. Of course sustained increases or "changes in larger-scale processes, such as fire, insects, droughts, and disease, [which] could decrease forest productivity," will require expertise in the disciplines of *forest management, natural resources, environmental science,* and *fisheries and wildlife sciences.*

> *Increased damage occurs in coastal and permafrost areas*—Climate change and the resulting rise in sea level are likely to exacerbate threats to buildings, roads, power lines, and other infrastructure in climate-sensitive areas. For example, infrastructure damage is expected to result from permafrost melting in Alaska and from sea level rise and storm surges in low-lying coastal areas.

None too attractive is the consequence of increased damage in coastal and permafrost areas as the seas rise and permafrost melts. The specialties of *physical oceanography, ocean biogeochemistry,* and *coastal oceanography* become essential to measuring the physical properties and activities of the oceans, as do *construction engineering, mechanical engineering,* and *civil engineering* to anticipate threats and repair damages to infrastructure.

> *Adaptation determines health outcomes*—A range of negative health impacts is possible from climate change. However, as in the past, adaptation is likely to help protect much of the U.S. population. Maintaining our nation's public health and community infrastructure, from water treatment systems to emergency shelters, will be important for minimizing the impacts of water-borne diseases, heat stress, air pollution, extreme weather events, and diseases transmitted by insects, ticks, and rodents.

As the 21st century progresses and the environment heats and dries, the impact on human health could be potentially devastating. Somewhat comforting is the document's claim that "adaptation is likely to help protect much of the U.S. population," although the qualifier *much* is disconcerting as is the fact that this adaptation is limited to the United States. Critical to adaptations that determine health outcomes is the development of specialists in *medicine, nursing, nutrition, human ecology, public health, psychology* (for help with individual adaptation), and *sociology* (for help with communal adaptation).

> *Other stresses are magnified by climate change*—Climate change is very likely to modify the cumulative impacts of other stresses. While it may magnify the impacts of some stresses, such as air and water pollution and conversion of habitat due to human development patterns, it may increase agricultural and forest productivity in some areas. For coral reefs, the combined effects of increased CO_2 concentration, climate change, and other stresses are very likely to exceed a critical threshold, causing large, possibly irreversible impacts.

In this quote, *conversion of habitat* means enhancement in agricultural and forest productivity while it also very likely means destruction of coral reefs. One impact of stress (not mentioned) will likely be the increased use of nuclear energy, as a comparatively clean energy source. The dangers of such a course have become evident through a variety of well-publicized events of meltdowns and near meltdowns of nuclear reactor cores. Nonetheless, nuclear sources of energy may become more attractive because renewable, nonpolluting energy sources (e.g., sun and wind power) are proving to be too limited to region and too little in their outputs of energy. Increased nuclear power means increased nuclear waste and more depositing of that waste in Nevada's Yucca Mountain, which was already discussed. The design, implementation, and impacts of that site have been written about professionally and publicly for 15 years, but to my knowledge, investigation has failed to extend to the waste generated by a growing dependence on nuclear power. What does this failure mean? It means that further study by *mining engineers, metallurgical engineers, geo-engineers, land use planners,* and many others already mentioned or not must be undertaken.

> *Uncertainties remain and surprises are expected*—Significant uncertainties remain in the science underlying regional changes in climate and their impacts. Further research would improve understanding and capabilities for projecting societal and ecosystem impacts. Increased knowledge would also provide the public with additional useful information about options for adaptation. However, it is likely that some aspects and impacts of climate change, both positive

and negative, will be totally unanticipated as complex systems respond to ongoing climate change in unforeseeable ways.

Sources: NAST 2000, 2001.

When we think of poets as prophets, as Wordsworth and many of his colleagues did, we cannot think about them predicting the uncertainties and
surprises of global warming. Certainly those poets of 19th-century Britain
predicted much. They observed Britain move with astonishing swiftness from
an agrarian and rural economy to an urban and industrial economy, for example, with steam engines leading and polluting the way. This change occurred
so quickly that many of them lived to experience it, just as global warming
will evidently do for us. Victor Frankenstein, who built Mary Shelley's prophetic monster, is pointedly a person with university training in *modern science*—in mathematics, chemistry, biology, physiology, and so on. Having created the monster, however, Victor then turns his back on it—to his own, his
family's, and society's peril. Victor Frankenstein thought little about uncertainties and surprises while building his creature and then thought obses-
sively about them after doing so. He should have thought about consequences before he built it; as part of his university experience, he should have
been trained to do so. Arguably (because of projects such as the development
of the atom bomb, where consequence was a major part of the discussion),
too little has been thought of the surprises and consequences inherent to the
building of monsters (say, combustion engines) since Watt's steam engine. I
confess that I enjoy almost as many of today's *monsters* almost as much as anybody else does (probably, I regret to admit, limited only by my inability to create or buy them myself), and I acknowledge that in terms of action I have often been a hypocrite. I am 52, I have lived fully, and I am almost ready to say
"let me up-shift my Solara to 100 miles per hour in ten seconds and then top
it out at 140, as Toyota claims I can." I still have plenty of deserted roads to
do so on. So many of us baby-boomers—the culprits in consumption largely
responsible for global warming—have children in their 20s and also grand-
children. It is important to think seriously about what we leave them with.

I italicized the disciplines and specializations needed to counter global
warming or climate change so the reader might get a sense of the number included and omitted. The number I included is 46—representative of a comprehensive university, a current tower of babel. Forty-six disciplines or more
were probably omitted. Towers of babel are precisely the institutions that, by
design, can meet the complexity, density, and seriousness of the problem.
There are no other institutions so capably equipped. The one language/one
imagination that Genesis asserts was taken from humans in punishment for

their hubris, however, has no potential to address the myriad challenges of global warming. Nor does Wordsworth's Poet, insofar as he or she by definition cannot be a hydrologist, climatologist, or oceanographer. We not only need specialists whose languages and imaginations reflect the multifaceted nature of the problem, but also those who worry about the uncertainties and surprises—the consequences of what they do. How might the development of these types of specialists, those who act with environmental imagination, be encouraged? One way is for disciplines to develop and teach codes of ethical behavior for students and professionals. The Code of Ethics of Engineers follows.

SOCIETY POLICY
ETHICS

ASME requires ethical practice by each of its members and has adopted the following Code of Ethics of Engineers as referenced in the ASME constitution, Article C2.1.1.

Code of Ethics of Engineers

The Fundamental Principles

Engineers uphold and advance the integrity, honor, and dignity of the engineering profession by:

   I. Using their knowledge and skill for the enhancement of human welfare;

  II. Being honest and impartial, and serving with fidelity the public, their employers and clients; and

 III. Striving to increase the competence and prestige of the engineering profession.

The Fundamental Canons

1. Engineers shall hold paramount the safety, health and welfare of the public in the performance of their professional duties.
2. Engineers shall perform services only in the areas of their competence.

3. Engineers shall continue their professional development throughout their careers and shall provide opportunities for the professional and ethical development of those engineers under their supervision.

4. Engineers shall act in professional matters for each employer or client as faithful agents or trustees, and shall avoid conflicts of interest or the appearance of conflicts of interest.

5. Engineers shall build their professional reputation on the merit of their services and shall not compete unfairly with others.

6. Engineers shall associate only with reputable persons or organizations.

7. Engineers shall issue public statements only in an objective and truthful manner.

8. Engineers shall consider environmental impact in the performance of their professional duties.

In the introductory chapter, I remarked that few disciplines offer their students a code of ethics to consider while, not after, they are learning to do what they will be doing as professionals. An obvious exception is the profession of engineering. I came on engineering's code of ethics in an accidental way. I observed a writing center tutor who was working with an engineering student required to write a paper comparing the ethical systems of a group of Western essayists. During his interaction with the tutor, this student mentioned the "Code of Ethics of Engineers," which he thought might be of use in writing his essay. After the session was finished, I asked the student about the degree of his exposure to this document. He remarked that, although he was not overexposed to "the canons," they were regularly shared and discussed in his engineering classes. He knew them well enough to consider using them in writing a paper for another class. Given my interest in codes of ethics for the writing of this chapter, I asked him to send me a copy through campus mail, which he quickly did.

Several points strike me as important in the document. First, there's a noteworthy insistence that professionals operate within the arena of their expertise, performing "services only in the areas of their competence." Second, engineers are charged emphatically with holding as "paramount . . . the welfare of the public" in performing their specialized activities, with avoidance of conflicts of interest and with truthful and objective public statements about their activities. Third, they must not only behave ethically throughout their own careers, but create conditions promoting ethical development for those engineers under their supervision. Fourth, they "shall consider environmental impact in the performance of their professional duties." Given the fact of global warming and engineers' positions to act for good or bad in that process, the consideration of environmental impact seems vital to their profession. I am sure that engineers do not always abide by or even consider such a code in the performance of their professional activities. Who has not performed their duties, at some point or other, without thinking about right or wrong or the consequences of what they are doing? Who has not acted out of personal gain or professional expedience? Almost no one. Even when both the negative and positive consequences of some performance of professional duties are deeply considered, again as with the atom bomb, authorities often decide that the positive outweighs the negative and go forward with development and deployment. Most of the time, however, potential consequences are less evident, such as with the steam or combustion engines, or computer technology, and development may proceed almost unreflectively until negative consequences cannot be ignored.

The problem has been and remains not that codes of ethics are ignored, but that almost no formal curricular venues exist for thinking about them. Regular exposure to a code of ethics similar to that for engineering students, especially if accompanied by pragmatic problem-solving activities, will have an impact on students as it obviously did on the student who sent the code for engineers to me. In an ideal world, consistent attention to such a code would cause students to apply ethics to their professional behavior—cause them to determine the consequences of their work, however small or large, to the people and the planet. Such prophetic attention is, however, impossible. Even in the world in which all of us live, a world disjointed, contradictory, multiple, and far from ideal, attention to a code of ethics should stimulate at least some thinking about consequence. And some thinking is better than no thinking.

The expertise made available to professionals through the assimilation of various specialized languages is necessary to solving a problem as complex and sinister as global warming. As true as this is, however, it is equally true that without the ability to talk to each other, to collaborate in a language understandable across specializations, the problem could only be approached in its parts. Such an approach would not be of much use to achieving a balanced and blended whole solution, much as Victor Frankenstein stitched together parts of different beings and came up with, not the perfect being hoped for, but a *filthy creation*. Victor toiled alone; he did not collaborate. What is needed, along with the languages which define disciplines, is one which crosses them so that groups of experts may communicate to one another what they are doing and how (and why) they are doing it. In merged disciplines (e.g., biochemistry or geophysics), the common language between them amounts in cognitive complexity to a disciplinary language. It *does* the merged disciplines' work. Moving outward from such disciplines into broader disciplinary relationships, a common language would describe the specialized activities to collaborators in a way which opens paths and provides contexts for their own activities. It is not disciplinary in the sense of supporting a particular specialization and guiding its work. Nor is it street vernacular. Between these two, this language probes disciplinary boundaries without entering them, is educated without being esoteric, and describes and shares the work of experts without doing it. In the sense of the Frankenstein myth, because of the input of others, specialists build better monsters. This common language would also allow them to talk *about* their work to a general audience.

Should there (or could there) be an academic forum for teaching a common or cross disciplinary language? Initially, the first-year composition sequence may appear to be a likely candidate, but first-year students are often unaware of language differences between disciplines or postsecondary structures. Before understanding the need for a common language, they have to acknowledge the multitude of discourse communities which make up a campus and how their entry into one of them is not only an academic but a cultural, historical, and personal event. They need to know that, as majors, their role is to learn a language by reading, writing, and speaking it. They need to be able to *do* the work before they can comment on whether it *should be done*. As first-year students, they probably have not made these discoveries yet.

Perhaps this course could be designed at the upper division level with a syllabus that treats professional ethics, common language, and collaborative problem solving. Based in the pertinent discipline and open only to majors, such a course might be designed to address many issues at once, and, doing so, its potential has great appeal. Its curriculum begins with discussion of language difference between disciplines and a metacognitive examination of how writers use language (and the values, purposes, and forms for writing) within the home discipline. Students share papers they have written for classes in their major, trace their progress as writers in the discipline, and look at student and professional writing from other disciplines. Faculty guest speakers from within and outside the students' disciplines are invited to the class to talk about their professional writing and their growth as writers. Students examine the publications of professionals who *do* the work in academic articles and write *about* the work in generalist articles. Small group work then focuses on the distinctions between these types of writing, and the contexts and audiences for each. Such a process must reveal to the class the multiple situations in which writers write, even within one discipline. By extension, it demonstrates the myriad situations in which scholars across campus may write, different but equal.

Students might be set to the collaborative tasks, with faculty guidance and input, of developing principles for ethical behavior within their disciplines and professions, using model codes from other disciplines (e.g., the engineering code) as a stimulus. Hundreds of codes of ethics exist, but their presence is lamentably unacknowledged by initiates. "Whistle blowers" could be called in to speak about their ethical choices and the consequence of those choices. A serious dilemma pervades our culture. Instead of heroes, whistle blowers are too often labeled somehow as traitors, "dirty rats" who betray their home departments, organizations, and companies. More often than not, these people have made wrenching choices that involve framing and then answering the questions, "I know how to do what is expected of me. I have the language and cognitive ability to do it, but should I be doing it? Does my (our) doing it advance or undermine my health, the health of my organization, or the health of the people and planet my organization must somehow, however vaguely, serve?" With global warming, large-scale economic fraud, massive disease and famine, war in Iraq, and so on, asking these questions should, *must* become perfunctory in postsecondary communities.

In this upper division course, students might also study examples of problems requiring multiple specialists, such as the development of the atom bomb. As the course's major project, small groups then examine any significant and controversial project within their state or region. They analyze the way in which the problem has been framed by various specialists, explain the proposed or ongoing solutions, assess the degree to which collaboration has occurred, and account for how stake-holders have had an influence on the process. After doing this research, they would offer their opinion on this local problem, critique the solution's efficacy, and reflect on their own group's collaborative effort. In Nevada, among many other issues of pressing importance, this means examining the Yucca Mountain nuclear waste facility. As I explained earlier, the creation of this facility opens itself as a problem to multiple disciplines: On the practical side, plumbing, welding, constructing, framing, policing, and so on; on the academic side, mining engineering, construction engineering, hydrology, biology, nuclear physics, chemistry, political science, sociology, and so on. Examining how these specializations collaborate within and between each other would be revelatory for students, and it might be readily facilitated through in-class and on-site interviews with specialists. Understanding how disciplines collaborate would help lead to some consensus about what a common language is and how it helps to solve complex problems.

I am intrigued by the notion of such a course and would enjoy teaching it to upper division English majors. In fact, I am in the process of proposing it to my Department and College curriculum committees. Nonetheless, I believe that adding another course to the curricula of every department is unrealistic. At UNR, we have a core curriculum requirement that includes a senior-level capstone course within the majors' departments. Perhaps, among that course's other requirements, the issues of difference between discourse communities, a disciplinary code of ethics, and a common language of collaboration might be included. UNR also requires seniors to take a capstone course outside their majors. These are the courses in which students have had such trouble because the languages in which they are taught (and the values, purposes, and forms for writing) often differ from their home departments. These are the courses in which faculty have publicly said, "These students don't know how to write," largely because they do not write in a way endorsed by their teachers. In UNR's situation, this course may be the best arena for discussing issues of difference and collaboration. I have been and will continue to be an advocate for inserting these issues into capstone courses.

WAC/writing center programs have an essential role to play in helping promote language users within disciplinary contexts. They are well positioned to encourage critical thinking activities, through their consulting with faculty and tutoring of students. Their situation makes it possible to promote a curriculum which eases students into specialization, knowing that "A traveler in a foreign land best learns the names of people and places, how to express ideas, ways to carry on a conversation by moving around in the culture, participating as fully as he can, making mistakes, saying things half right, blushing, then being encouraged by a native speaker to try again" (Rose, 1989, p. 142). The fundamental qualifier is that consultants collaborate with their constituents in a way which empowers faculty to make assignments and students to write them, without agendas that debilitate that process.

Compelling evidence exists to suggest that writing to learn, if it is understood in its process-expressivist orientation, belongs much more to composition studies than to any other discipline. The complementarity that WAC experts claim is shared between learning to write in the disciplines and writing to learn depends not on logic or common sense, but on the passionate commitment of compositionists and those they convert in the disciplines, on composition's sense of ownership of writing, and on the success of composition teachers in their own classes. It is hard to argue with such success. Nonetheless, the immediacy of a problem such as global warming, with its obvious complexity and nearly certain impacts, suggests that the time to celebrate should end; numerous specialists must not only have the expertise to formulate the problems and offer solutions and the ability to collaborate within and between their communities, but also have the inclination to reflect on their activities. WAC/writing center programs can and must play a role in the process of developing professionals who are at once experts in the disciplines and stewards for the planet.

Appendix A

1) From the *American Journal of Agricultural Economics*, August 2002

LOCAL VERSUS GLOBAL SEPARABILITY IN AGRICULTURAL HOUSEHOLD MODELS: THE FACTOR PRICE EQUALIZATION EFFECT OF LAND TRANSFER RIGHTS

Michael R. Carter and Yang Yang

Commonly employed global tests for separability between production and consumption decisions are theoretically inappropriate when the market failures creating non-separabilities differentially constrain some, but not all households. Simulated maximum likelihood estimates using Chinese panel data reject restrictions implied by a global separability test in favor of regime-specific or local separability tests. The estimates also show that a global approach to separability obscures the significant effect that less-encumbered land transfer rights have on shadow factor price equalization across households and allocative efficiency. The findings on transfer rights suggest a resolution to the debate in China on further property rights reform. *Key words*: household models, land rights, Chinese agriculture, separability.

2) From *The American Naturalist*, 160, 2, August 2002

A Mechanism for the Evolution of Altruism among Nonkin: Positive Assortment through Environmental Feedback

John W. Pepper, Santa Fe Institute, Santa Fe, New Mexico, 89501

Barbara B. Smuts, Department of Psychology, University of Michigan, Ann Arbor, Michigan 48109

Submitted January 10, 2001; Accepted January 18, 2002

ABSTRACT:

The evolution of altruism often requires genetic similarity among interactors. For structured populations in which a social trait affects all group members, this entails positive assortment, meaning that cooperators and noncooperators tend to be segregated into different groups. Several authors have claimed that mechanisms other than common descent can produce positive assortment, but this claim has not been generally accepted. Here, we describe one such mechanism. The process of "environmental feedback" requires only that the cooperative trait affects the quality of the local environment and that individuals are more likely to leave low-quality than high-quality environments. We illustrate this dynamic using an agent-based spatial model of feeding restraint. Depending on parameter settings, results included both positive assortment (required for the evolution of altruism) and negative assortment (required for the evolution of spite). The mechanism of environmental feedback appears to be a general one that could plan a role in the evolution of many forms of cooperation.

3) From *College English* 1989

A Common Ground: The Essay in the Academy

Kurt Spellmeyer

> . . . *the objectivity of dialectical cognition needs not less subjectivity, but more.*
>
> —T. W. Adorno (*Negative Dialectics*)

In his essay "Of the Education of Children," Montaigne recalls an encounter with two scholars who, on the road to Orleans, were followed closely by a third traveler, La Rochefoucauld:

One of my men inquired of the first of these teachers who was the gentleman that came behind him. He, not having seen the retinue that followed him, and thinking that my man was talking about his companion, replied comically: "He is not a gentleman; he is a grammarian, and I am a logician." (125)

If the essay as a distinct genre begins with Montaigne, it also begins as an assault upon the scholasticism he alludes to in this passage. Through his account of the two self-absorbed pedants, Montaigne makes light of the conception of knowledge that distinguishes so exactly between the grammarian and the logician, and he introduces, as an alternative to such distinctions, the example of La Rochefoucauld, the "gentleman," by which he does not mean a member of the ruling class, but instead the questioner whose pursuit of understanding has carried him beyond the limitations of the customary. The new system of education proposed by Montaigne in his essay is designed to repair precisely that fragmentation of experience—into grammar, logic, theology, rhetoric, and so forth—which characterized scholastic discourse, and which arose from still another fragmentation, between the "high" language of court and college and the "low" language of the street and the home. Unlike Montaigne's two erudite travelers, a person of genuine sophistication, a person like La Rochefoucauld, surmounts these divisions because he measures them against an experiential unity no single discipline can encompass. Indeed, Montaigne repeatedly warns that the conventional branches of learning, because they are by nature specialized and mutually exclusive, obscure not only the complexity of real life, but also the coherence. As an antidote to the tautological circularity, which is a danger for all discourse, he commends the test of personal experience. "Let" the student "be asked for an account not merely of the words of his lesson, but of its sense and substance, and let him judge the profit he has made by the testimony not of his memory, but of his life" (110).

4) From *The Plant Cell*, August 2002

A Major Light-Harvesting Polypeptide of Photosystem II Functions in Thermal Dissipation

Dafna Elrad, Department of Biological Sciences, Stanford University, Stanford, California, 94305

Krishna K. Niyogi, Department of Plant and Microbial Biology, University of California, Berkeley, Koshland Hall, Berkeley, California 94720-3102

Arthur R. Grossman, Department of Plant Biology, Carnegie Institution of Washington, 260 Panama Street, Stanford, California 94305

Under high-light conditions, photoprotective mechanisms minimize the damaging effects of excess light. A primary photoprotective mechanism is thermal dissipation of excess excitation energy within the light-harvesting complex of photosystem II (LHCII). Although roles for both carotenoids and specific polypeptides in thermal dissipation have been reported, neither the site nor the mechanism of this process has been defined precisely. Here, we describe the physiological and molecular characteristics of the *Chlamydomonas reinhardtii* *npq5* mutant, a strain that exhibits little thermal dissipation. This strain is normal for state transition, high light-induced violaxanthin deepoxidation, and low light growth, but it is more sensitive to photoinhibition than the wild type. Furthermore, both pigment data and measurements of photosynthesis suggest that the photosystem II antenna in the *npq5* mutant has one-third fewer light-harvesting trimers than do wild-type cells. The *npq5* mutant is null for a gene designated *Lhcbm1*, which encodes a light-harvesting polypeptide present in the trimers of the photosystem II antennae. Based on sequence data, the *Lhcbm1* gene is 1 of 10 genes that encode the major LHCII polypeptides in Chlamydomonas. Amino acid alignments demonstrate that these predicted polypeptides display a high degree of sequence identity but maintain specific differences in the N-terminal regions. Both physiological and molecular characterization of the *npq5* mutant suggest that most thermal dissipation within LHCII of Chlamydomonas is dependent on the peripherally associated trimeric LHC polypeptides.

5) From *Nature*, 419, 2002

Evidence from the AD 2002 Izu Islands earthquake swarm that stressing rate governs seismicity

Shinji Toda, Active Fault Research Center, Geological Survey of Japan, AIST, Tsukuba 305-8567, Japan

Ross S. Stein, US Geological Survey, MS 977, Menlo Park, California 94025, USA

Takeshi Saglya, Geographical Survey Institute, Tsukuba 305-0811, Japan

Magma intrusions and eruptions commonly produce abrupt changes in seismicity far from magma conduits that cannot be associated with the diffusion of pore fluids of heat. Such swarm seismicity also migrates with time, and often exhibits a 'dog-bone'-shaped distribution. The largest earthquakes in swarms produce aftershocks that obey an Omori-type (exponential) temporal decay, but the duration of the aftershock sequences is drastically reduced, relative to normal earthquake activity. Here we use one of the most energetic swarms ever recorded to study the dependence of these properties on the stress imparted by a magma intrusion. A 1,000-fold increase in seismicity rate and a 1,000-fold decrease in aftershock duration occurred during the two-month-long dyke intrusion. We find that the seismicity rate is proportional to the calculated stressing rate, and that the duration of aftershock sequences is inversely proportional to the stressing rate. This behaviour is in accord with a laboratory-based rate/state constitutive law, suggesting an explanation for the occurrence of earthquake swarms. Any sustained increase in stressing rate—whether due to an intrusion, extrusion or creep event—should produce such seismological behaviour.

Appendix B
Why Is It Important to Advance Critical Thinking Skills?

PERRY'S DEVELOPMENTAL SCHEME

dualism: division of meaning into two realms—Good versus Bad, Right versus Wrong, We versus They, All that is not Success is Failure, and the like. Right Answers exist *somewhere* for every problem and authorities know them. Right Answers are to be memorized by hard work. Knowledge is quantitative. Agency is experienced as "out there" in Authority, test scores, the Right Job.

multiplicity: diversity of opinion and values is recognized as legitimate in areas where right answers are not yet known. Opinions remain atomistic without pattern or system. No judgements can be made among them so "everyone has a right to his own opinion; none can be called wrong."

relativism: diversity of opinion, values, and judgement derived from coherent sources, evidence, logics, systems, and patterns allowing for analysis and comparison. Some opinions may be found worthless, while there will remain matters about which reasonable people will reasonably disagree. Knowledge is qualitative, dependent on contests.

relativism with commitment: an affirmation, choice, or decision (career, values, politics, personal relationship) made in the awareness of Relativism. Agency is experienced as within the individual. "I must be wholehearted while tentative, fight for my values yet respect others, believe my deepest values right yet be ready to learn."

BELENKY'S DEVELOPMENTAL SCHEME

received knowledge: a perspective from which women conceive of themselves as capable of receiving, even reproducing, knowledge from the all-knowing external authorities but not capable of creating knowledge on their own.

subjective knowledge: a perspective from which truth and knowledge are conceived of as personal, private, and subjectively known or intuited.

procedural knowledge: a position in which women are invested in learning and applying objective procedures for obtaining and communicating knowledge.

constructed knowledge: a position in which women view all knowledge as contextual, experience themselves as creators of knowledge, and value subjective and objective strategies for learning.

Appendix C
Toward Identifying Critical Thinking

J. Bean: To grow as thinkers, students must develop the mental habits that allow them to experience problems phenomenologically, to dwell with them—to understand, in short, what makes a problem problematic. To a large extent, these mental habits are discipline-specific, since each discipline poses its own kinds of problems and conducts inquiries, uses data, and makes arguments in its own characteristic fashion. But some aspects of critical thinking are also generic across disciplines. (*Engaging Ideas*)

J. Kurfiss: Thinking critically requires an investigation whose purpose is to explore a situation, phenomenon, question, or problem to arrive at a hypothesis or conclusion about it that integrates all available information and that can therefore be convincingly justified. (*Critical Thinking*)

M. Waldo: Framing and solving problems, seeing multiple points of view on complex issues, analyzing processes or information, making informed arguments—such activities characterize critical thinkers ("On Assigning and Assessing Writing in Criminal Justice")

M. Belenky et al.: Constructivists seek to stretch the outer boundaries of their consciousness—by making the unconscious conscious, by consulting and listening to the self, by voicing the unsaid, by listening to others and staying alert to all the currents and undercurrents of life about them, by imagining themselves inside the new poem or person or idea that they want to come to know and understand. Constructivists become passionate knowers, knowers who enter into a union with that which is to be known. (*Women's Ways of Knowing*)

S. D. Brookfield: The two central activities of critical thinking involve identifying assumptions and exploring alternative ways of thinking and acting. (*Developing Critical Thinkers*)

R. W. Paul: Critical thinking involves entering imaginatively into opposing points of view to create dialogic exchange between our own views and those whose thinking differs substantially from our own. ("Dialogical Thinking . . .")

V. R. Ruggiero: Critical thinking is any mental activity that helps formulate or solve a problem, make a decision, or fulfill a desire to understand. It is a searching for answers, a reaching for meaning. (*The Art of Thinking*)

J. Golub: the ability to analyze, classify, compare, formulate hypotheses, make inferences, and draw conclusions is essential to the reasoning processes of all adults. The capacity to solve problems, both rationally and intuitively, is a way to help students cope successfully with the experience of learning within the school setting and outside. (*Activities to Promote Critical Thinking*)

P. Freire: The critically transitive consciousness is characterized by depth in the interpretation of problems; by the substitution of causal principles for magical explanations; by the testing of one's "findings" and by openness to revision; by the attempt to avoid distortion when perceiving problems and to avoid preconceived notions when analyzing them; by refusing to transfer responsibility; by rejecting passive positions; by soundness of argumentation; by the practice of dialogue rather than polemics; by receptivity to the new for reasons beyond mere novelty and by the good sense not to reject the old just because it is old—by accepting what is valid in both old and new. (*Education for Critical Consciousness*)

Appendix D

From *How Writing Shapes Thinking*, Applebee and Langer (1987)

First, the more that content is manipulated, the more likely it is to be remembered and understood.

Second, the effects of writing tasks are greatest for the particular information focused upon during the writing.

Third, writing tasks differ in the breadth of information drawn upon and in the depth of processing of that information that they invoke.

Finally, if content is familiar and relationships are well understood, writing may have no major effect at all.

Conclusion: The Implications of Writing as a Means of Thinking in the Undergraduate Curriculum

As the chapter has tried to show, teaching thesis-based analytical and argumentative writing means teaching the thinking processes that underlie academic inquiry. To use writing as a means of thinking, teachers need to make the design of writing assignments a significant part of course preparation and to adopt teaching strategies that give students repeated, active practice at exploring disciplinary questions and problems. Additionally, it is important to emphasize inquiry, question asking, and cognitive dissonance in courses and, whenever possible, to show that scholars in a discipline often disagree about answers to key questions. By teaching a problem-driven model of the writing process, teachers send a message to the Skylers of the world that good writing is not a pretty package for disguising ignorance. Rather it is a way of discovering, making, and communicating meanings that are significant, interesting, and challenging (Bean, 1996, p. 35).

Appendix E
Sample Assignments

For Biology 376 (Ornithology)

WRITING ASSIGNMENT NUMBER 1

Your neighbor is an editor for the *Reno Gazette Journal*. In a conversation with her last week you mentioned you are taking an Ornithology course at UNR. She is a nature-lover and has long wanted to start a nature column for the general reader. Consequently, after you made the mistake of mentioning your "bird class," she immediately asked you to write an article on "How Birds Fly" as the initial topic for her column. She is convinced you are now an "expert" on the subject, and would do an excellent job. Besides, she offered to pay you $100 (as long as we're imagining here, we might as well imagine BIG).

You accept the challenge. However, keep in mind that you are writing for a general audience, not a class of biology majors or picky professors. Feel free to be creative, and don't feel confined to only the material discussed in class; additional sources of information are OK. In your article, explain such topics as: (1) the concept of an airfoil and how a bird's wing is structured to resemble an airfoil; (2) how a bird's wing acts as an airfoil to generate lift; 3) how a bird's primaries act as oscillating propellers to generate propulsion; and (4) how different wing types are adapted for different lifestyles of birds (you don't necessarily have to mention the topics in this order; do it whatever way you think best).

Limit your article to 2 single-spaced, typed pages or less (or 4 double-spaced typed pages). You will be graded on (1) the accuracy of your explanations; (2) the clarity, development, and completeness of your explanations; (3) the appropriateness of your article for the general public; and (4) the quality of your writing (including such basics as proper sentence structure, punctuation, spelling, continuity of thought, etc.).

Your article will be graded on a 20-point scale. A top grade (20) indicates your article explains the essentials of bird flight clearly to a general audience. A "middle" article (10–15) will demonstrate to someone who already understands the phenomenon that you probably understand it too, but the readers of your newspaper would probably be confused. A "low" article (5–8) demonstrates either a lack of understanding on your part or is written so poorly that it makes little sense.

The assignment is due on THURSDAY, MARCH 7, at the beginning of class. No late assignments will be accepted. All papers MUST BE TYPED. Put the title of the article at the top of the first page, centered, with your name centered below it, like this:

HOW BIRDS FLY
by
Mary Peterson

Then skip a line and begin the text. Good luck, and have fun with it. Who knows? If you do a good job, it could be the start of a glorious career, and the hundred bucks won't hurt either (don't you wish).

You can work together with a friend if you want, to help clarify ideas, but your paper should be written entirely in your own words. Identical papers from more than one person will be unacceptable (a grade of zero).

Biology 314   Ecology & Population Biology   Fall 1998

Essay Assignment: Controversies in Ecology

Many of you are thinking about careers that will require you to write clearly and persuasively. The only route to better writing is practice. I've designed an essay assignment that should help you improve your writing ability. Just as importantly, this assignment should help you develop your critical thinking skills.

More specifically, why is this essay assignment important for meeting the goals of Biology 314? First, this is one way to gain a deeper understanding of how the scientific process really works—probably more valuable than listening to a series of lectures about it. Second, it is important to know that the frontiers of science, particularly ecology, are "fuzzy." There is disagreement about interesting and important issues. I've chosen topics for the assignment which illustrate this. Third, at this stage of your education you need to begin to learn how to read and critically evaluate original research papers in science, not just rely on textbook summaries. This is important not only for those of you who plan to become scientists, but for everyone who wishes to be an effective citizen (think about the scientific issues that you read about in the newspaper—behind many of these issues are important debates that are often glossed over or ignored by reporters).

Objective

Your main objective in this essay will be to critically evaluate contrasting arguments and evidence about an ecological phenomenon. Because each of you has different interests within the broad scope of ecology, you may choose to write about one of several different specified topics (see handout entitled "Topics for Essay Assignment"). For each topic, I provide key references, although you may use a library search to find others that may be useful as well.

Audience

Your essay should be written to persuade your peers of your point of view. For purposes of this assignment, your peers are fellow students of ecology with some knowledge of basic biology.

Form and Content of the Essay

Your essay should include the following components:

1. A concise but clear and descriptive title.
2. A summary of the alternative arguments in the key papers you read.
3. A statement of your opinion about the controversy reflected in these papers.
4. Reasons for your opinion
   a. What's wrong with the evidence or arguments on the other side of the issue? Why?

   b. What is especially convincing about evidence or arguments on the side you support? Why?

   c. Are there other kinds of arguments or evidence about the issue that you can add to the debate? These may be based on other reading, your own experience, or your imagination. In using the word "imagination" here, I don't mean to suggest that you should suspend critical thinking. Be creative, but logical.

   d. What are some possible counter-arguments to your position? It can be very effective in a critical essay such as this to introduce some key counter-arguments and then make a logical counter-counter-argument to each; i.e., strengthen your position by exposing the flaws in objections to it.

5. A brief summary of the main theme of your essay.

6. A section of Literature Cited, in which you list all references which you cite in the body of the essay.

You need to do all these things in no more than five pages! This means that editing and rewriting are important. Once you know what you really want to say and have it down on paper in a rough draft, you can usually figure out how to say it in fewer words.

In thinking about organizing your essay in terms of this outline, please keep in mind that you don't necessarily have to first summarize the key ideas in the papers you read, and then describe and defend your own opinion. Depending on the topic, it may be more effective to interweave your summary of the ideas and your evaluation of them.

Don't feel that you have to discuss every substantive issue in the papers which form the basis for your essay. It will probably be more effective to pick one or two key points of disagreement between the authors of the papers, state why you think these are especially important or interesting, and discuss them in some depth.

Use of the Literature

Your essay may be based solely on the key references that I provide for your topic. However, if you find other relevant papers you may wish to cite their results or ideas to support your arguments or shed light on the general topic under consideration. However, you **MUST** give appropriate credit to the authors of any papers you use. This means using quotation marks around direct quotes from these papers or expressing their results or ideas in your own words if you don't use direct quotes (preferably the latter—direct quotations are used sparingly in scientific papers). In either case, you should cite the sources in the text like so:

Beavers exhibit a small but significant decline in body temperature in winter (Smith et al., 1993).

or

Smith et al. (1993) showed that the body temperature of adult beavers declined by about 1°C in winter.

All references which you use in your essay and cite in the text should be listed in alphabetical order in a section called Literature Cited at the end of the paper. Use the format of citations of key references for the various topics as a model of how to list references in the Literature Cited section. Don't list any references in the Literature Cited which aren't explicitly cited in the text.

Procedures

The first draft[1] of your essay is due on Monday, 16 November, at 9 am. We will use the week of 16–20 November to meet in small groups to discuss the topics of your essays. In order to schedule these meetings, I need to know no later than Monday, 2 November what topic you have selected and your schedule during the week of 16–20 November. Therefore, please complete the topic-selection and scheduling questionnaire to turn in at the beginning of class on 2 November.

I will return your first draft with comments about content and writing style on 23 November. Based on these comments as well as ideas that came up during the group discussion, you should prepare a final draft of your essay to be turned in on 7 December, the last day of regular class.

Grading

I will evaluate your essay on the basis of style (overall organization, paragraph and sentence structure, grammar, spelling, word choice) and content (identifying and discussing the most important aspects of the topic, avoiding irrelevant issues, supporting your ideas with logical arguments and appropriate examples, creativity). In reading your essay for content, I will ask myself how effectively your have dealt with the items listed in the section called *Form and Content of the Essay*. Style and Content count equally in the final grade. The first draft is worth 8% of the total course grade, the final draft is worth 20%. Participation in discussion of your topic during the week of 16–20 November counts as part of the grade of the first draft.

---

[1]Note that this is not necessarily the first draft that you write, but the first that you turn in.

Summary of Important Dates

Monday, 2 November, 9 am	Topic-Selection and Scheduling Questionnaire Due
Monday, 16 November, 9 am	First Draft of Essay Due
Week of 16-20 November	One-hour Meeting to Discuss topics (times and places to be announced)
Monday, 7 December, 9 am	Final Draft of Essay Due

Biology 314   Ecology & Population Biology   Fall 1998

Topics for Essay Assignment

Please choose **one** of these topics for your essay. The key references listed for each are available on reserve in the Life and Health Sciences Library.

1. **What determines the northern range limits of wintering birds in North America?**

Root, T. 1988. Energy constraints on avian distributions and abundances. Ecology **69**:330–339.

Repasky, R. R. 1991. Temperature and the northern distributions of wintering birds. Ecology **75**:2274–2285.

Root, T. L., and S. H. Schneider. 1993. Can large-scale climatic models be linked with multiscale ecological studies? Conservation Biology **7**:256–270.

Root (1988) argues that limits on metabolic rate determine the northern limits of many species of birds that winter in North America. Repasky (1991) analyzes the correspondence between range limits and temperature isotherms somewhat differently, presents additional data, and looks at Root's data in a different way. Root and Schneider (1993) include a brief section in which they rebut Repasky's critique of Root's earlier paper. They also discuss implications of these results for reducing effects of global climate change on species distributions. If you are interested in animal physiological ecology or in studies on large-scale problems using correlation methods, this would be a good topic to select.

2. **Is there adaptive adjustment of the sex ration of offspring by female pigs?**

Meikle, D. B., L. C. Drickamer, S. H. Vessey, T. L. Rosenthal, and K. S. Fitzgerald. 1993. Maternal dominance rank and secondary sex ratio in domestic swine. Animal Behaviour **46**:79–85.

Mendl, M., A. J. Zanella, D. M. Broom, and C. T. Whittemore. 1995. Maternal social status and birth sex ratio in domestic pigs; an analysis of mechanisms. Animal Behaviour **50**:1361–1370.

Meikle, D. B., S. H. Vessey, and L. C. Drickamer. 1997. Testing models of adaptive adjustment of secondary sex ratio in domestic swine. Animal Behaviour **53**: 428–431.

Mendl, M., A. J. Zanella, D. M. Broom, and C. T. Whittemore. 1997. Studying birth sex ratio in domestic pigs. Animal Behaviour **53**:432–435.

Study of sex ratios from an evolutionary perspective has been an active and exciting area of research in recent ears. A purely mechanistic viewpoint suggests there should be only random departures from 50:50 sex ratios, at least at the time of conception. The evolutionary perspective suggests that, under certain conditions it may be more advantageous for females to produce sons than daughters, and vice versa under other conditions. Furthermore, the evolutionary perspective suggests that mechanisms can evolve to produce such skewed sex ratios if they contribute to higher fitness. These papers by Meikle et al. and Mendl et al. illustrate one example of these kinds of studies. Their work produced different results and interpretations—which set of authors is more convincing to you and why? Don't be put off by the fact that this research is about pigs—these papers provide a window on an important general area of research in contemporary biology, as well as plenty of controversy to digest and discuss.

3. Do herbivores benefit plants?

Belsky, A. J., W. P. Carson, C. L. Jensen, and G. A. Fox. 1993. Overcompensation by plants: herbivore optimization or red herring? Evolutionary Ecology **7**:109–121.

Lennartsson, T., J. Tuomi, and P. Nilsson. 1997. Evidence for an evolutionary history of overcompensation in the grassland biennial *Gentianella campestris* (Gentianaceae). American Naturalist **149**:1147–1155.

Herbivores eat plants, so in general their impacts on plants would be expected to be negative. Yet there has been much interest in recent years in potential beneficial effects of some grazing herbivores on some species of plants.

In part, this interest stems from an evolutionary perspective—how could a mutualism between plants and animals that eat plants evolve? In part, it comes from a management perspective - is there some level of grazing which actually benefits grasslands, for example? This topic has been really controversial. The two key papers I'm suggesting are a review by Belsky et al. (1993) which is negative about the general idea and a more recent study by Lennartsson et al. (1997) which purports to show evidence of beneficial effects of grazing on a particular plant species in Sweden.

4. Is an observational or experimental approach most effective for understanding the role of predators in intertidal communities?

Menge, B. A. 1976. Organization of the New England rocky intertidal community: role of predation, competition and environmental heterogeneity. Ecological Monographs **46**:355–393.

Edwards, D. C., D. O. Conover, and F. Sutter III. 1982. Mobile predators and the structure of marine intertidal communities. Ecology **63**:1175–1180.

Menge, B. A. 1982. Reply to comment by Edwards, Conover, and Sutter. Ecology **63**:1180–1184.

Simple removal or caging experiments have played an important role in understanding what determines the distributions of species in rocky intertidal communities. Menge (1976) describes these kinds of experiments in detail. Edwards et al. (1982) question Menge's interpretations, based on their own observations that suggest that Menge may have failed to account for effects of an important mobile predator (a species of fish) in the design of his experiments. Menge (1982) mounts a vigorous defense of his own work and of experimental field ecology in general.

5. "Are large predators keystone species in Neotropical forests?" (Wright et al., 1994)

Terborgh, J. 1992. Maintenance of diversity in tropical forests. Biotropica **24**:283–292.

Wright, S. J., Me. E. Gompper, and B. DeLeon. 1994. Are large predators keystone species in neotropical forests? The evidence from Barro Colorado Island. Oikos **71**:279–294.

Asquith, N. M., S. J. Wright, and M. J. Clauss. 1997. Does mammal community composition control recruitment in Neotropical forests? Evidence from Panama. Ecology **78**:941–946.

A keystone species is one that has a major impact on the structure and function of its ecosystem, such that if the keystone species is removed, there are major changes in species composition, physical appearance, and ecological processes of the ecosystem. Sea otters along the Pacific coast and beavers along streams in North America are classic examples of keystone species. Whether large mammalian predators play a similar role in tropical forests is less clear. These papers by Terborgh (1992), Wright et al. (1994), and Asquith et al. (1997) don't offer starkly opposite views of the issue, but they provide some conflicting evidence that could stand to be carefully examined by several of you who may be interested in large mammals and in questions about how ecosystems work.

6. What benefit do birds get from living in colonies?

Brown, C. R. 1988. Enhanced foraging efficiency through information centers: a benefit of coloniality in cliff swallows. Ecology **69**:602–613.

Shields, W. M. 1990. Information centers and coloniality in cliff Swallows: statistical design and analysis—a comment. Ecology **71**:401–405.

One fundamental issue in behavioral ecology is how individuals of some species live in social groups. This is an important issue because there are some automatic disadvantages of group living, such as increased competition and increased likelihood of parasite or disease transmission, so researchers have generally assumed that there must be some compensating advantages, or else groups wouldn't form (individuals of most species do not live in social groups). Brown (1988) tested one common hypothesis for group living—that individuals increase their foraging efficiency by following others to feeding sites. Shields (1990) described several problems with Brown's methods and interpretations. Some of Shield's criticisms involve statistical issues that you may not have the background to appreciate, but the majority of his points are about more fundamental issues of research design. This essay topic shows how difficult it can be to design effective research projects to answer questions about social behavior, because it may not be possible to do simple, clear cut experiments. Don't necessarily avoid this topic because of the statistical issues. Reading and thinking about these papers will be a good way to learn some important basic principles of designing research in ecology.

(This assignment, written by Steve Jenkins of UNR's Biology Department, is the most thorough I have seen, especially with regard to student writers explaining opposing points of view and then taking a position with regard to the pertinent issue. It has a distinct advantage over many other assignments demanding equally complex thinking and writing tasks for success. It provides the sources for multiple points of view, sources with which Steve is obviously familiar, and it then offers synopses of these sources. It entices students into complex and creative thinking and directs them on how to express it, based on disciplinary interests and constraints. It assumes their own interest as its context, and their peers as its audience. Doing so, it rightly assumes their engaged "voice," though Steve would not ask for it. While extremely demanding for Steve in its labor of design, students know what they are supposed to do, why they are doing it, and for whom. It offers support along the way. Steve's assignment thus becomes easier and fairer to grade when the final copies come in. As a model assignment for upper division students, within the context of opposing points of view, it would be difficult to find an equal.)

PACE PROGRAM IN SOCIAL WORK
"FAMILIES: POLITICS AND PROCESS"

1. Your 25 year old sister has been having problems with her most recent relationship. In particular she wants to have more closeness in their relationship while her partner keeps distancing himself whenever she "pursues" him. You have talked with her several times on the telephone, and she is aware that you now are a family "expert" (at least relative to her) because of the courses you have taken in this area. One of her friends believes that it is an issue of his unwillingness to "commit" to a relationship, while her other friend believes this is a way for him to maintain "power" in this relationship. Your sister writes you to ask what you think is going on. She wants not only your "professional" view of which explanation fits the best but also some theoretical rationale because she is developing a greater interest in this area. Please provide for your dear sister a theoretical explanation which you think best fits the situation as you know it (you will have to fill in some details here) and why one particular friend has best identified the problems you think are going on here. (Ehrenreich, Swidler, Galvin & Brommel, and other relevant articles.)

2. Congratulations! You recently have been elected to the Washoe County Commission! Now, as new commissioner, the other members ask that you, because of your expertise in the family area, develop a proposal which the Commissioners could use for the entire community to enhance families in Washoe County. They also have asked two other family professionals to approach this task from their particular theoretical point of view, which is different from yours. Your task, as they describe it, is to outline: a) what problems or concerns you would address from your theoretical perspec-

tive, b) why those problems or concerns are important from your point of view, and c) what possible solutions you might propose from your view point. Because the other commission members are fairly sophisticated, also please make reference to materials they might read which would be helpful to them in understanding your key points.

Sample assignments for P.J. Hill's Economics 105 Class

1. You are enrolled in an art history class at MSU in which the instructor says that Michelangelo's Pieta is a "priceless" work of art. You note that, in terms of your economics class, this has certain implications about the demand curve for the Pieta. Write a short essay to your instructor, using the concept of demand to comment on her statement.

2. Many years ago, McDonald's started opening earlier and serving breakfast. One friend says that this is just another example of the greed of large corporations: "They weren't satisfied with the profits they already had—instead they wanted to make even more." Another friend disagreed: "It was an effort to make the customers happy—most fast food restaurants don't serve breakfast; in doing so McDonald's is performing a real service for the people who want a quick, reasonably priced breakfast." Who is correct? Write a short essay to your friends that will help them solve this disagreement.

3. A wealthy individual buys a thousand acres of land adjacent to Gallatin Field (Bozeman's airport). He plans to raise registered quarter horses. Three years later he sues the airport authority, claiming that noise from planes is making his horses nervous, significantly reducing their value and consequently lessening his income. You are the district Court judge who hears the suit. Using the economic approach to the pollution, write a brief summary of your ruling and the reasons for it.

Appendix F
Samples of Student Physics Papers

Dear Brother,

1. How are things with you? Not so good by the sound of it. I am sorry you think I gave you a bum steer on that recipe I sent you for soft boiled eggs. If you let me explain, you will know that your sister does know what she is talking about.

   In Reno a three minute egg has to be cooked a little longer for some very good reasons. Since Reno is at a higher elevation, our atmospheric pressure isn't as much as it is in the Big Apple. Meaning that since we are higher up here in Reno, gravity has less pull on the air here. How does this relate to boiling an egg for more than three minutes you ask? Well since there is less atmospheric pressure here, water in Reno boils easier and at a lower temperature; 97 Celsius which is 143 Fahrenheit the temperature you are more familiar with. This compares with 100°C at sea level or 212°F. Obviously then, since you are boiling the egg at a lower temperature, you are going to have to boil it longer to achieve the same results.

   Another reason we have to boil our eggs longer, brother, is because the specific heat of water is really high—meaning it really takes a lot of heat to raise the temperature of water to it's boiling point. Remember, water does boil easier here in Reno, but since it boils easier and at a lower temperature, it takes longer to get a high enough boiling temperature to boil the eggs.

I hope I cleared things up for you, Brother. If you have any questions you know where to reach me. Take care of yourself and write soon.

Pat

2. Dear Brother,

You asked about the eggs and why they boiled at a lower rate in Reno. Well the reason is because of the altitude. Which is what makes the air pressure. The pressure in Reno is less therefore the altitude is greater, which makes the water boil quicker. You see, the water boils quicker in higher places than in lower places. Reno is higher than New York because of it's altitude thus making the water boil faster. When water boils faster it takes longer for an egg to cook because their isn't as much heat in it.

Pat

3. Dear Brother,

I guess I really blew it in your eyes. My only excuse seems to be that I forgot to take into account the distance we are apart and the difference in our altitudes.

The difference in altitude is an important factor in how we cook eggs and why our eggs in Reno tend to take longer to cook. This is all dependent on atmospheric pressure. You know, the stuff we measure with a barometer. You see, Brother, the higher up we go the less pressure there is per square inch. This is because the molecules at a higher altitude are not as close together as those at sea level. That is why when you are at a higher elevation, like in the mountains, you feel like the air is thinner. Unfortunately, most recipes are figured out for sea level, where the atmospheric pressure is the greatest.

Back to the eggs. . . . To reach a boiling point, you have to have an equal balance between those molecules that are leaving the liquid as vapor pressure and those in the air, atmospheric pressure. So, when you boil your water, your molecules in New York are held tighter than ours, because of the greater atmospheric pressure pushing down on the water. You have to get the water to a higher temperature to release the energy of the molecules in the water, so that it creates steam. Our water can be boiling like crazy, but the temperature still isn't high due to the lesser pressure we have here in Reno.

Colder water doesn't cook eggs as fast. The total amount of heat in the water doesn't matter because the flow depends on the temperature.

I hope you haven't completely given up on your sister yet, and that this will help you understand. My mistake, however, unintentional, did get you to write . . .

4. Dear Brother,

People in Reno definitely know how to cook a good three minute egg. It is just that due to certain factors the cooking time is a little longer here than in New York. One factor is the relationship of atmospheric pressure to altitude, another is the effect of pressure on boiling point, and also the relationship of heat content of water to temperature. So read on brother and I'll try to explain these factors so you will be able to understand.

As altitude increases the atmospheric pressure decreases. The less the atmospheric pressure, the less pressure there is to hold in the water molecules and they escape faster, so they vaporize faster with less energy. Reno has a higher altitude than New York so the atmospheric pressure is lower, and the boiling point of water is lower. The boiling point of water is Reno is 97° C (or 206.6° F) and water boils at 100° C (or 212° F) in New York. As you can see, since the pressure is lower, the boiling point of water is lower and there is less energy. When the boiling point of the water is lower then the heat content is lower. In essence, the heat is not as hot at a higher altitude as it would be at a lower altitude. To compare the difference in boiling points, try to imagine setting your stove at a lower setting and waiting for it to boil rather than setting it on high and waiting for it to boil.

So Brother, your little joke was actually true. What it all boils down to (pardon my little joke!) is that the boiling point of water in Reno is not as hot as the boiling point of water in New York, so it takes longer to cook a three minute egg. This all due to the altitude difference.

Your brother,

Pat

5. Dear Brother,

I just received your letter regarding three minute eggs. So you will know that I am learning something in college, I will try to explain.

Actually your joke about boiling water being colder in Reno is close to the truth. First, let's look at boiling. Imagine yourself standing barefoot on a hot plate. At first it's cool and comfortable, but as the temperature goes up you have to jump around to not burn your feet. Finally you jump off to get away from the hot plate. It's the same with water. As it gets hotter, the water wants to leave the heat source. When it leaves, we say it's boiling. Now imagine yourself on the same hot plate with 100 lbs. of bricks on your head. (Oh, come on, just imagine it!) You certainly won't be able to jump as high or far as you did before. It would take a hotter hot plate to make you leave. Once, again, it's the same with water. If water has a large force holding it down, it won't leave the hot plate as fast either. In fact when it does leave, it is at a higher temperature than when it has a small force pushing it down. So we know brothers will jump off hot plates at different temperatures depending on how much weight is holding them down and water will boil at different temperatures also depending on how much weight is holding it down.

Can it be that the weight holding a brother (and water) is greater in New York than it is in Reno? Amazingly the answer is yes. The weight is greater in New York than in Reno because New York is near the ocean and Reno is in the mountains. In fact, Reno is 4,000 feet above New York. To put it another way, Reno is forty stories above New York. So there are forty stories more air over New York than over Reno. New York folks have to go around all day carrying 4,000 ft. more air on their head than Reno folks. Anyway, the extra weight of air in New York makes water boil at a higher temperature in New York than in Reno.

Since water boils at a higher temperature in New York it doesn't take as long to cook an egg in New York as it does in Reno. This occurs because the rate at which heat flows into the eggs depends on the difference in the temperature of the water, the faster the heat flows into the eggs to cook them. It doesn't matter how much heat the water contains.

So you see, I've learned a lot in college. First, how to cook. Second, how to write, and third, how to please my brother (not unlike pleasing certain professors). I hope I've answered your questions and now you can sleep at night.

Your brother, Pat.

Appendix G
Writing Center Phone Survey

Gathering data campuswide on the kinds of writing required of students, and faculty perceptions of the quality of student writing.

1. Do you generally teach upper division, lower division, or a combination of these students during an academic year?

2. Which of the following types of writing do you require in at least one of your classes? Please reply yes or no to the items on the following list:

a. writing that analyzes or critiques information	yes	no
b. in-class writing excluding exams	yes	no
c. essay exams	yes	no
d. writing reviews or summaries of information	yes	no
e. writing that demonstrates problem solving	yes	no
f. writing that requires argument or persuasiveness	yes	no
g. writing that requires the synthesizing of information	yes	no
h. writing that requires considering multiple points of view	yes	no
i. lab reports	yes	no

3. In how many of your lower division classes do you require at least one of those types of writing?

    All   More than half   Less than half

4. In how many of your upper division classes do you require at least one of those types of writing?

   All   More than half   Less than half

5. Over the last three years, have you required more writing from lower division students, less writing, or the same?

6. Over the last three years have you required more writing from upper division students, less writing, or the same?

7. Do you feel that upper division students in general are better writers than lower division students?

8. To be more specific about which areas upper division students in general show more capability than lower division students in writing, I'm going to read a list of writing abilities. For each item on the list, please tell me to what degree upper division students demonstrate more competence than lower division students

a. ability to problem solve in writing

   great   moderate   small   none

b. ability to reflect your assignments' requirements in their writing

   great   moderate   small   none

c. ability to assert an argument in writing

   great   moderate   small   none

d. ability to support an argument in writing

   great   moderate   small   none

e. ability to achieve sentence-level correctness (punctuation, spelling, grammar)

   great   moderate   small   none

f. ability to reflect complex thought in writing

   great   moderate   small   none

g. ability to write logically about a subject

   great   moderate   small   none

h. ability to synthesize information in writing

   great   moderate   small   none

9. In general, do you see any writing improvement by your lower division students over the course of a semester?

      yes   no

10. In general, do you see any writing improvement by your upper division students over the course of a semester?

      yes   no

11. What do you see as 1-2 strong points in your students' writing? 1–2 weak points?

12. How have the writing components in the Core courses affected the quality of writing students are doing in your courses (over the last 5–10 years)?

13. Do you encourage your students to use the Writing Center?

Appendix H
Visitor Response Sheet
UNR Writing Center

DATE:_____ TUTOR'S NAME:_____

Your thoughtful response allows us to continually improve the quality of our services as well as give recognition where recognition is due. Thanks for your time!

Please respond to each of the following:

Have you been to the Writing Center before?   YES
                                                                               NO

    If "yes," would you say that you visit the WC on a regular
    basis (more than three times each month)?   YES
                                                                               NO

Is this particular visit to the WC a requirement for a course?   YES   NO

Which of the following best describes the writing that was considered during the appointment?

    Brainstorm Essay   Incomplete Draft   Journal Response   Lab Report
    Resume/Vitae   Personal Statement   Thesis/Dissertation   Other:_____

If this writing is for a class in which you are currently enrolled, please specify the course:_____

Did your tutor begin your appointment on time?   YES
                                                                   NO

Did your tutor meet your expectations?   YES
                                                                   NO

Please elaborate.

What was a strength or benefit gained from your visit today?

What suggestion(s) could you offer to improve the quality of your tutoring session?

What suggestion(s) could you offer to help improve the quality of the Writing Center?

References

Applebee, A., & Langer, J. (1987). *How writing shapes thinking*. Urbana, IL: National Council of Teachers of English.

Balester, V. (1992). Revising the "statement": On the work of writing centers. *College Composition and Communication, 43*, 167–171.

Barnett, R., & Blumner, J. (Eds.). (1999). *Writing centers and writing across the curriculum programs: Building interdisciplinary partnerships*. Westport, CT: Greenwood.

Bartholomae, D. (1995). Writing with teachers: A conversation with Peter Elbow. *College Composition and Communication, 31*, 62–71.

Bazerman, C. (1988). *Shaping written knowledge: The genre and activity of the experimental article in science*. Madison, WI: The University of Wisconsin Press.

Bean, J. (1996). *Engaging ideas: The professor's guide to integrating writing, critical thinking, and active learning in the classroom*. San Francisco: Jossey-Bass.

Belenky, M., Clinchy, B., Goldberger, N., & Tarule, J. (1986). *Women's ways of knowing: The development of self, voice, and mind*. New York: Basic Books.

Berkenkotter, C., & Huckin, H. (1995). *Genre knowledge in disciplinary communication: Cognition, culture, power*. Hillsdale, NJ: Lawrence Erlbaum Associates.

Berkenkotter, C., Huckin, T. H., & Ackerman, J. (1994). Social context and socially constructed texts. In C. Bazerman & D. Russell (Eds.), *Landmark essays on writing across the curriculum* (pp. 211–231). Davis, CA: Hermagoras.

Berlin, J. (1988). Rhetoric and ideology in the writing class. *College English, 50*, 477–494.

Berthoff, A. (1978). *Forming/thinking/writing: The composing imagination*. Rochelle Park, NJ: Hayden Book Company.

Bizzell, P. (1986). Foundationalism and anti-foundationalism in composition studies. *Pre/Text, 7.1–7.2*, 37–56.

Blair, C. (1988). Only one of the voices: Dialogic writing across the curriculum. *College English, 50*, 383–389.

Britton, J. (1972). *Language and learning*. London: Penguin.

Bruffee, K. (1984). Collaborative learning and the "conversation of mankind." *College English*, 46, 635–652.

Burnham, C. (2001). Expressive pedagogy: Practice/theory, theory/practice. In G. Tate, A. Rupiper, & K. Schick (Eds.), *A guide to composition pedagogies* (pp. 19–35). New York: Oxford University Press.

Coles, W., & Vopat, J. (Eds.). (1985). *What makes writing good.* Lexington, MA: Heath.

Dartmouth Conference. (1966). Dartmouth College.

Dawson, D., Goin, P., & Webb, M. (2000). *A doubtful river.* Reno, NV: University of Nevada Press.

Detweiler, J., & Peyton, C. (2000). Developing a language for discussing writing: Composition in occupational therapy. In *Innovations in Occupational Therapy Education 2000* (pp. 113–137). Bethesda, MD: American Occupational Therapy Association.

Dias, P. A., Freedman, P., & Medway, P. (1999). *Worlds apart: Acting and writing in academic and workplace contexts.* Mahwah, NJ: Lawrence Erlbaum Associates.

Eagleton, T. (1996). *Literary theory: An introduction* (2nd ed.). Minneapolis, MN: University of Minnesota Press.

Elbow, P. (1970). *Writing without teachers.* New York: Oxford University Press.

Elbow, P. (1996). Writing assessment: Do it better, do it less. In E. M. White, W. Lutz, & S. Kamusikiri (Eds.), *Assessment of writing: Politics, policies, and practices* (pp. 120–135). New York: The Modern Language Association.

Elbow, P. (1991, 1998). Reflections on academic discourse: How it relates to freshmen and colleagues. In V. Zamel & R. Spack (Eds.), *Negotiating academic literacies: Teaching and learning across languages and cultures* (pp. 145–169). Mahwah, NJ: Lawrence Erlbaum Associates.

Emig, J. (1971). *The composing processes of twelfth graders.* Urbana, IL: National Council of Teachers of English.

Faigley, L. (1986). Competing theories of process: A critique and a proposal. *College English*, 48, 527–542.

Faigley, L. (1995). *Fragments of rationality: Postmodernity and the subject of composition.* Pittsburgh: University of Pittsburgh Press.

Fishman, S., & McCarthy L. (1992). Is expressivism dead? Reconsidering its romantic roots and its relation to social constructionism. *College English*, 54, 647–661.

Foucault, M. (1972). *The archeology of knowledge and the discourse on language.* New York: Pantheon.

Freire, P. (1990). *Education for critical consciousness.* New York: Continuum.

Fulwiler, T., & Young, A. (Eds.). (1990). *Programs that work: Models and methods for writing across the curriculum.* Portsmouth, NH: Heinemann.

Gage, J. (1984). The 2000 year-old strawman. *Rhetoric Review*, 3, 100–104.

Geertz, C. (1983). *Local knowledge: Further essays in interpretive anthropology.* New York: Basic Books.

Geisler, C. (1994). *Academic literacy and the nature of expertise: Reading, writing and knowing in academic philosophy.* Hillsdale, NJ: Lawrence Erlbaum Associates.

Genesis 11:5–9. *The Bible.* King James Version.

Gere, A., & Smith, E. (1979). *Attitudes, language, and change.* Urbana, IL: National Council of Teachers of English.

Gradin, S. (1995). *Romancing rhetorics: Social expressivist perspectives on the teaching of writing.* Portsmouth, NH: Boynton/Cook.

Graff, G. (1992). *Beyond the culture wars: How teaching the conflicts can revitalize American education.* New York: W. W. Norton.

Grimm, N. (1999). *Good intentions: Writing center work for postmodern times*. Portsmouth, NH: Boynton/Cook.

Gusdorf, G. (1965). *Speaking (la parole)* (P. Brockelman, Trans.). Evanston, IL: Northwestern University Press.

Hairston, M. (1982). Winds of change: Thomas Kuhn and the revolution in the teaching of writing. *College Composition and Communication, 33*, 76–88.

Harris, J. (1989). The idea of community in the study of writing. *College Composition and Communication, 40*, 11–22.

Harris, J. (1996). *A teaching subject: Composition since 1966*. Upper Saddle River, NJ: Prentice-Hall.

Hillocks, G. (1986). *Research on written composition*. Urbana, IL: National Conference on Research in English.

Hirsch, E. D. (1982). Remarks on composition to the Yale English Department. In J. Murphy (Ed.), *The rhetorical tradition and modern writing* (pp. 13–18). New York: Modern Language Association.

Horney, K. (1970). *Neurosis and human growth: The struggle toward self-realization*. New York: W. W. Norton.

Howard, R. M. (2001). Collaborative pedagogy. In G. Tate, A. Rupiper, & K. Schick (Eds.), *A guide to composition pedagogies* (pp. 54–70). New York: Oxford University Press.

Johnston, S. (1996). *Basic writers and peer tutors: An ethnographically-oriented case study*. Dissertation. Reno: University of Nevada.

Jones, R., & Comprone, J. (1993). Where do we go next in writing across the curriculum? *College Composition and Communication, 44*, 59–68.

Judy, S. (1976). On clock watching and composing. In R. Graves (Ed.), *Rhetoric and composition: A sourcebook for teachers* (pp. 70–78). Rochelle Park, NJ: Hayden.

Kent, T. (Ed.) (1999). *Post-process theory: Beyond the writing-process paradigm*. Carbondale, IL: Southern Illinois University Press.

Kirsch, G. (1993). *Women writing the academy: Audience, authority, and transformation*. Carbondale, IL: Southern Illinois University Press.

Kirscht, J., Levine, R., & Reiff, R. (1994). Evolving paradigms: WAC and the rhetoric of inquiry. *College Composition and Communication, 45*, 369–380.

Knoblauch, C., & Brannon, L. (1984). *Rhetorical traditions and the teaching of writing*. Portsmouth, NH: Boynton/Cook.

Kuhn, T. (1970). *The structure of scientific revolutions*. Chicago: The University of Chicago Press.

Langer, S. (1957). *Philosophy in a new key: A study in the symbolism of reason, rite, and art*. Cambridge, MA: Harvard University Press.

Lave, J., & Wenger, E. (1991). *Situated learning: Legitimate peripheral participation*. Cambridge, England: Cambridge University Press.

Lewin, D. (1994). A tutorial on Klumpenhouwer networks, using the chorale in Shoenberg's Opus 11, no. 2. *Journal of Music Theory, 38.1*, 79–101.

Macrorie, K. (1970). *Uptaught*. Rochelle Park, NJ: Hayden.

Mahala, D. (1991). Writing utopias: Writing across the curriculum and the promise of reform. *College English, 53*, 773–789.

McLeod, S. (2001). The pedagogy of writing across the curriculum. In G. Tate, A. Rupiper, & K. Schick (Eds.), *A guide to composition pedagogies* (pp. 149–164). New York: Oxford University Press.

McLeod, S., & Maimon, E. (2000). Clearing the air: Wac myths and realities. *College English, 62*, 573–583.

Moffett, J. (1968). *Teaching the universe of discourse.* Boston: Houghton-Mifflin.

Moran, C. (2001). Technology and the teaching of writing. In G. Tate, A. Rupiper, & K. Schick (Eds.), *A guide to composition pedagogies* (pp. 203–223). New York: Oxford University Press.

Murray, D. (1968). *A writer teaches writing.* Boston: Houghton-Mifflin.

Newkirk, T. (1997). *The performance of self in student writing.* Portsmouth, NH: Boynton/Cook.

North, S. (1984). The idea of a writing center. *College English, 46,* 433–446.

North, S. (1987). *The making of knowledge in composition: Portrait of an emerging field.* Portsmouth, NH: Boynton/Cook.

Ohmann, R. (1974). *English in America.* New York: Oxford University Press.

Parker, W. (1967). Where do English departments come from? *College English, 28,* 339–351.

Peak, K., & Waldo, M. (1997). On assigning and assessing students' prose: A discipline-based approach. *Journal of Criminal Justice Education, 8,* 75–81.

Perry, W. (1981). Cognitive and ethical growth: The making of meaning. In A. Chickering & Associates (Eds.), *The modern American college: Responding to the new realities of diverse students and a changing society* (pp. 76–116). San Francisco: Jossey-Bass.

Piaget, J. (1959). *Language and thought of the child* (M. Gabain, Trans.). London: Routledge & Kegan Paul.

Prior, P. (1998). *Writing/disciplinarity: A socio-historic account of literate activity in the academy.* Mahwah, NJ: Lawrence Erlbaum Associates.

Roen, D., Brown, S., & Enos, T. (Eds.). (1999). *Living rhetoric and composition: Stories of the discipline.* Mahwah, NJ: Lawrence Erlbaum Associates.

Rose, M. (1989). *Lives on the boundary.* New York: The Free Press.

Russell, D. (1990). Writing across the curriculum in historical perspective: Toward a social interpretation. *College English, 52,* 52–71.

Russell, D. (1991). *Writing in the academic disciplines, 1870–1990: A curricular history.* Carbondale, IL: Southern Illinois University Press.

Shaughnessy, M. (1977). *Errors and expectations: A guide for basic writers.* New York: Oxford University Press.

Shen, F. (1998). The classroom and the wider culture: Identity as a key to learning English composition. In V. Zamel & R. Spack (Eds.), *Negotiating academic literacies: Teaching and learning across languages and cultures* (pp. 123–134). Mahwah, NJ: Lawrence Erlbaum Associates.

Smith, L. (1988). Why English departments should "house" writing across the curriculum. *College English, 50,* 390–395.

Spellmeyer, K. (1989). A common ground: The essay in the academy. *College English, 51,* 262–276.

Tobin, L. (2001). Process pedagogy. In G. Tate, A. Rupiper, & K. Schick (Eds.), *A guide to composition pedagogies* (pp. 1–18). New York: Oxford University Press.

Tomer, J. L., Wall, M. C., Reid, B. P., & Cline, J. I. (1993). Photofragmentation dynamics of 2-chloro-2-nitrosopropane. Scalar correlations of velocity and angular momentum. *Chemical Physical Letters, 216,* 286.

U.S. Environmental Protection Agency web site: http://www.epa.gov/globalwarming/publications/car/index.html.

Vygotsky, L. (1962). *Thought and language* (E. Hanfmann & G. Vakar, Trans.). Cambridge, MA: The MIT Press.

Waldo, M. (1985). Computers and composition: A marriage made in heaven? *Collegiate Microcomputer, 4,* 351–357.

Waldo, M. (1986). Romantic rhetoric for the modern student: The psycho-rhetorical approach of Wordsworth and Coleridge. *Rhetoric Review, 4,* 64–80.

Waldo, M. (1988). More than "first aid": A report on the effectiveness of writing center intervention in the writing process. *Issues in College Learning Centers, 5,* 13–22.

Waldo, M. (1993). The last best place for writing across the curriculum: The writing center. *Writing Program Administration, 16,* 15–26.

White, E. M. (1990). Language and reality in writing assessment. *College Composition and Communication, 41,* 187–200.

Why Johnny Can't Write. (1975, December 8). *Newsweek,* pp. 58–65.

Wordsworth, W. (1965). Preface to the second edition of the *Lyrical Ballads* (1800). In J. Stillinger (Ed.), *Selected poems and prefaces by William Wordsworth* (pp. 445–464). Boston: Houghton-Mifflin.

Author Index

Subject Index